D1489437

Treasures
of the
Tropic Seas

Treasures
of the
Tropic Seas

RENÉ CATALA

Facts On File Publications
New York, New York • Oxford, England

PUBLIC LIBRARY. PLAINFIELD. N. J.

folio
574.92
C27

TREASURES OF THE TROPIC SEAS

Copyright c 1986 by Times Editions

All rights reserved. No part of this book may
be reproduced or utilized in any form or by
any means, electronic or mechanical,
including photocopying, recording or by an
information storage and retrieval systems,
without permission in writing from the Publisher.

First published in the United States by Facts On File, Inc.
460 Park Avenue South, New York NY 10016

**Library of Congress
Cataloging-in-Publication Data**

Catala, René.
Treasures of the tropic seas.

Translation of: Offrandes de la mer.
Bibliography: p.
Includes index.
1. Station de biologie marine Aquarium de
Nouméa (New Caledonia) 2. Marine
biology — Tropics. I. Title.
QH95.59.C3713 1986
574.92'072093'2 86-13461
ISBN 0-8160-1590-2

Printed by Tien Wah Press, Singapore
Typesetting by Superskill, Singapore

To my wife, the wonderful Stucki,
whose tenacity, intelligence and taste
have made it possible for our shared
enterprise, the Aquarium of Noumea,
to be maintained to the highest levels
of both science and beauty during
20 years of unflinching devotion.

871321X

Pages 8 and 9: The brilliant effect of *Bantamia merleti* Wells under
ultra-violet irradiation. The natural color is brown with a reddish center.
Rare in New Caledonia: from depths between 20 and 40 meters.
Pages 10 and 11: The effects of ultra-violet light on
Trachyphyllia jeoffroyi Audouin whose natural colors range from
brown to reddish and gray. Very common in New Caledonia,
from shallow waters to a depth of 30 meters.

CONTENTS

Sponges gathered from between
20 and 40 meters in the lagoon of
New Caledonia. Axinellinae family

Opposite page: above, *Lobophyllia hemprechii* coral in daylight; below, the same species fluorescing. This page: above, *Galaxia sp.* coral under ultra-violet light; below, *Catalaphyllia plicata*, also under ultra-violet.

INTRODUCTION

A French edition of *Treasures of the Tropic Seas*, published in 1980, had numerous pages devoted to the *Station de Biologie Marine*, better known as the Aquarium of Noumea. This establishment, which is not only a scientific and educational center but also a major tourist attraction for New Caledonia, was founded in 1956 by the author and his wife. It soon gained an excellent international reputation, mainly as a result of the Catalas' spectacular discovery in 1958 that certain madrepores fluoresce if exposed to ultra-violet rays.[1]

Five years of nearly daily underwater excursions to various depths had actually led them to suspect such a phenomenon, but their intuition had to be tested by carrying out further research with more general implications.

They began a thorough investigation into a project which seemed to be fraught with difficulties. Would it be possible to create in an aquarium an environment acceptable to the marine invertebrates found in the lagoons of New Caledonia, and on its surrounding reef, in order to obtain their maximum lifespan? Priority was given to corals, soft-corals and other animal colonies and the results soon surpassed even the most optimistic prognoses.

It became evident that the excellent biological equilibrium in the aquarium was responsible for the survival of specially selected varieties of fish which were thought to be both interesting and rewarding to observe. Indeed, thanks to environmental conditions which closely resembled those of their natural habitat, most specimens remained in good health and showed astounding longevity (sometimes 20 years and more).

In the two decades of its existence during which it was founded and managed solely by the author and his wife, the Aquarium of Noumea inspired numerous publications. Books, encyclopaedias, reviews, magazines and articles, sometimes written by world authorities, have chronicled the history and development of the aquarium and its positive impact on many aspects of marine biology.

The first edition of this work concentrated on the aquarium's structure and equipment, the difficulties encountered at the outset and the results which were finally achieved. It would be untimely to reiterate these facts once again. Let us simply remember two significant points: it was essential to combine certain vital factors; sea water in uninterrupted circulation, with a perfect supply of oxygen and correct salinity; illumination of the tanks by daylight only, so as to preserve the daily and seasonal cycles. Under these favorable conditions the concrete walls of the tanks were generally covered by marine plants and animals, such as grow on the old hulls of sunken ships.

This marvelous world of innumerable sea creatures proved to be an ideal support system for countless micro-organisms, of which plankton consistently provides the main source of nourishment for the tanks' inhabitants, invertebrates and fish alike. What a contrast to the distressingly bare walls of other aquaria throughout the world! Alas, most of them do not have access to free flowing, and therefore constantly renewed, sea water and find themselves obliged to resort to tricks of artificial decor and perspective or other illusions which only serve to mislead the inquisitive layman. The Catalas always felt that nature in its splendid diversity does not need improving.

And then came the lucky day when some animal — crab, sea urchin or fish — scraped at the natural lining of the tank so thoroughly that a small bare spot appeared on the concrete wall. There a coral larva found a suitably solid base and attached itself. As the months and years went by they could see this madrepore grow and build its branches. Later other corals and different kinds of soft-corals established themselves similarly and prospered, providing the ultimate proof of the perfect biological balance in the tanks. Surely these colonies in the aquarium are the greatest treasures that the sea could have offered us.

---

1 Catala, R., *Academie des Sciences*, Paris, vol. 247, November 1958, pp. 1678-79.
Catala, R., *Nature* (London), vol. 183, April 1959, p. 949.
Catala, R., *Carnaval sous la mer*, Sicard, Paris, 1964.

Sponges

ponges form an extraordinary world with the beauty of their colors, the strangeness of their forms, the complexity of their structure and the peculiarity of their physiology. With the exception of only one freshwater family they are marine, and there are so many thousands of species that even specialists differ in their estimates of the exact number. Some scientists, having spent some time at the Aquarium, are surprised at the biological conditions here that allow healthy growth of so many sponges.

People are absolutely astonished to find themselves in a world totally unknown to them — which is quite understandable because these sponges normally live at depths of between 20 and 40 meters. According to some, the colors of these "plants" cannot be natural (meaning they are too beautiful to be true) and we are often asked how many times a year we have to repaint these "things". Others cannot believe that sponges are animals because "they don't move". We are no longer surprised by such comments when, in fact, it is not so long ago (only about the middle of the last century) since the strictly animal nature of sponges has been proved by naturalists. The term zoophytes, (zoo = animal: phytes = plant) used formerly to designate sponges, indicates the naturalist's hesitation in deciding whether they were plant or animal, so they used both.

Sponges are classified as superior to the unicellular protozoa (amoeba, foraminiferans, radiolarians, etc.) but inferior to the multicellular coelenterates (jellyfish, sea-anemones, corals, etc). One could simply describe a sponge as a bag equipped with a large top opening, or osculum, and multiple smaller side openings, (ostia). It is through these ostia that the life-sustaining current of water enters the sponge and, after having circulated the interior of the body, leaves again through the osculum, known as the exhalent opening. Some sponges can have many oscula, as the examples in photographs **2** (*Haliclona*), **17** (*Dendrilla*) and **21** (*Axinissa*) show. Professor Pavans de Ceccati[2] quotes the case of certain sponges of the Bahamas where the total water flow was measured at around two liters a minute, and an average of 2,800 liters a day.

Professor Robert Barnes[3] studied a small

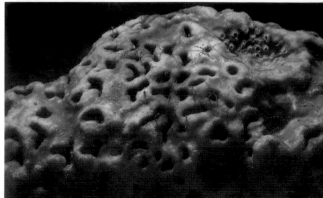

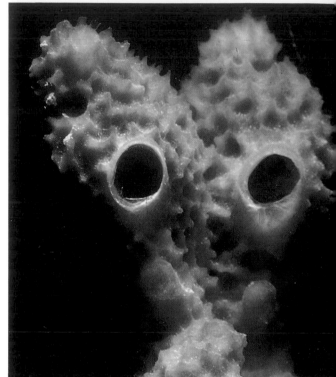

2   Pavans de Ceccati, M. *Les spongiares, La Vie des Animaux*, Larousse, Paris, 1969.

3   Barnes, Robert. *Invertebrate Zoology*. W.B. Saunders Company, Philadelphia, 1968.

1 Deep-water sponges (20–30 meters) give a glimpse of the diversity of form and color.

2 *Haliclona sp*. The two large openings (*oscula* or exhaling pores) through which water that has circulated inside the sponge is expelled. The water enters through the *ostia* or inhaling pores (numerous much smaller openings).

3 *Cliona schmidti*, a sponge with violet-colored encrustation which is very widespread in coral habitats. See also photograph 53 in the chapter Mollusks and 156 in the chapter Fish.

4 *Cliona sp*. with numerous large exhaling pores (*oscula*). The tissues of these sponges are particularly tightly packed.

6 *Stelospongia sp*. Sponges with an extremely rough exterior texture which can reach a height of one meter.

Page 17: A cup-shaped *Haliclona sp*.

7

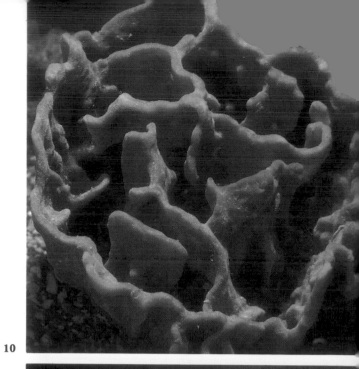

10

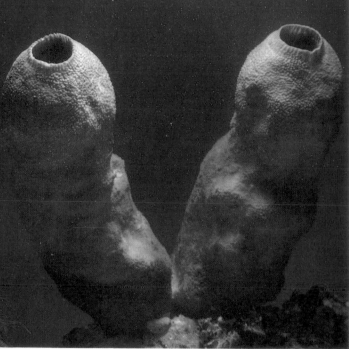

8

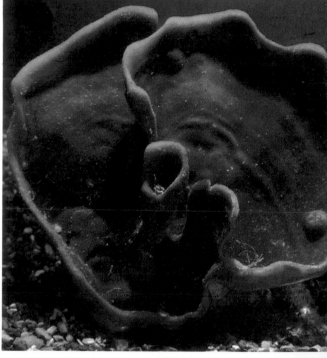

11

9

7 *Stelospongia sp.* A close-up of the distal extremity showing the unique *osculum*.

8 A hard, corny sponge which has not yet been identified. It looks like a *Stelospongia* in shape, but the outside texture is much less rough.

9 *Haliclona sp.* with a large *osculum* at its base.

10 and **11** *Phyllospongia sp.* seem to be two species belonging to the same genus. They are smooth to the touch and wax-like in appearance.

12 *Axinella carteri*. A fragile species which is less resistant than many others in the Aquarium.

12

13 *Haliclona sp.* Looking like a large and extremely thin dark purple cup, this sponge exhibits a very beautiful reddish fluorescence under ultra-violet light.

14 These bright yellow sponges with multiple branches belong to the family *Dictyoceratidae.*

15 This branched sponge of the *Haliclonidae* family is very fragile. Slightly turbid water can quite often prove fatal to it.

16 *Verongia sp.* The walls of this species are very thick, for a sponge with a diameter of only 15 centimeters, and the texture is extremely hard.

17 *Dendrilla rosea.* Small-sized organisms often shelter behind the large *oscula*: Mollusks (gastropods), echinoderms (ophiuroids) etc ...

18 *Haliclona (?).* These large "leaves" have a smooth texture and wax-like appearance.

13

16

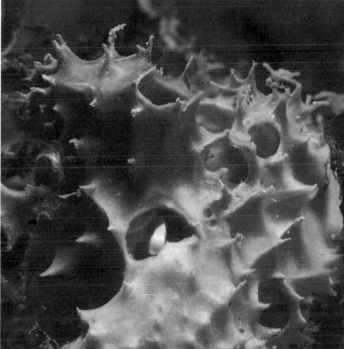

14

17

15

18

species of *Leuconia*, which has a diameter of one cm and is 10 cm high, and showed that its little body pumps 22,5 liters of water a day at a current speed of 8,5 cm a second through the osculum.

This brief summary only touches on the extraordinary functions that make up a sponge. They look like a simple collection of cells, but just how many body functions must they carry out? Some are muscular, some nervous, some glandular, some epithileal and others still are reproductive. There are, in fact, male sponges and female sponges. But they can also multiply by simply budding off a new sponge. On the other hand, in cases of fragmentation, the sponges are gifted with great powers of regeneration. There are even cases where two sponges growing very close to one another can unite and become one.

The external wall, ectoderm, is made up of flat cells, and the internal wall, the endoderm, by whip cells, the choanocytes. The choanocytes vibrating whips beat day and night in the same direction, drawing water in through the ostia and out the top through the osculum. The continual current of water assures oxygenation of the sponge and its feeding by the filtering of nutritive particles. The ectoderm and the endoderm are separated by a sort of jelly, the mesoglea. (The anatomy of the polyp of a coral shows the same arrangement of these three layers).

It is the amoeboid cells of the mesoglea that differentiate themselves, some for the production of sperm and some for the production of eggs. Fertilization is effected inside the sponge. It gives place to larvae called planula (like those of the coelenterates).

This is only a partial description of the remarkable physiology of sponges. The curious reader should consult the specialized references in the Bibliography.

Sponges are supported by an amazing diversity of stiff spicules. These are composed of little needles of calcium carbonate in the calcareous sponges but are of silica in the sponges called silicious sponges. These spicules are secreted by amoebocyte cells, and their considerable number forms the sponge's framework of support. Seen under a microscope they are of a magnificent diversity of form and size. Curved or straight needles, on one or many axes, some spicules resemble anchors, some resemble forks, others stars or snow-crystals. The many types of spicules have been catalogued and named according to the number of axes they have — the monaxon, tetraxon, triaxon, polyaxon, etc. Because of their consistency of form — and also because of their good preservation — these spicules serve as a base for identifying sponges and also permit scientists to assign them a place in the classification (we shall see in the chapter devoted to coelenterates that identification of the Alcyonarian "soft corals" is also made according to the supporting spicules).

In some sponges, the spicules are supported by an organic protein cement called spongine. The density of this substance, minimal in certain cases, forms in others a thick cover around bundles of spicules. The texture of the tissue molded in this way is often so compact that it offers incredible resistance to the best-sharpened knife. Certain species of these hard sponges, for example *Hircinia*, also contain considerable quantities of gravel, sand and various foreign bodies that have been swept in by the circulating water current. Finally, there are some sponges which lack spicules altogether, these being replaced by a fibrous tissue close to the composition of horn.

The classification adopted by specialists divides sponges into three classes:

First is the class of Calcareous Sponges. They are exclusively marine, living in all the seas of the world, and are found only in shallow depths. It seems that they cannot tolerate areas that are diluted by fresh-water run-off.[4]

The second class, the Demospongia, consist of both fresh-water and marine sponges. The family Spongillidae live exclusively in the fresh waters of lakes, ponds and small, tranquil rivers. According to Hyman[5], some *Cladorhiza* in the subdivision of *Monaxonida* belonging to this class of *Demospongia* have been brought up from ocean depths of 6,000 meters.

The third class is the Hexactina, consisting for the most part of sponges living at depths between 450 meters and 900 meters. But, Hyman also tells us — and Barnes[6] confirms — that certain species have been dredged from a depth of three miles (5,400 meters).

---

4 Hyman, Libbie Henrietta. *The Invertebrates*. McGraw-Hill Book Company. New York. London, 1940, p. 323.

5 Hyman, as above, p. 343.

6 Barnes, Robert. *Invertebrate Zoology*. W.B. Saunders Company Philadelphia 1968, p. 69.

19 *Gellius sp.* The diaphanous *oscula* are showing a maximum prolapse in this photo. This sponge lives in symbiosis with an algae of the genus *Codium*.

20 *Clathria sp.* has exceptionally numerous branches. It is very widespread in the Lagoon.

21 *Axinissa sp.* Several large *oscula* can clearly be seen.

22 A sponge which has not yet been identified.

23 A large specimen of a *Clathria sp.*

24 *Dysidea sp.* The structure of this sponge determines that it offers hiding places to many small-sized organisms (especially crabs).

26 *Haliclona sp.* Very large *oscula* with serrated or toothed edges can be seen.

25 *Haliclona sp.* Very fragile. The yellow mark is the beginning of a necrosis which will extend over the whole sponge in two or three days.

27 *Spirastrella sp.* A massive, hard sponge which is very rare.

28 *Chladochalina sp.* A smooth sponge with a wax-like appearance.

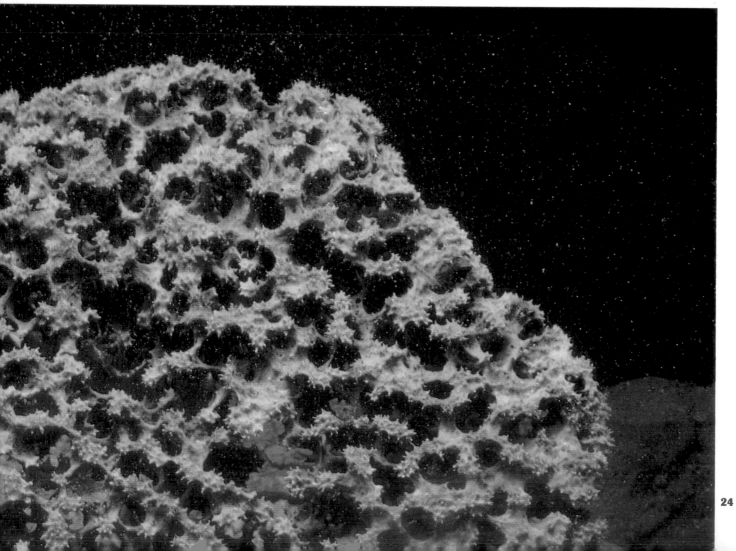

miles (5,400 meters).

Some Hexactina even exist in the polar waters. Pavans de Ceccati[7] writes of "underwater divers who found, under the Antarctic ice, some species of sponges whose size and form offered the same advantages as those of an armchair".

The enumeration of all the different types of *spicules*, establishing the essential characters of the sponges belonging to these three classes, goes beyond the scope of the present work. On the other hand, some observations are worthy of mention.

While certain sponges measure only a few millimeters in height and in width, others reach considerable sizes. The specialist Odette Tuzet[8] quotes the case of the *Hircinia gigantea* attaining a diameter of a meter and a weight of 60 kilograms. Other authors make mention of specimens whose weight exceeds 200 kilograms. I remember an enormous "pouffe" which, at less than four meters depth at low tide, was lying in the open on one of the banks of the bays close to the Aquarium. Some young people had had the idea of transporting this enormous sponge onto the beach. There were four of them toiling hard to move it. While it was still in the water they had some success, but when it broke surface it was a different story. Full of water this mass was too heavy and, in spite of the help of many bathers called in to assist, they could roll it only to about ten meters from the shore. During this very difficult maneuver the divers made many stabs and many cuts into the bundle of compact fibers and it was then that an unbelievable amount of organisms emerged. They came out, by the thousands; worms, crustacea, brittle stars and even small fish ... enough to keep many specialists of the different animal groups busy for many weeks. In all this multitude of animal life a species of pure white pistol shrimp (*Alpheidae*) was the most abundant. Many other observers had earlier noted the high proportion of these crustacea. Hyman quotes the case of Pearse who, in 1932, was able to count 16,352 specimens of a pistol shrimp called *Synalpheus* in the interior of

7   Pavans de Ceccati, M. *Les spongiares, La Vie des Animaux,* Larousse, Paris, 1969.
8   Tuzet, Odette. *Spongiaires Zoologie*. Encyclopédie de la Piéiade, Paris, 1963.

29

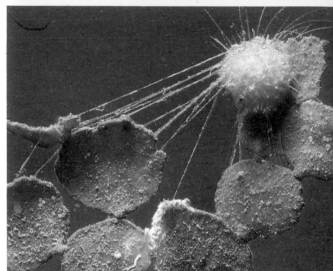

30

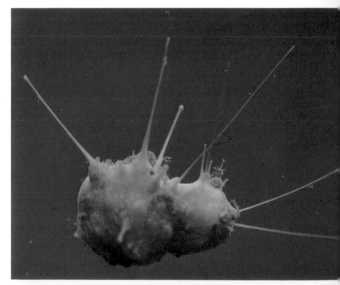

31

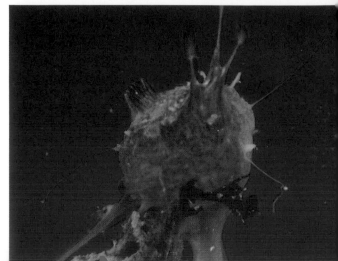

32

29 *Tethya sp.* fixed on the algae *Halimeda tuna* showing production of filaments (rhizoids).

30 *Tethya sp.* The rhizoids solidly mooring the sponge to several support elements.

31 *Tethya sp.* Another individual emitting rhizoids.

32 *Tethya sp.* On the top left hand corner is a fully open *osculum*. At the base of the sponge, both on the right and left, several rhizoid anchors can be seen.

33 *Tethya sp.* Reproduction. The weight of the new sponge has bent the carrier filament. The "baby" *Tethya* is now in contact with the substrate.

34 A mixture of sponges (*Prionas, Verongia, Dysidea* and *Tethya*) growing on the valves of a living razor-shell (*Pinna vexillum*).

35 *Siphonochalina sp.* which has grown on a *Chlamys* bivalve.

33

34 and 35

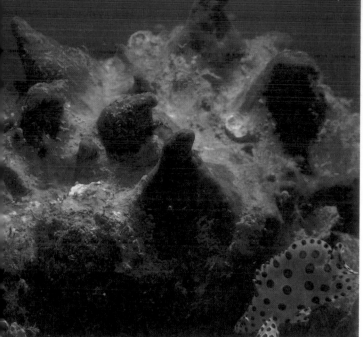

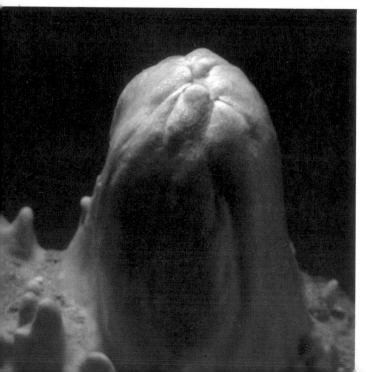

only one sponge, *Spheciosponqia*. One can imagine the uproar that such a number of "pistol shrimps" made when one hears the loud bang produced by the nippers of just one individual!

I also remember that at the time this big *Hircinia* was cut it gave off an acrid odor resembling acetic acid mixed with ammonia. I often had to overcome aversion to this unpleasant smell when preparing samples destined for the Museum National de Paris. And while mentioning our famous museum in rue Cuvier, I must express my gratitude to Professor Claude Lévi, not only for the many identifications of sponges that he made, but also for all those fascinating scientific discussions we had during his stay at the Aquarium. It is a great satisfaction to be able to finally put names on sponges that one has known for so long; it is another thing to be informed about so many facts that only such specialists know.

Moreover, preparations of samples of sponges are very instructive: As soon as certain species are submerged in the fixative liquid their color begins to leach out into it. When placed in a new "clean" solution, they continue to lose their color; and so it goes on until the assistant becomes weary of trying to maintain clear liquid. The same thing goes for the *Cliona schmidti*, sponges containing a superb violet coloring. Other sponges hold unpleasant surprises. I remember some large samples of dog-eared sponge which I decided to dry in the sun. For days they let out an incredible amount of mucus through their two oscula. The same exudation happened with the amazing *Stelospongia* whose size sometimes reaches one meter. Illustration **6** shows a complete specimen and picture **7** shows a closer shot of its unique osculum. To the touch, these sponges are unpleasantly rough. Other species, on the contrary, feel soft, downy and velvety. Some very smooth ones, like certain *Phyllospongia (***10** & **11***) Haliclona* (**13** & **18**) and *Acanthella* (**42**) feel waxy.

Some are very thick walled and as hard as wood, such as the *Verongia*, which have the appearance of large wine glasses (**16**). Others are thin and delicate like the very elegant mauve goblets of *Haliclona (***13**) which only keep their form as vases in calm water. The divers, who bring them up from depths of between 25 and 40 meters, have to handle them with care to bring them back intact. Out of the water they sag on

36

37

38

36 *Sporastrella vagabunda*. Very often parasitized by multitudes of worms.

37 A great mixture of sponges fixed on ideal supports — sheaths of the giant sea-worms, *Eunice tubifex*.

38 *Sporastrella sp*. Similar to the form with the large open aperture in plate 8, but its external texture is smooth.

39 *Timea sp*. One of the most beautiful deep-water sponges (25–30 meters). Rarely collected.

40 A sponge of the *Haliclonidae* family (common). Often inhabited by hundreds of small ophiuroids. (Refer to chapter on Echinoderms).

39

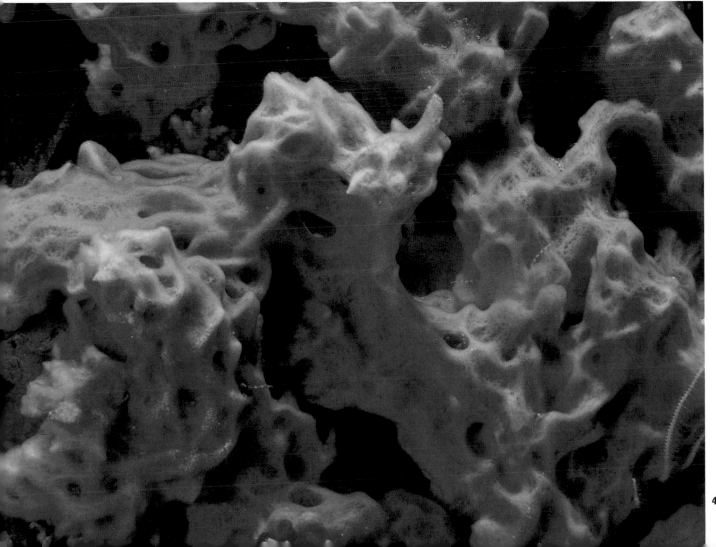

40

each other like sheets of wet newspaper. It is interesting to note that these *Haliclona* sponges fluoresce under ultra-violet radiation (wavelength of 3,650 angström) to show a superb reddish fluorescence. We did not have time to exactly identify the nature of this photoluminescence. Is it caused by the symbiotic micro-algae fluorescing or is it due to the same process as occurs in the fluorescent corals where special pigments are included in the actual tissues? Here is a very appealing area of study for someone who has at his disposal a set-up similar to that in our aquarium and can keep some sponges as fragile as this alive. It would also be interesting to look for the cause of a phenomenon that we have noticed often over many years. We have observed a progressive discoloration of these same *Haliclona* which become completely white in a few months. In the chapter devoted to coelenterates we shall see that some corals (for example some *Trachyphyllia* Coelenterates, **5** & **6**) when placed in abnormal conditions of very weak luminosity, lose their colors as their micro-algae (Zooxanthelles) disappear. With the *Haliclona* sponges it is difficult to attribute their discoloration to the same process since they are exposed to normal daylight and, at certain hours, are in direct sunlight. It is worth pointing out that these sponges, having remained white for many weeks, sometimes recolor themselves to recapture their original beautiful mauve hue.

Other sponges of the family Haliclonidae are represented in **9** and **25**. Some amazing "finger" shapes are noticed among the *Clathria* (**23**). Another with very extended "fingers" is the fragile *Haliclona* (**26**). Photo **19** shows a sponge of the *Gellius* type, and here one sees the remarkable diaphanous oscula on the end of about ten of its chimney-like extensions. This sponge lives in symbiosis with an algae of the *Codium* type. An intimate union develops between algae and the sponge which it envelops.

"Charming little *Tethya*... I don't know your name but I like you a lot already and you intrigue me greatly!" We are talking about little sponges that look like raspberries. There are many in the family and the task and pleasure of giving them their new species names will be left up to Professor Claude Lévi. Some that we have in the Aquarium at a depth of 25 meters are bright red, some whitish while others are milk-curd yellow. The most remarkable fact about these sponges,

 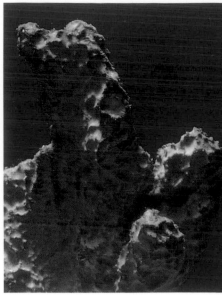

41   **42**

which vary in size from a small pea to a walnut, is that they produce numerous filaments on all the sides of the sphere, (the rhizoides **29**), which extend out to fix themselves at different points and so become mooring cables. These supports can be empty bivalve shells, fragments of dead corals, rocks or even algae, as in picture **30** which shows mooring lines on the thick and hard lobes of a *Halimeda tuna*.

The only obvious movements animating these sponges are very slow contractions of the oscula which open and shut. A great many authors previously believed that sponges cannot move themselves about. But we were astonished to note the mobility carried out by the *Tethya*. To firmly establish this movement, we put some on a perfectly horizontal glass "track" hard against the side of one of the tanks in the laboratory; behind them, and to serve as a "railing", was a smooth ruler. A soft lead pencil marked their exact place each evening. By the next morning they had moved and a new pencil mark would be made, and so on, every 12 hours. Usually the movement was around one centimeter, but sometimes the *Tethya* had advanced by two or three times as much and at other times it had not moved at all. In this last case we noticed the reinforcement of two or three rhizoides. A dissection under the microscope showed that it was not a question of a number of rhizoides joining together, but rather of one alone having thickened in less than 24 hours from the size of a silk spider's thread to that of a pencil lead. The "rope" became a "cable" (**32**).

41   *Megalopastas sp.* A common sponge. A favorite with spider-crabs when disguising themselves. (See chapter on Crustacea).

42   *Acanthella sp.* Very beautiful species, thick and smooth with a wax-like appearance (rarely collected).

We wanted to know whether the sponges moved at random, or only because of the regular thrust of the current, so we closed the small water valves in the laboratory tanks to allow minimum flow for survival. Despite this reduction of water flow for 24 hours — which was fatal for many other species — the *Tethya* still moved from one to two centimeters. But we couldn't draw firm conclusions because the fine bubbles of the ventilators create a micro-current by themselves. Therefore we closed these taps as well. During the 24 hours passed in this still water our *Tethya* remained perfectly stationary and the thickness of their rhizoides didn't increase. That seems quite conclusive. And as it was vital for the survival of these small, fragile beings to re-open the water valves we changed the direction of the current and increased its force. The different influences of an undirectional current and a changing current on the rhizoides is very interesting to observe. The first created a more rapid thickening of the "mooring ropes" and the second an increase in the number of anchor filaments in the directions from which the currents were coming. We began to take notes on the resistance of the "cables" and the weights they could support before breaking. But, as so often happens, other occupations forced us to shelve these observations until some future date. Quite a pleasant job for someone with all the time in the world to get engrossed.

We kept the *Tethya* alive for several months which allowed us to observe their very interesting reproductive technique. For each one of the small spheroid protuberances with which the sponge is abundantly provided, and which give it something of the appearance of a raspberry, one can detect a slight swelling which makes one think that a tiny bud is going to free itself from the mother mass. But this swelling is still far from detaching itself because it is held by a filament similar to the rhizoides I have just mentioned. The filament lengthens a little more each day, carrying the baby *Tethya* at its extremity. After two or three days the weight of the new little sponge bends the filament towards the bottom. It then attaches itself there by producing new rhizoides, while the carrier filament disappears. Photograph **33** couldn't be made any clearer because of the slight coating of algae that had grown on the window pane during these few days. Any cleaning attempt before taking photographs would have caused these very fragile suspensary ligaments to rupture.

Even though I know very little about this group of sponges — one would need a complete lifetime to master such a vast subject — I will give an idea of the diversity of base supports on which the sponges attach themselves. I have just spoken about some of the "dead" supports with reference to the *Tethya*, but many living organisms serve as anchors... firstly the sponges themselves. One quite often sees a mixture of different sponges which slowly interpenetrate among each other. In other examples, small, discrete patches of different sponges install themselves on the main mass of sponge. The astonishing diversity of the shades of all these sponges offers colorful palettes.

Other living supports seem to normally have sponge coverings, such as the valves of the *Chlamys* bivalves of which there will be a discussion in the chapter on mollusks. We have never seen *Chlamys* which were not coated with sponges, the more common ones being the *Siphonochallina* (**35**) and the *Mycale*. The amount of sponge cover is sometimes so cumbersome for these bivalves that they become unbalanced during "flight", at the end of which they fall lopsided. The shells of other bivalves are more or less covered with sponges, as is shown by the razor shell *Pinna vexillum* (**34**). Certain sponges also attach themselves on the coelenterates, and we have seen cases where one sponge of the *Zygomycale* species would overgrow a large deep-water gorgonian to complete suffocation. When a minute region on these animal colonies (gorgonia, antipathaires, etc.), becomes roughened, it is immediately the point chosen by a sponge to attach itself to. And once installed it overwhelms its host.

In the chapter about crustacea one will see how sponges are precious camouflage for the spider-crabs, and discover the funny way in which sponge crabs use them to disguise themselves. To finish, I must mention the supporting structure that I consider the most remarkable — the parchment-like sheath of the giant sea-worm, *Eunice tubifex*, which is found embedded in the bottom of muddy sands between 20 and 40 meters (**37**).

Coelenterates

The continual increase of knowledge inevitably brings with it some important modifications to classification. Certain authors would consider Cnidaria as a sub-branch of Coelenterates and would therefore also consider that this last term no longer has any zoological value. They would prefer me to call this chapter Cnidaria. But I have kept the term Coelenterates in consideration of those who have my book, *Carnaval sous la mer*, and are not familiar with the subtleties of scientific names. In this way they will be able to link the organisms I am going to write about in this chapter to those which formed the subject of chapters I to IV in my previous work.

I want to make it clear that the present book is, above all, a biological work and makes no claim to be a zoological treatise. Those wanting to go further into scientific nomenclature should consult some of the specialized works listed at the end of the book.

I will therefore limit myself by giving a table at the end of the chapter, showing the classification that corresponds to organisms illustrated here.

In *Carnaval sous la mer* I made quite an extensive study of coelenterates since corals occupy a very big section in this branch. On the other hand, the discovery that my wife and I made in 1957 of the superb effects of fluorescence of certain madrepora corals when submitted to ultra-violet rays was most exciting. I explained their exuberance and the unceasing work of the minute animal organisms, the polyps (**1, 2, 3**) which have built up over the ages reefs of considerable size and importance in many regions of the globe. Of course, I gave the classic example of the most famous amongst them, the Great Barrier Reef which stretches out over a distance of 2,400 kilometers of the east coast of the Australian continent with widths varying from 10 to 140 kilometers. And, making reference to the 800 kilometers of coral reef which surround New Caledonia, I pointed out that, in this region, the three types of reef formation can be found together: the barrier reef which, in the very open sea, stands up to the violence of ocean waves with its solid ramparts, the fringe reefs bordering directly on the coasts or on the periphery of small islands and the annular reefs which are the atolls. The most typical of the annular reefs for this region is the atoll Entrecasteaux.

On the subject of antiquity of corals, I mentioned those which survive in fossil form over hundreds of kilometers in the Ardennes, the Vosges, the Morvan, the Lower Alps, the Isère, etc., and I said that, in these calcareous masses (many of which have transformed themselves into marble), the geologist often finds the same species that live today in warm seas.

Having listed the essential factors which condition the life of corals; light, temperature, salinity, clarity, I always emphasized the strictly animal character of these organisms.

Of course, all zoologists know this, but the general public continues — obstinately — not to see anything there except "plant-life". I know this because, for 20 years at the Aquarium, we have shown visitors many displays of coelenterates (corals, alcyonarians, gorgonians, antipathairians, etc.) and the great majority still go into ecstasies in front of "all these plants" and some even ask, "do you transplant them with their roots?"). I hasten to add that one cannot easily dispel this belief because the majority of books, reviews, magazines and other publications maintain this confusion between animals and plants. So you find chapter headings or captions such as "aquatic floral festival", "sea flower", "underwater bushes", "coral forests", and, the ultimate of this botanic lyricism, "the coral in flower".

But even in science it is not so long ago that zoologists recognized the strictly animal nature of corals and other coelenterates.

It was Jean-André de Peyssonnel who first established in 1723 that "coral flowers" were none other than little animals. In a manuscript, which was never published and is conserved in the library of the Museum of Natural History in Paris, he wrote: "I saw the opening of the coral in bowls full of sea-water and I observed that what we believed to be the flower of this so-called plant was only, in fact, an insect similar to a small sea nettle or octopus... The calyx of this so-called flower is the body itself of the animal, expanding or coming out of the cell." Louis Figuier[9] later wrote: "A naturalist of great fame, the Count de Marsigli, made a discovery which seemed to establish — with a scandal — the real origin of this product of nature. The Count de Marsigli announced having discovered the flowers of the

---

9 Figuier, Louis. *Zoophytes et Mollusques*. Hachette, Paris, 1866.

1 *Goniopora lobata*, a colonial coral with its polyps totally extended.

2 *Alveopora catalai*. The coral polyps (or madrepores) have a crown of six tentacles (hexacorals), while soft-corals have eight or multiples of eight.

Page 33: *Rhizostoma sp.* jellyfish whose tentacles play host to shoals of trevally.

3 A close-up of a coral polyp. These tiny creatures build the immense coral reefs over thousands of years.

4 An area of one of the large tanks in the Aquarium. From left to right: a sea-squirt, *Polycarpes* (orange), soft-corals *Spongodes merleti*; in front, the base of the largest one and a specimen which is retracted; a pale yellow sponge; the long tentacles of a large sea-anemone; a vermilion sponge. The bottom is full of underwater plants (*Caulerpes*).

5 *Trachyphyllia jeoffroyi*, a solitary coral (one giant polyp alone). Its genuine color is due to the micro-algae, zooxanthelles.

6 The same coral, quite alive despite the total loss of its zooxanthelles.

7 A parasite of certain corals: the polychaete worm *Spirobranchus giganteus* (gill bouquets and the operculum of its gallery).

coral…. 'How could one doubt that this coral be a plant since one had seen its flowers blooming?' He continued: 'The observations of Peyssonnel destroyed a discovery which had aroused unanimous admiration'. Therefore Peyssonnel's work was very badly received by naturalists of the day. Réaumur stood out above all in the battle that was waged against the young innovator. He wrote to Peyssonnel, sarcastically: 'I believe, like you do, that nobody until now has taken it into their head to look at the coral as a work of insects. One cannot dispute this novel and unusual concept. But the corals never seemed to me to be built by small sea nettles or octopuses as you understood!'"

In addition to the brief historical account that I gave about this "discovery" in *Carnaval sous la mer* I also have in my possession a 22 page memoir, by Bernard de Jussieu presented at the Royal Academy on November 14, 1742.

He wrote: "The newness of this remarkable observation provoked some other botanists to examine coral and other marine plants more accurately; M Peyssonnel, doctor in Marseille, was the one who applied himself most to observing them and, particularly intrigued by that which had excited the curiosity of the Count de Marsigli, he noted that what had appeared as flowers to this famous physicist were really animals or marine insects similar to the sea nettle. He confirmed this impression by several observations made during his travels in Africa, in the same place where one goes coral collecting. These observations by M Peyssonnel seemed so remarkable to M Réaumur that, in an excerpt that he gave in 1727 in the Memoirs of the Academy, he felt obliged to spare the author by not naming him."

All this might have been merely "interesting" but Louis Figuier makes a more serious footnote: "Peyssonnel, sad and disgusted by the bad reception given to his works, abandoned his researches. He also abandoned science and the company of men and went to grow old in obscurity in the West Indies as a marine surgeon," and, continues: "While Peyssonnel lived, forgotten, his scientific works that had been recognized in Paris were a complete but sterile triumph for him. Réaumur gave to the animalcules which live in coral the name *polyps* and *polypier* to the hard parts which they use as a cover or support."

5

6

7

And this term polyps is still in existence today to identify the frail constructors of coral reefs. These polyps are, in fact, small actinia or sea-anemones. They are distinguishable, however, by their ability to secrete calcium carbonate which serves them as both skeleton and protection. These minute organisms are of a very simple structure. The polyp is, in fact, an extremely fine fleshy tube made up of an external casing, the ectoderm, an interior lining, the endoderm, and an intermediate layer, a sort of jelly called mesoglea.

The small cylindrical column is fixed to its substratum by the basal disc, and has the oral disc (peristome) on its upper part in the centre of which the slit mouth is situated. All prey captured by the tentacles is brought to this mouth, and then into the stomodaeum, which one can compare to an oesophagus, then into the digestive cavity called coelenteron (from the Greek *koilos*, cavity and *enteron*, intestine).

It is in this external layer of the ectoderm that you find the cells called cnidoblasts, small oval or round capsules containing the stinging cnidocyst (= nematocyst) **A**, small microscopic javelin bathing in a liquid toxin. This javelin is coiled like a spring and when it contacts a foreign body it is projected towards the exterior of the capsule. There are numerous types of cnidocysts, of which the javelins assume many forms varying from the simple filament to the prickly harpoon with sharp hairs. Under the microscope one sometimes sees a considerable number of these cells pressed against each other, like rockets on a rocket-launcher, all ready for the release of their projectiles. One can imagine the effect produced on a marine organism receiving a number of these poisoned darts all at the same moment.

In the endoderm layer one finds the zooxanthellae, microscopic unicellular algae whose presence is extremely useful in oxygenating polyps through photosynthesis. Some scientists believe that their presence is indispensable to the good health of coral. We are not certain because, at the Aquarium, corals of numerous species are not any worse off after having lost their zooxanthellae following long periods in weak natural light. Photographs **5** and **6** show the same coral, *Trachyphyllia jeoffroyi*, as it was when it had just been brought up from 20 meters filled with zooxanthellae to which it owed

its beautiful coloring, and then completely discolored following the disappearance or death of symbiotic micro-algae. However, it remained in excellent health.

When put back in conditions of long daily hours of sunlight, these corals "reinfect" themselves with zooxanthellae and then, little by little, their original coloring reappears.

The reproduction of corals — like that of many other coelenterates — is carried out by a sexual method (sperm fertilize the eggs which develop into larvae called planules) **B** and also by the asexual method (budding of the polyp). To this double chance of fecundity is added the remarkable power of regeneration of these organisms and the rapidity of tissue healing if injured. This is a subject to which I shall return later.

Although thousands of planules are released each year by an incalculable number of polyps, the great majority are either destroyed by many predators or carried away by the currents to areas that are unsuitable for their survival. After a free swimming period, which varies according to the species, the planule becomes heavy and, little by little, sinks to the bottom. It can only attach itself to become a polyp, the prime stage of a fixed coral, if the substratum is solid, clean and free of muddy-sand sediments. The ideal substrates are rocks, pebbles, dead coral, oyster or other chance collectors. But sometimes it attaches itself to the most unexpected objects, as was the case for this larva *Trachyphyllia jeoffroyi* which latched onto a Bic ballpoint pen that had fallen out of a passenger's pocket onto sand 30 meters deep. This "Bic-coral" lived for a long time in one of our tanks where it intrigued visitors (**12**). One could add a great deal on the larvae of all the coelenterates — like that of an *Antipathes* which came to attach itself in the knobbly hollow of a coral. This little "animal flower-pot" is a *Montipora foveolata* (**13**). Once attached, the larva passes from the planule to the polyp stage. It first constructs a calcareous plate adhering to the support which the animal secretes under its foot, and this rises progressively as the pedestal thickens. Then little blades, the radial septa, are built and will all be joined to a small circular wall, the theca **C**. In many species an axial stem called columella rises in the center. The whole of these diverse calcareous pieces, and some others that

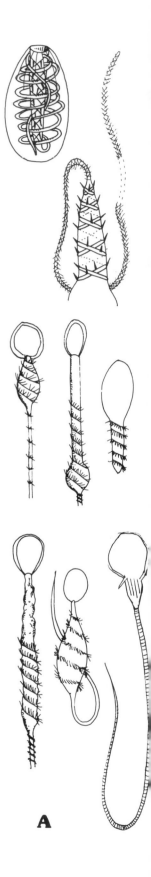

A

8 and 9

8 A branching coral (*Acropora formosa*) growing from a larva which spontaneously attached itself to the cement wall of a tank.

9 A closer view of the same coral four years later. Its ramifications are approaching the surface.

10 A deep-water (25–30 meters) octocoral, commonly called "iron wire gorgonia". The tiny polyps are retracted.

11 The coral *Euphyllia grandis*. In the center, a "lid" of mucus surrounds a gangrenous area that had been wounded.

12 A young *Trachyphyllia jeoffroyi* coral whose larva had attached itself to a BIC pen (found at a depth of 30 meters).

13 *Antipathes sp.* (octocoral) whose larva has fixed onto the cankered center of a *Montipora foveolata* coral.

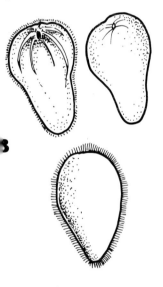

10 and 11

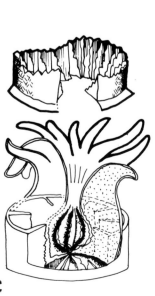

12 and 13

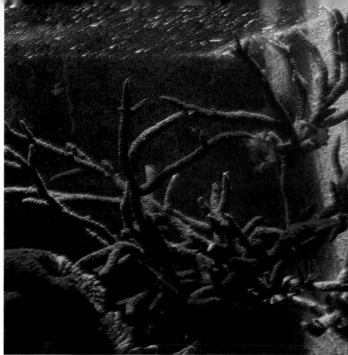

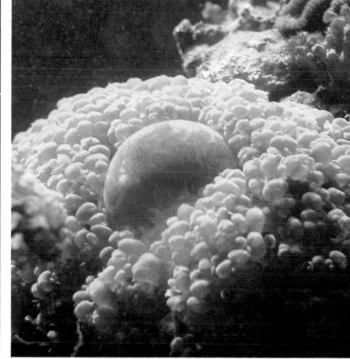

14

15

16

17

would take too long to describe here, constitute the calyx. Specialists base the classification of corals into families, genera and species on the differences of character of these skeletal elements.

The reader who is interested in growth and multiplication of corals and, more generally, in the formation of coral reefs, can easily satisfy his curiosity in many books, several of which are quoted at the end of this volume. In addition to what I have written about them myself in *Carnaval sous la mer*, I will add a few observations made since then at the Aquarium.

The growth of corals varies according to the family to which they belong. Among certain *Porites*, the size of the coral colony increases only a few centimetres each year; among others, as is the case with the *Acropora formosa* (**9**), the branches will grow 20 centimeters and more in the same period. From the outset the division of polyps is also more rapid in some corals than in others. Many times an oyster, a pebble or some other substrate was brought to the Aquarium on which there was still only one polyp, or a few. We were therefore able to follow their division. The four polyps of a *Goniopora lobata* (**1**), brought up from about 20 meters, gave 212 polyps in 18 months, which was extremely rapid. On the contrary, the division of a *Turbinaria turbinata* (Mollusks, **9**), which increased from five to 39 polyps in the same period was very slow.

To obtain protective camouflage, spider-crabs sometimes attach polyps of the coelenterate *Palythoa* (**31**) on their carapaces. To clarify certain points of the technique used by these spider-crabs, I cut some *Alveopora* polyps as close as possible to their base. The operation needs microsurgical scissors and manipulation of great speed because these small organisms retract so rapidly into their calices. In less than three weeks they had completely regenerated a mouth and crown of tentacles.

From this and other experiences, I am always astonished at the brief time in which several species of corals heal their flesh following an incision with a very fine scalpel. I believe that there is material here for interesting research of more far-reaching significance than simply the knowledge of the physiology of these invertebrates.

Another observation — probably unpublished — deals with the manner in which

14 A *Hymenocera elegans* shrimp trapped by a *Trachyphyllia* coral which will have absorbed it in two days time (see the same species of shrimp intact in Crustacea, photograph 67).

15 A colony of *Spirobranch* worms having hollowed out their gallery in a coral. On the bottom, to the left, a crinoid (Echinoderms).

16 A *Symphillia sp.* coral (*Musidae*), parasitized by barnacles (crustacea cirripeds).

17 A *Goniopora* coral whose polyps have been nibbled by a *Phestilla* sea-slug.

18 A *Spongodes merleti* soft coral with its white polyps totally extended and a *Catalaphyllia plicata* coral. In the left corner, a red *Axinissa* sponge.

19 Two *Phestilla melanobranchus* nudibranchs (but yellow-orange in color!) having nibbled at the polyps of a *Goniopora* coral. A few corals, on the bottom right, haven't been touched yet. Numerous egg layings have been attractively festooned by these sea-slugs.

18

19

certain corals succeed in limiting the risk of gangrene which is sometimes produced when a wound becomes infected. Photograph **11**, even though not perfectly sharp because of the very thick slab of glass, shows a small "dome" of mucus secreted in the center of a *Euphyllia grandis* to enclose an area of infection which was two months old. This would also be a very interesting research project for someone who did not have the worry of running the Aquarium and could have plenty of time to devote to these experiments. When they find themselves exposed at the time of low spring tides all corals exude some mucus — a defensive reaction or even a protection. This secretion shelters the polyps from the air and yet maintains enough humidity to survive. It is strange that when one even touches certain coral species underwater, without injuring them in any way, they produce an abundance of mucus.

Even though we had to neglect many observations and forego many experiments that would have been of great interest, we must consider ourselves very fortunate that some corals were born spontaneously in some of our large tanks and that they are continuing to grow there. Such an event would have seemed impossible a few years earlier. To our great astonishment, no attachment of coral larvae has ever been seen on the walls of our tanks. We have no doubt that excellent biological conditions existed there when we successfully kept corals installed 14 years earlier healthy. The good conditions also allowed regularity of attachment and seasonal development of a large number of algae of different species and also, to our annoyance, an abundance of organisms which clogged the pipes bringing in sea-water.

Further proof of the richness of sea-water was finally seen in the chambers of our large reserve tank where abundant planktonic fauna developed. Having survived the terrible maelstrom created by the turbines of the powerful pumps, they would arrive (probably a little groggy) in this wave of hyper-oxygenated water and stay to develop into healthy adult animals. There were crustacea, mollusks, echinoderms, worms, and sometimes some coelenterates such as the stinging *Plumaria* and some *Antipathes*, but never any corals. In addition to this crowd of invertebrates, some attached and others mobile,

20

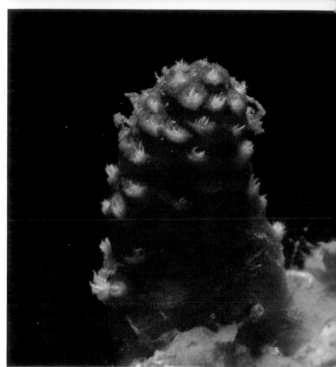

21

22

23

20 A few polyps of the *Alcyonium catalai* with air bubbles in the column of one of them. "A mystery story".

21 *Alcyonium catalai*. During the day the polyps are retracted.

22 When darkness comes the polyps begin to emerge from their calices.

23 During the night the polyps are in total extension. Notice the fineness of the small pinnules on the tentacles.

24 The whole colony in full bloom. A polyp, on the left, seems to be detached — an illusion due to the extreme transparency of its column. On the right, a small yellow colony of *Leucetta* sponges.

24

larval fish would also sometimes arrive. Only rarely did fish at the larger fry stage get through and they would grow thanks to the continual presence of plankton. It was logical that, in the long run, this absence of attachment of coral larvae would transform our perplexity into an obsession. It wasn't until many years later, after multiple attempts at difficult and complicated processes, that we had the intense satisfaction one day of noticing a small brown plate against the wall of a large tank, which was the beginning of the calcareous pedestal secreted by a planule. Some time later, the appearance of a swelling in the centre of this plate showed the beginning of a first polyp. Then there was the lengthening and thickening of the "stem" and finally, during the months and then years, the formation of lateral ramifications. This coral, *Acropora formosa* (ah! the predestined names!) is shown as it was after two years (**8**), then two years later (**9**) and today (July 1976) it continues to grow and become more beautiful. As photograph **9**, shows its higher branches were continuing to draw nearer to the surface and we wondered whether they would reach it and then inevitably die on contact with the air. Nothing of the kind happened. When they reached one-and-a-half centimeters from the surface, these vertical branchings stopped growing and it was the horizontal ones from below that spread out and divided in a more exuberant development. (The pictures of them here are not perfectly sharp because this *Acropora* had attached itself in a corner and the photograph could only be taken at an angle through the glass.

We were very concerned about this coral. Because of the lack of water turbulence in our tanks (in the sea there are waves), the base hadn't strengthened sufficiently and it had grown too quickly. Each additional growth of the coral branches increased the weight of the whole colony and we were worried that this coral would one day break from its pedestal. The idea of placing a prop could have appeared tempting, but would have proved impracticable because we would risk causing the dreaded accident ourselves. When I say we, it is really my wife I mean because she is the only person allowed in this tank called "The Tank of Sponges" (**4**). She places one foot in it carefully, then the other, moving with infinite caution in the luxuriant jumble of extremely fragile and sometimes

venomous organisms. The slightest false movement... She is the one who replaces a sponge that a fish has maltreated or installs new ones with superb variegation (**7**). And she is also the one to whom the duty of wielding the "lawnmower" falls when the green meadow of the shallow-water *Caulerpes* algae (**4**) that she transplanted becomes too thick and calls for skilfull work with scissors. And it is also her duty to constantly clear the brown algae from the glass slabs which multiply so rapidly that in less than eight days the visitors would no longer see anything through them. This was a task that was even more delicate when the growth of this precious *Acropora* made the passage of the hand between it and the pane more difficult each week. Stucki tried to arrange a certain number of massive corals wedged with stones so that the top of the pile would come almost to the level of one of the "master branches" with the hope that other branches would come to rest on it. But this was unsuccessful. We suspect that the polyps were aware that the surface of the water was very close and behaved as if all contact with a living body or rock would be fatal at the place of impact, inhibiting their ultimate growth.

And that leads me into a very interesting observation. The foot disc of a large sea-anemone, attached under the sand at the bottom of the concrete of this tank, had always maintained itself in the same place. Therefore this sea-anemone had never disturbed its neighbouring organisms. One day it shifted itself slightly, bringing its long tentacles into contact with two branches of our *Acropora*. This irritating contact provoked a curious reaction on the part of the coral polyps, manifesting itself by an accelerated production of calcium. One was in the form of a little club, the other like the scabs of certain plant-life and others like those of little crab *Hapalocarcinus* which lives in the interior of the branches of similar coral. The coral expert who followed the progress of our "spontaneous corals" with most infatuation, was the eminent Professor J.W. Wells of Cornell University, and he wanted to make a very thorough examination (X rays, dissections, etc.) of the growths of the defense reactions. But how could one break off the particular pieces without jeopardizing the life of the whole colony? This charming friend understood the argument and is now waiting for the day when this coral is dragged down by its

25 A soft-coral, *Sterecanthia stuckiae*, in the light of day.

26 The same octo-coral fluorescing under ultra-violet rays.

27 *Alcyonium catalai* with a yellow "trunk" (the color is not important for identification), to the right a *Tubastraea* coral with polyps completely retracted at the bottom of their calices (see them in full bloom in photograph 67).

25 an

44

28 The top part of the soft-coral *Umbellulifera striata* (see *Carnaval sous la mer*, page 53 and fig. 19 which shows the strange way of multiplication by natural hiving off).

29 Beautiful polyps belonging to an unidentified soft-coral brought up from a depth of 35 meters.

30 *Millepora sp.* (commonly known as "fire coral" because of the toxicity of its nematocysts) which isn't a madrepore but a hydrozoaire (Photo: B. Conseil).

31 Colony of *Palythoa*.

32 *Spongodes merleti*, a type with a slender form (able to reach a height of 60 centimeters). they are generally solitary.

33 *Spongodes merleti*, a type in the form of a ball and small in size (10–15 centimeters), often in very dense populations.

28

31

29

32

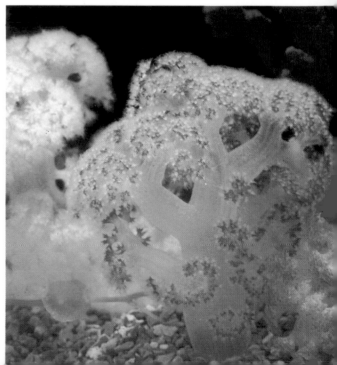

30

33

34 Soft corals of the *Sarcophytum* genus. In the subject to the left, looking like a mushroom, the polyps are retracted. The one on the right has all its polyps extended. Looking at a polyp face on, one can see the eight tentacles of the octo-corals.

35 A soft-coral (*Dendronephthya*) and the expansions at the base of its "trunk".

34

35

excessive weight, allowing him to make his detailed examination of the pieces in question.

This observation of the virulence of sea-anemone coming into contact with corals leads me to tell you about a discovery made over a number of years. A small littoral reef near the Aquarium was greatly enriched with corals of diverse families. From place to place one could see some anemones with their symbiotic fish *Amphiprion*. From one year to the other, we could determine the numerical increase of these sea-anemones. As they spread over a wider area, the corals proved to be less numerous, until the day came when they had almost all disappeared.

Back at the Aquarium we have observed over many years the attachment of other corals of different types. Certain ones continued to grow, others unfortunately suffered accidental or natural damage. The achievement of these coral attachments "in vitro" is so remarkable that I will record here, for the interest of specialists, the corals born spontaneously in our place; *Acropora formosa* (fam. Acroporidae), *Acropora patula* (fam. Acroporidae), *Culicia rubeola* (fam. Rhizangiidae), *Echinopora lamellosa* (fam. Faviidae), *Pocillopora sp.* (fam. Pocilloporidae), *Seriatopora histrix* (fam. Pocilloporidae), *Tubastraea aurea* (fam. Dendrophylliidae).

This last developed from larva born of a specimen brought up from 30 meters which had been installed in this tank for two years. It lived only 19 months.

One day my old friend and colleague from the Museum, the dear Bala (diminutive of his name which became a general nickname), gave me a joyous surprise by coming to the Aquarium. A famous entomologist, his vast knowledge also extends to the marine world. We gave him a detailed tour of all the tanks. Arriving at the one where the already famous *Acropora* and other corals were growing, he said:

"Tell me Kala" (another nickname that I have always had), "I recently read your article in the magazine *Atlas*. You reported the legitimate joy that you and Stucki had with this success but you remain silent on the actual details of this achievement. You will tell me, won't you?"

And I replied to Bala: "All the other discoveries, results of years of cautious experiments, we will give up quite willingly to those who, eventually, take over here. But you will forgive me for wanting to keep this little story of spontaneous corals secret for a little longer."
— "A long time?"
— "Listen, Bala, being a member of the Academy of Sciences, you will be well placed to be the first to hear about it. The day when we have disappeared, the permanent secretary of your illustrious group will open the envelope in which all is explained and you will be the first to agree that there was no wizardry."

— "Yes, I understand", said Bala who looked at me sharply and simply added: "All the same, don't let us wait too long."

Corals are strictly carnivorous. They can content themselves with micro-plankton (zoo-plankton), but certain species are perfectly capable of eating prey of considerable size in relation to their own size. It is a great godsend for them when a fish, dumbfounded at having been disturbed during its sleep, stumbles into their tentacles which grasp him immediately. *Carnaval sous de mer* has already shown two remarkable illustrations of such captures so I will restrict myself here to referring to a shrimp, *Hymenocera elegans*, which was caught during the night and whose body is already in the mouth of a *Trachyphyllia jeoffroyi* (**14**). If you look at it in the chapter on crustacea (**66**) and note how beautiful it is you will realize what a piteous state this coral put it in in a few hours. But these feasts remain accidental incidents.

But the corals are also victims of predators of which the most ferocious is the abominable *Acanthaster planci* (Echinoderms **1**). The incredible spread of this large starfish has caused immense damage in certain regions of the Pacific. Magnificent reefs have thus been destroyed by this voracious echinoderm.

Outside of this predator which is capable of destroying entire reefs, there exist a few organisms capable of penetrating the most compact skeleton of the corals without, however, putting their life in danger. Like some of the sea-worms which hollow out their galleries from which only their superb variegations of their multicoloured branchiae show. For example, the multitude of *Spirobranchus giganteus* installed

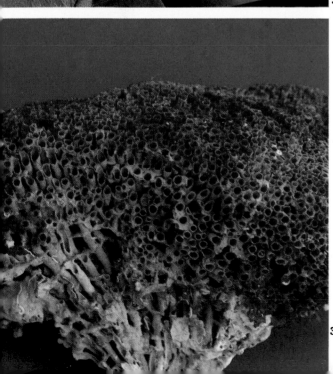

36 A soft-coral, *Siphonogorgia squarrosa*, found at a depth of 20 meters.

37 Fluorescence of an endemic plant of the primitive forest (*Tapeinosperma*).

38 Skeleton of the octo-coral *Tubipora musica* looking like organ-pipes.

39 Octocoral *Cavernularia sp.* with its fine polyps completely extended.

40 The same specimen, carefully removed from the sand and all curled up.

41 The same again, having taken its foot out from the sand to move position (the polyps remain open).

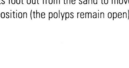

42 The coral *Polyphyllia talpina* so named, perhaps because of the muzzle-like form (talpa = mole) of the long, central protuberance.

43 The coral *Fungia actiniformis* whose long tentacles resemble those of certain sea-anemones.

42

43

forever in a large coral of the family of the *Poritidae* (**15**). Another example of the parasitism of corals is given by the barnacles (Cirripede Crustacea) that photograph **16** shows us a coral of the family of the Mussidae encrusted in a *Symphillia*. I must also mention the damage affecting some isolated corals such as the *Turbinaria* (Molluscs **9, 10, 11**), that are much sought after by small nudibranches of the family of Eolidae which also feast on the polyps of the *Goniopora* (**19**).

One cannot ignore the appetite that our parrot-fish show for the tips of coral branches which their powerful teeth break clear to crunch and, in all probability, to absorb the zooxanthelles micro-algae with which the polyps of these corals are crammed. In the sea that doesn't have much importance because these fish only break a small number of branches on a coral and then pass to another. But in an aquarium like ours, no matter how big our tanks, these fish break the tips of all the branched corals and provide us with a task we could well do without since we have to frequently replace them. Fortunately the corals are very common species and the task of replacement is worth it because, among other attributes, these parrot-fish have such sumptuous colours.

In certain years we have also noticed a curious disease attacking the polyps of corals, in particular among the *Seriatopora* and the *Pocillopora*. In a colony of about 100 polyps several dozens of them, sometimes half, show a very characteristic paling. At the same time these polyps are afflicted by an obvious sickness which is detected by an extreme slowness of retraction when touched with a fine point. It is possible that this deficiency can be attributed to a loss of *zooxanthelles* and that there is, therefore, insufficient photosynthesis. But if this were the explanation, one would wonder why certain polyps of the same colony are deficient while others, quite close, are not. The same phenomenon of "indisposition" of a certain number of polyps is also noticed in many neighboring colonies, and without any obvious pollution being detected in the area observed. There, again, is a very interesting research topic for anyone who would like to study the pathology of these corals.

As well as serious damage done by the abominable *Acanthaster*, after the wounds inflicted on corals by man in certain regions (cf. chapter on Damage) and those which were the result of an oil spill, there is the terrible damage done by typhoons.

Blind providence kills many billions of marine organisms which, in a few hours, disappear forever. Thus it is ruin and devastation down to 20 meters and sometimes more, due solely to the force of the typhoon's enormous waves. The ravages are without comparison to those that the same typhoon can make on land. (I have personally seen violent typhoons in Madagascar followed by such strong and brutal flooding that rivers, such as the Faraony, rose 24 meters in 15 hours!) At the time of typhoon "Colin", which raged in January 1969 in New Caledonia, the under-sea devastation was total in the outer, most exposed marine areas. And I think in particular of the example of a region close to the barrier-reef where life had reached the greatest intensity and beauty. The harmonious array of corals, of which many multicolored species had overlapped on each other, presented a real fairytale spectacle. A precise memory of this strange kaleidoscope was made more difficult because of the unceasing movements of the living fauna creating a different arrangement at each instant. The multiple shades of the fixed and mobile organisms were bathed in steely-blue, varying with the depth and degree of light. It wasn't only the hue but also the shimmering effects of the light: all the mobility of this environment made it vibrant; wind ripples on the surface above made glistening lines across the bottom which constantly streaked the corals, rocks and algae, lighting up the bronze or silver sides of the wandering fish, and reflecting rainbows on the iridescent domes of the pulsating, translucent jelly-fish. The exceptional visibility, stretching out to the luminous fuzziness of the horizon and the shimmering lights caused by the surface ripples, added to the perpetual activity of all these elements, creating an astonishingly subtle atmosphere. If we looked up towards the surface a few meters it appeared to us like a mackerel sky and the waves which stirred it created a misty quivering. It was a little like the vibrations of air layers on overheated ground.

In this harmony of patterns of light, of forms and of colors in the middle of this fairyland setting, where many optical subtleties combine, we experienced the total satisfaction of aesthetic perfection.

And, it is this "*luogo d'incante*" that 12 hours of typhoon demolished from top to bottom to depths of 30 meters. Some divers who had regularly explored these regions, and who had to wait for the water to clear of suspended rubbish, came back aghast. The rocky plateau which, over the course of many decades, had been the support of a prodigious accumulation of organisms, was literally bare. "Like tiling", they were saying, and all life had disappeared from it.

Certainly nature, in its power of restoration, can slowly develop new biotopes, but it needs several decades for such a world of animal associations to be fully re-established. Here we show a certain number of pictures of organisms which lived in the tanks of our aquarium and which recall, for us, the memory of so many underwater wonders of those glorious sea-beds.

Let us admire those colonial Hexacorals of *Dendrophyllia* and *Tubastraea* (**67**) whose tentacles only open out at night. The same goes for *Cyranina lacrymalis*. Photograph **45** shows its retracted tentacles during the day and photograph **46**, its extension during the night. This last illustration allows us to see in the cloaca centre, an opening serving at the same time as both mouth and anus. In **47** we see another specimen of the same species. The extreme thinness of the bodies allows us to see the calcareous septa of the skeleton through them when they are full of water.

The book *Carnaval sous la mer* dedicated such a large number of superb color plates to the effects of fluorescence that I will now limit myself to showing only the effects of fluorescence of *Cynarina* (**48**) and those of another beautiful coral, *Merulina ampliata*. Photograph **51** shows it in the light of day and **52** in fluorescence under ultra-violet while photograph **53** shows some of these calices also in fluorescence and close-up.

These examples show that corals endowed with fluorescent abilities under ultra-violet irradiation don't only offer — as has been believed by certain authors who have never seen fluorescent corals alive — "a little more sparkle to the colors than in natural light", but many colors that are completely new and unexpected. Because of our vast experience, we know this

44 A deep-water *Cerianthus sp.* with very long, stinging tentacles. Bad luck for the fish which inadvertently brushes them.

45 A solitary *Cynarina lacrymalis* coral, retracted in the daylight hours.

46 The same specimen with its tentacles opened out at night.

47 Another *Cynarina* in the light of day. Thanks to the extreme thinness of the flesh, transparency shows the calcareous pieces (septa) of the skeleton.

48 The same individual fluorescing under ultra-violet rays.

45 and 46

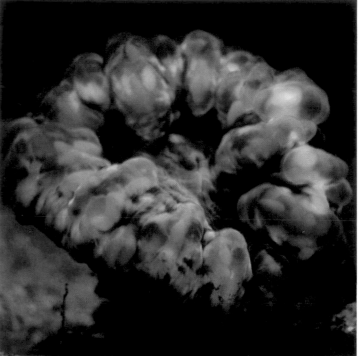

47 and 48

49 and 50

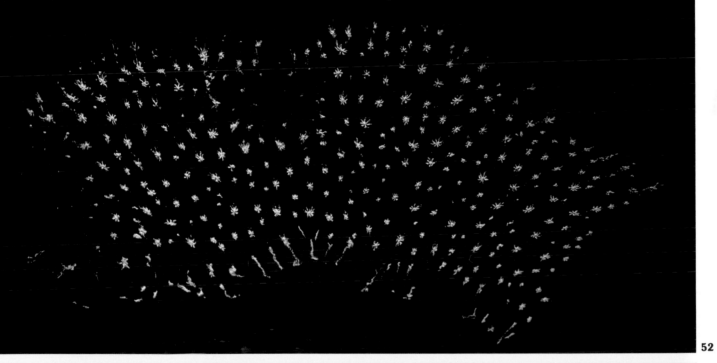

49 *Parascolymia vitiensis* in the light of day (found at 35 meters).

50 The same coral fluorescing under ultra-violet rays. These were new and quite unexpected colors.

51 A *Merulina ampliata* coral in daylight.

52 The same one fluorescing. Its intensity cannot be reproduced in print.

53 Close-ups of a few calices.

51

52

53

54

55

56

better than anyone.

The coral represented in **42** is *Polyphyllia talpina*. Other specimens do not have this central prominence in the form of a proboscis and have been identified by experts as belonging to the same species. But it is probable that the first specimen, examined in 1816 by Lamarck, must have had the same prominence for him to have given it the name *talpina*, since this protrusion would have looked like the snout of a mole (*Talpa* or *Talpina*). The specimen represented here lived more than ten years at the Aquarium. It was one of the numerous examples of those corals whose very fine bodies are tightly filled with water on certain days and on others scarcely filled and flaccid.

Another member of this large family of Fungiidae is the *Fungia* in picture **43**. It is a solitary coral and is, in fact, only one giant polyp. One notices its numerous tentacles in full extension. These are sometimes so elongated that they give this coral the look of a sea-anemone. Many people who are not experts on corals, but are nevertheless familiar with marine invertebrates, have been mistaken about them and found themselves quite surprised that the organism they had taken for a sea-anemone had such a weight. Their scientific name is, furthermore, *Fungia actiniformis* (*Actin* = anemone, *formis* = similar to). The skeleton of these corals is always quite heavy for their size. These *Fungia* owe their name to the resemblance of their calcareous gills to the radial gills of certain fungal mushrooms. As I have mentioned before, the young *Fungia* are attached to rocks by a peduncle of a few centimeters. With growth, it snaps off by the simple increase of weight of the calcareous mass. The coral then falls on the bottom where it leads a free life and, among certain species, is even capable of movement.

In regard to the fluorescence of corals, my wife and I had had our suspicions for more than ten years before our Aquarium of Noumea, with its special installations, gave us the proof (and how brilliant it was!). One of the first deep-growing corals that we saw reacting to the irradiations of a Wood's lamp has already been shown in fluorescence in the *Carnaval sous la mer* (pl. III, fig. 4). Here I give another illustration of it, but in daylight only (**68**). In the above-mentioned book I called this coral *Euphyllia*

54 *Alicia sp.* as it is during the day. (Here it has temporarily fixed itself on the encrusting sponge *Cliona schmidti*).

55 The same organism during the night, with its column totally extended and tentacles bending in the direction of the current.

56 The tentacles capture some micro-plankton (larvae of *Artemia* shrimps). Spiral movement.

57 The basal disc is attached to the glass pane of the tank. Notice the translucence of the foot and the column.

58 A deep-water Zoantharian (not identified), close relation of the *Alicia*. Average diameter of half a meter.

59 The same one in the first hours of night. The column can reach a height of 45 centimeters and the whole animal can sting dangerously.

58 an

60 *Antipathes sp.* found at a depth of 35 meters. The only specimen in 20 years, it measured close to one meter high.

61 *Cirrhipathes sp.* (commonly called "wire gorgonia"). The polyps of this octo-coral are too small to be easily visible from this distance.

62 *Antipathes spiralis* (partial view), polyps in semi-expansion. The fish *Forcipiger longirostris* gives us an idea of the size.

60

61

62

picteti Bedot, but in this book it carries the name of *Catalaphyllia plicata* Wells. Although such name changes are normal for specialists, they often seem most peculiar to the general public. A brief account is therefore essential to show again how arduous the identification of certain organisms can be.

In the communication presented at the Academy of Sciences[10] and also sent to *Nature*[11] to record the date of the discovery of the fluorescence of corals, we had given the generic name of *Flabellum* to this coral. At that time many authors, such as Gardiner[12] in 1905 and Yonge[13] in 1930, had used that name. Initially I thought it might be *Pectinia jardinei* Saville-Kent (1893) because of the resemblance to a water-color in his famous book[14] which today is out of print, and which I had the chance of acquiring in a sale in Australia. But in a 1955 publication, John W. Wells[15] of Cornell University (U.S.A.) called it *Euphyllia picteti*. I am quite certain that all the other coral specialists in the world have followed his immense scholarship. He identified almost all the coral skeletons from the Aquarium, and it was one of these fluorescent corals that did not always seem to agree with the original description that was the most intriguing. So intriguing that he decided, in September 1970, to come and stay with us. We were overjoyed to receive him because, in addition to the scholarship of this very great man, he has quite charming simplicity. On the eve of his departure, he asked us if we had any *Euphyllia picteti* skeletons to entrust to him because he wanted to make a closer study of this coral now that he had seen several living specimens. Several months later he completed a revision of that order of Scleractinia which led him to create a new genus which, very elegantly, he dedicated to me..." in small recognition of his contributions to the study of the tropical marine

10   Catala, R. Comptes rendus de l'Académie des Sciences. Paris. vol. 247, November 10, 1958.
11   Catala, R. *Fluorescent effects from coral irradiated with ultra-violet rays*. *Nature*, London, vol 183, p. 949, April 4, 1959.
12   Gardiner. *Fauna and Geography*. Maldive and Laccadive Archipelago, vol 2, p. 954 pl. 63 fig. 28–29.
13   Yonge, CM. *A Year on the Great Barrier Reef*. Putnam, London, New York, 1930, p. 132, pl. 39.
14   Saville-Kent, W. *The Great Barrier Reef of Australia*, W.H. Allen and Co., London, 1893.
15   Wells, J.W. *Report of the Great Barrier Reef Committee*, vol. 6, p. 26.

63 *Dofleina armata.* We took advantage of this sea-anemone going under the sand to put down a few black stones so as to obtain a better color contrast. See the emission of sperm.

64 The same anemone with its foot deeply fixed on the rocky subsoil. Only the tentacles emerge, and these are often confused with the sand.

63

64

fauna, the new genus is named in honour of Dr. Catala". In this publication he states that this genus *Catalaphyllia* embodies two species, *C. plicata*, represented here, and *C. fimbriata*[16], this last one being described by Matthai in 1928 and whose skeleton exists in the Paris Museum.

In another publication Professor Wells[17] wrote: "Grave difficulties have arisen in absorbing the remaining genera in the colonial forms, and evidence has accumulated that several of these should be recognized as valid genera. The present paper, stimulated particularly by the study of a number of solitary mussids from New Caledonia sent by Dr. R. Catala of Noumea, to whom the writer expresses his appreciation, is an attempt to rectify some of these errors of judgements."

It is in this publication that the splendid coral *Parascolymia vitiensis*, which formerly appeared on the dust-jacket of *Carnaval sous mer*, was studied and I repeat it to show the difference in coloring between the same organism seen in the daylight (**49**) and in fluorescence under ultra-violet (**50**).

It is logical that we have illustrated this book with the most remarkable octocorals to have lived at the Aquarium. In the "theatre of gorgonia" (**65**) these magnificent animal colonies shelter a whole world of other organisms which are described in other chapters in this book. One can admire the thin branches of the beautiful soft coral *Spongodes merleti* (**18**) and another representative of the class of Anthozoa, the *Alcyonium catalai*. This octocoral resembles the *Corallium rubrum* (red coral of the jewellers) of the Mediterranean and it doesn't begin to open out its polyps until late evening. It is satisfying to be able to show the progression of this opening out (**20** to **24**). Specialists will be interested by photograph **20** which shows a few air bubbles in the interior of a polyp: I haven't found any explanation for the presence of these bubbles. Contrary to hard corals, octocorals do not have a skeleton and multiple small calcareous bodies,

16   Matthai, G. *A monograph of the recent meandroid Astreidae*. Catalogue of Madreporian Corals. British Museum (Natural History). Vol. 8, 288 pp., 72 pl.

17   Wells, J. W. *The Recent Solitary Mussid Scleractinians Corals*. Zoologishe Medeingen. Deel XXIX Uitgever voor Het Rijkmuseum, Leiden, Holland, 1964.

60

65

the spicules, form the support framework for their tissues. As in the case of sponges, it is the form of these microscopic spicules that allows the specialist to classify these soft corals. Mme. Tixier, of the Museum of Natural History of Paris, who identified the soft corals of the Aquarium and who kindly dedicated one of them to me, told me that the actual color wasn't significant in the classification of these organisms. That is why the *Alcyonium catalai* (**24**) and the one represented in **27** are both the same species, despite such different shades on their trunks. Another soft coral that this expert dedicated to my wife is also quite rare; *Sterecanthia stuckiae* (**25**) has the special characteristic, which is not usual in this group of organisms, of reacting to ultra violet-rays by producing fluorescence of great intensity (**26**). The soft coral *Solenopodium steckei* has also been reported to show superb fluorescence.[18]

It would not occur to anyone, especially someone not acquainted with systematics, to doubt an identification made by a great expert like Mme. Tixier, and this is supported by the following fact: some years ago a very beautiful species of soft coral was brought to the Aquarium for the first time; it had been found between 20 and 25 meters, and covered quite a vast area with remarkable density. I show two specimens here, one pink and one white (number **33**). As this was the first time in 20 years of diving that we had seen this soft coral, we thought that it was perhaps an unknown species, or, in any case, not known in the New Caledonian region. To our great

surprise the expert who had determined the new species of *Spongodes*, formerly dedicated by her to Doctor Merlet, gave us the same identification for our new soft coral. Instead of the streamlined look of the early *merleti*, our specimens are in the form of balls. I have tried to show the two types next to one another under the numbers **32** and **33**. Another illustration can be seen in number **18**, but better still in *Carnaval sous la mer* (Pl. XVI, fig. 1). These different illustrations clearly show the different shapes of these two types of soft corals. It is important to add that both do not react to light in the same manner, nor at the same hours, the slender *Spongodes merleti* retracting in full daylight. They are generally quite scattered and often very distant from each other, but the ball-shaped ones are found in great numbers and, as I have already said, in thick density. This is a good example of the contradiction between taxonomy and behavior.

We also show a close-up of the polyps of a specimen that we only found once at 30 meters (**29**) and have not yet identified.

Certain species of soft corals have their polyps fully opened out during the day and others during the night only. But, whether diurnal or nocturnal, their sensitivity to vibrations and to touch is about the same. As soon as a foreign body disturbs the polyps, they retract immediately, followed by all the others in succession, and do not open out again for 20 minutes or perhaps more than an hour. The young soft corals of the genus *Sarcophyton*, shown in photograph **34**, resemble little mushrooms because they have just retracted after a passing fish brushed them. Very close by another specimen of the same species is totally extended, untroubled by external brushing.

And I should point out to the experts that certain soft corals demonstrate quite an astonishing ability to move about, advancing even more slowly than the movement we observed among anemones. One of these migrations was carried out on the glass pane of a tank and this wanderer moved about 40 centimeters in around five months.

66

18 Catala, R. *Carnaval Sous la mer.* Pl. V, fig. 1 and 2.

65 A glorious array of deep-water gorgonians and antipatharians reconstructed in a large tank at the Aquarium.

66 *Stylaster* (red on a blue background).

67 *Tubastraea* corals (on the left) and *Dendrophyllia* with their polyps in full nocturnal extension.

68 *Catalaphyllia plicata* in daylight. The thick flesh of this coral makes super fluorescence appear under ultra-violet rays. (Refer to *Carnaval sous la mer,* pl. XIII).

69

72

70

71

69 A *Nemanthus (?)* sea-anemone which is quite common between 22–30 meters at "Fosse aux canards" in New Caledonia.

70 A sea-anemone (unidentified) with a very large column. Doesn't seem very common. Depth = 10 meters.

71 A pimply sea-anemone (*Actinodiscus?*), found at a depth of 35 meters at Banc Gail.

72 An unidentified sea-anemone. It is a swimmer and moves with the aid of its tentacles vigorously beating the water.

Another observation may be of interest to experts on soft corals: on several occasions we noticed that some specimens whose base had been damaged at the time of their collecting produced expansions during the ensuing months in the Aquarium to give themselves better mooring. Photograph **35** of a Nephtidae gives a good idea of this curious phenomenon and shows half-a-dozen of these extra expansions. (No wonder that the visitor who thought that these animal colonies were plants, said to us: "You see, they are growing roots!")

Finally, let me point out the ability of certain soft corals to fix themselves to rock supports when their growth spreads out in layers. They are like buds or tiny petals and sometimes there are chance resemblances which are most amusing! One day, in 1961, Yves Merlet was on an exploration outing on the outer edge of the large reef and brought up a superb soft coral from 20 meters which we have never seen since. It is, however, known from another region of the Pacific and was identified by Mme. Tixier as *Siphonogorgia squarrosa* (**36**).

The same evening, my wife returned from one of her Sunday excursions in the primitive forest — a happy time when she still had the leisure to escape for a few hours to take photographs of native flowers. Seeing this soft coral in one of the laboratory tanks, she said, laughing: "Look, I found the same one in the forest!" [*Tapeinosperma*, family of Myrsinacidae[19] (**37**)]. An amusing coincidence.

Having mentioned the movements of certain soft corals, I show three illustrations of a

19   Identification Dr. McKeen.

73 Serpules. These are sedentary tubeworms bearing no relation to coelenterates, but their long tentacles are often confused by amateurs with small sea-anemones. Note the extreme fineness of the pinnules on the tentacles.

74 An unidentified sea-anemone which is a swimming species. Being very fragile its tentacles (which look like the tendrils of nudibranchs) detach easily.

73

74

65

75

76

77

75 A *Physobrachia sp.* sea-anemone with a couple of *Amphiprion* symbiotic fish.

76 A unidentified sea-anemone which is a dangerous stinging species.

77 A *Stoichactis* sea-anemone. Its basal-disc is attached to the glass panel. Totally stretched out its diameter measures half a meter.

Cavernularia because of its strange behavior. This organism lives in the muddy-sandy sea floor from which only the upper half protrudes, carrying multiple and remarkably thin polyps (**39**). Not to bruise the fragile tissues of this animal, the diver must gently dig around the foot and slide his hand under. On its arrival in the Aquarium, this beautiful *Cavernularia* was in sorry shape. To see this poor thing in its flabby state (**40**), the public could never imagine that it would soon re-establish its full vigor and be crowned with a glory of polyps. Sometimes — and we have never understood the reason for this — the animal takes its foot out from the ground and, remaining turgid, penetrates the sand again some distance away (**41**). The white-greyish polyps of *Tubipora musica* hide the interesting structure of the internal skeleton. Photograph **38** shows the parallel tubes on one side, which justify the name of the genus (*Tubipora*) and, on the other side their particular arrangement like organ-pipes which gives it its specific name (*musica*).

Among the very beautiful creatures of the world of coelenterates there are the Cerianthids (**44**), living in soft tubes from which they extend their long tentacles at certain hours in an elegant spray giving these organisms the look of luminous fountains. But woe betide the fish which accidentally contacts these filaments. The toxicity of their nematocysts is relentless.

I will finally show a typical photograph of the *Umbellulifera striata* (**28**) which was only sketched in *Carnaval sous la mer*. The two illustrations complement one another so much better than the simple text of *Carnaval* (p. 51-53) which reported the curious reproduction method of this beautiful soft coral.

Most anemones are little known or not known at all. And that is not surprising since, in contrast to their quite superb shapes while alive, once placed in liquid preservative they become shabby little things looking stunted and relatively discolored. Photographs **69** to **77** show specimens which all come from depths of 20 to 40 meters. In the Aquarium most of them thrive well, sometimes even too well, dividing frequently and encroaching on the more fragile neighboring organisms. The anemone *Physobrachia* (**75**) often shelters those very pretty fish, *Amphiprion,* which are very popular with aquarists. The superb *Dofleina armata* (**64**) is a remarkable anemone whose foot disc is attached under the sand. It

78 *Cassiopeia sp.* One of the most graceful jellyfish with a high frequency of propulsion beats.

79 *Thysanostoma sp.* Exceptionally long tentacles (80 centimeters). Only one specimen of it in the Aquarium in 20 years.

80 *Rhizostoma sp.* These enormous jellyfish often shelter a complete shoal of trevally which swim between the thick, stinging tentacles. (Also see Fish, 73 to 77).

78

79

80

withdraws entirely at will, especially when its dangerous stinging tentacles have been able to seize prey. Against the sand background this *Dofleina* loses much of the beauty of its flesh coloration so the photographer had to resort to a little stratagem to get better contrast. Having made the animal retract by gently touching it with a stick, he set out a few black stones on the periphery of its little hollow (**63**). When the anemone regained surface its tentacles were forced to spread out over this dark background. The little cloud that one notices is an emission of sexual products. It recurs at frequent intervals during more than an hour and, if the water is perfectly calm, this generous emission makes the water quite milky.

Another anemone, which we cannot identify, has a particularly dangerous sting. It is the one represented by number **76** in this chapter.

In *Carnaval sous la mer*, figure 3 of plate 1 shows a coral against which a fish had swum after being dazzled by the beam of an eletric torch. The same type of accident happens at night when one of the natural night-prowlers like the crabs, rock lobsters and other crustaceans, abruptly wakes a fish which stumbles onto such anemones while blindly saving itself. It is immediately struck down by the toxins of the nematocysts and will be digested in a few hours. But when these stinging organisms don't accidently find prey of this size they feed on plankton. The best example of the anemone's stinging, plankton-catching, net was provided for us by an organism of exceptional beauty which, after years of searching, we eventually recorded on film. Let me tell you how.

After the war, the Americans and Australians offered me a splendid ketch, the famous "*Evaleeta*," for the use of the Oceania French Institute I had just created. So I accepted — why not? One day, in 1947, we decided to clean its hull of the thick encrustation: long thin algae, minute bryozoa, hydrozooids and little gorgonians, sheets of small corals, sponge felting and many other fouling organisms in such abundance that one couldn't find a square centimeter without occupants. In amongst this mass of fixed organisms, hundreds of small animals were crawling: shrimps, spider-crabs, crabs, copepods and mantis shrimps; and also strange and beautiful sea slugs. Among the echinoderms were small sea-urchins, brittle stars, starfish and many other organisms including the teredo (so famous sadly because they bore into the hardest of boat timbers).

Amongst all of this marine life we carefully detached a small gelatinous mass (54) which we couldn't identify. By chance we placed it on the bottom of a small vitreous tank under our veranda, and morning and evening we supplied it with a bucket of fresh sea-water — the Aquarium of Noumea didn't exist then. One night we were surprised to see that this formless "thing" had become the most blossoming coelenterate one could imagine. It was identified by that great Swedish specialist of invertebrates, Professor O. Calgren, as the rare *Alicia* (57). This *Alicia* retracted in daylight but, once night came, expanded into a high translucent column and on its wall several types of budding of the prettiest effect appeared. This column was crowned with very long filamentous tentacles falling elegantly to its base. It was an object of great beauty. But as soon as light was projected on the tank the tentacles would first retract into the column which, in turn, would further retract until it became just the small gelatinous mass that we had detached from the boat.

After the Aquarium was fully functioning I do not know how many boat hulls we inspected; some in the open waters, others pulled to shore still dripping. We had begged The Nickel Company to warn us each time boats were pulled up on the careening slipways and we were especially interested in boats that had stayed at sea for a long time or had been outside of our territorial waters. On these occasions the cooperative official in charge would alert us. Certainly, not remembering the ode to Sestius, he did not cry "*trahuntque siccas machinae carinas*" of Horace, but instead called into his telephone: "Come quickly with your helpers, we have already begun to scrape off all that confounded rubbish!" Then, with our scrapers, knives, tweezers, jars and other containers, formalin, alcohol and not forgetting thick rubber gloves, we would set off hoping that the cleaners wouldn't do their jobs too rapidly because this "confounded rubbish" was always hiding many treasures... but never an *Alicia*. So we thought that the rare specimen from the schooner "*Evaleeta*" must have come from the warmer waters of the New Hebrides, since she had called there for several days.

Twenty years passed and we hadn't thought any more of the *Alicia*. Then, one day in July 1967, a team of young divers who had collected in some extremely rich zones, came back with a beautiful collection of alcyonarians, deep-water corals and also algae. On one of these I noticed, completely by chance, a few minute gelatinous objects. They were so small — the size of a small pea — and so retracted also that I didn't dare rejoice too early. Night came and I recognized very young individuals of this famous *Alicia* as they opened out. One of them doubled in size after a month's growth in the laboratory because I had taken care to feed it several times a night with the larvae of *Artemia* shrimps. I waited with patience for this remarkably translucent creature to be photographed to best effect. Photograph **55** shows the "hair to the wind", tentacles ready to seize any planktonic organisms passing within their reach. After pouring a quantity of *Artemia* larvae into the water, photograph **56** records beautifully the spinning movement of all the tentacles entwining them and carrying them in turn to the mouth in the centre of the crown.

Photograph **57** shows an *Alicia* whose foot disc is pressed like a suction cap to the glass of the tank which can move by very slow advances in the manner of many anemones. But we sometimes observed a method of moving that was quite peculiar and rapid. The fully stretched column of the *Alicia* curves over to grip the bottom with all its tentacles and then the suction-cap comes unstuck and the tentacles suddenly contract to make the foot loop over close to them. This action reminds one of looping caterpillars.

Many years afterwards, a diver brought up from 25 meters a disk-shaped organism the size of a large plate and perhaps of a close genus of the *Alicia*. In fact, for some time it remained as a fleshy mass of a general dark color scattered with pinks, bottle-greens and grays. It was installed by chance in the magnificent jumble of the famous tank called "The Sponges" and we only removed it just in time because it was very dangerous for the person cleaning that tank. The slightest contact causes a dermatitis of the worst kind lasting about a week. Conditions for photography were too bad to take better pictures of this organism (**58-59**).

Among other soft coelenterates in the order of the Zoanthidia, we find the genus *Palythoa*(**31**) which always present themselves as a carpet of

81 *Velella sp.* There are certain years when they are blown ashore in the millions by the wind.

82 *Velella sp.* The thin vertical blade of a cartilaginous appearance acts as a small sail or *velella*.

83 *Velella sp.* An amusing resemblance to flying saucers.

84 *Velella sp.* Three jellyfish held together by surface tension.

81

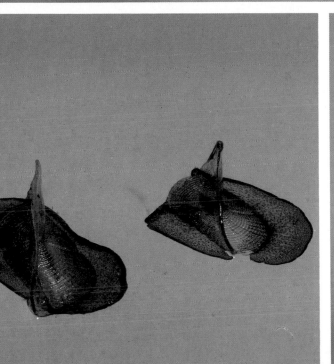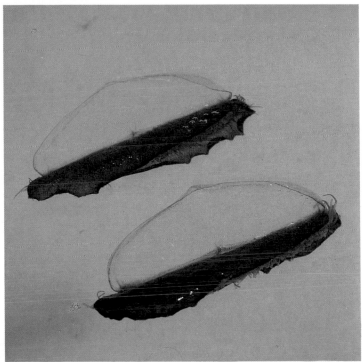

82 and 83

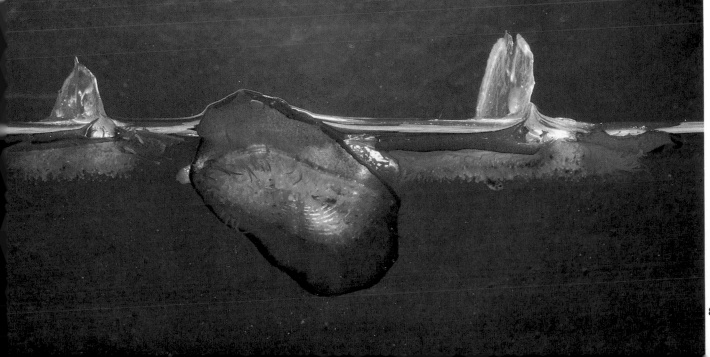

84

close-packed individuals. Certain species are met at depths of 35 to 40 meters, others in shallow water where they sometimes form such thick populations in very calm zones that the ecologist talks about "Zoanthid zone".[20] During the whole time that these *Palythoa* are uncovered at low tide, their tentacles are totally retracted and the graceful crowns are mere stumps. With the next flood tide they soon regain their slender elegance as photograph **31** shows. These *Palythoa* feed on micro-plankton and one cannot help but notice their amusing resemblance to the carnivorous plants *Drosera* and *Diona*.

In the chapter on crustacea, we write about camouflaging of the spider-crabs *Maia*, and show that sometimes they make use of *Palythoa* to cover themselves completely. Such crustacea disappear entirely under these living costumes which open out or retract their tentacles at the same hours of the day and night (Crustacea, **24**).

The zoanthids also include Antipatheria whose general appearance resembles certain gorgonians. With their horny skeleton and their extremely slender polyps, some are abundantly branched, like the colony already photographed in picture 18 of *Carnaval sous la mer*. Others look

---

20   Catala, R. *Contribution à l'étude écologique des îlots coralliens du Pacifique Sud*. Bulletin Biologique de la France et de la Belgique. Vol. LXXXIV. Paris, 1950.

85

86

87

88

89

85 *Physalia physalis* showing the pneumataphore, a small sustenance balloon filled with air, and tentacles (fishing filaments). (Photo: F.G. Myers).

86 *Physalia physalis*. A detail of the tentacles which are extremely toxic, even for man. (Photo: F.G. Myers).

87 *Physalia physalis*. Micro-photo (× 200) of the cnidoblasts (nematocysts). One cell is empty of its cnidocyst. (Photo: Keith Gillet).

88 A jellyfish of the *Tamoya* genus which is a delicacy for inhabitants of the Gilbert Islands on the Pacific equator.

89 Drying the edible part (*manubrium*) of these jellyfish in the sun.

70

like large feather dusters (**60**) but the most curious are undoubtedly the *Antipathes spiralis* and the *Cirrhipathes sp.* (commonly called "wire gorgonia"), represented by numbers **61** and **62**. Like most of the group these "spiral springs" are found at depths varying between 25 and 60 meters.

The class of Scyphozoa includes all the jellyfish. For those who haven't seen any except those stranded on the beach, these little heaps of protoplasm don't appear to have any attraction. But, living and intact, what is more graceful than these pulsating, translucent, animated umbrellas? Examples are *Cassiopeia* (**78**) with short tentacles or the *Thysanostoma* (**79**) which amazes us not only because of the uncommon length of its tentacles but also because of their thickness which gives them the look of large woollen plaits. Certain species are known to be deadly killers. This is the case of a Cubomedusae of the genus *Chironex*. Another jellyfish that is almost as dangerous is the *Physalia physalis*, commonly called "Portuguese Man-o'-War". It can float on the surface of the water thanks to an air-filled bladder (the *pneumatophore*) which supports a

large number of fishing threads able to reach several meters in length. This floating, transparent and iridescent balloon is an extremely pretty thing with its violet filaments which wind and unwind. But, to touch, what horror! Contact with the filaments brings terrible pain and nearly all those who have spent years of research in the sea have accidentally experienced this ordeal. Authors agree that the toxicity of these *Physalia* has even caused human deaths. Fish that have suffered the misfortune of coming into contact with this network of filaments never escape. We have seen several examples of this, both at sea and at the Aquarium.

Not being satisfied with the photographs that I had taken of this particular jellyfish, I called on my colleagues and friends at the Australian Museum, Keith Gillet and F. G. Myers, who kindly obtained the three negatives reproduced here. The first (**85**) shows us an entire specimen, its pneumatophore filled with air and trailing long tentacles. The second (**86**) is a close-up of its prehensile filaments. The third (**87**) allows us to see the cnidoblasts magnified 200 times. This shows the cnidocyst (nematocyst) coiling up in the

interior of the round capsules. One of the capsules is empty as its nematocyst has already been ejected.

During some seasons of the year another floating sinophonophore is sometimes seen in countless numbers; this is the "By the Wind Sailor", *Velella* (**81** and **82**) whose float is flatter than *Physalia* and surmounted by a small translucent crest acting as a sail (from which its name comes). In certain years these cover the sea surface in millions. If a storm blows up they become stranded on the beaches. These little translucent bluish beings, of some five to six centimeters in diameter, are very elegant and I have always regretted not having found the time when they were so abundant to film these fleets of little "boats". Some of the photographs look like two flying saucers (**83**) while others look like a large bomber, due to the fact that the surface tension of the water has brought three little boats side by side.

Having dealt with the beauty and peculiarities of jellyfish, as well as their terrible stings, I must now say something about the edible qualities of one eaten in the Gilbert Islands.[21] They call it *Te Baïtari* and it belongs to the genus *Tamoya* of the family Carybdeidae. Each month, seven days before the full moon, the receding high tides leave some of these edible jellyfish on the reef. In fact, it is only the internal part (*manubrium*) which is eaten. The natives prepare them by scraping the gelatinous exteriors with a knife (**88**). What remains is hung out on string suspended between two coconut palms or stakes (**89**). This dries in the sun for two or three days and, after this very simple operation, the little strips have a consistency of tripe or large tripe sausages. They are cooked on sunken ovens above very hot pebbles until crisp.

21   Refer to Catala R. *Etude sur l'économie des Iles Gilbert, Mission pour la Commission du Pacifique Sud* (project E6), National Academy of Sciences, National Research Council, Washington D.C., 1957.

Branches of Coelenterates or Cnidaria

The main characteristics of these invertebrates are: **a)** organisms consisting of tissue which is not constituted into organs (L.H. Hyman); **b)** Either the fixed or polyp type or the mobile or medusa type; **c)** Tentacles equipped with stinging cells (cnidoblasts or nematocysts) which can be mortally toxic to man (Cubomedusa, Physalia); **d)** Polyps with six tentacles (or multiples of six) e.g. the Hexacorals (corals), polyps with eight tentacles (or multiples of eight) e.g. the Octocorals (gorgonians)

Principal divisions

Class	Order	Type		
Hydrozoa	Hydroïdia Milleporia Stylasteria Siphonophoria	Plumularia sp. Millepora sp. Stylaster sp. Velella sp. Physalia sp.	no 18 page 172 no 30 page 46 no 66 page 62 no 81 page 69 no 85 page 70	
Scyphozoa	Acalephes	Rhizostoma sp.	no 80 page 67	
Anthozoa	Alcyonairia Stolonifera Gorgonacia Pennatulacia Cerianthairia	Alcyonium catalai Tubipora musica Melithaea ocracea Cavernularia sp. Cerianthus sp.	no 24 page 43 no 38 page 49 no 34 page 179 no 39 page 49 no 44 page 53	
Sub-class Zoanthairia	Actiniairia Zoanthidia Antipthairia (Madrepora or "true" corals)	Physobrachia sp. Dofleina armata Actinaria sp. Palythoa sp. Cirrhipathes spiralis Antipathes sp. Acropora formosa Alveopora catali Catalaphyllia plicata Cynarina lacrymalis Merulina ampliata Polyphyllia talpina Trachyphyllia jeoffroyi	no 75 page 66 no 63 page 59 no 76 page 66 no 31 page 46 no 61 page 58 no 60 page 58 no 8 page 39 no 2 page 35 no 68 page 63 no 47 page 54 no 51 page 55 no 42 page 50 no 5 page 37	

Mollusks

Although this chapter is limited to a single group, the marine mollusks, we are confronted with an astonishing array of sea creatures with a seemingly never-ending variety of shapes, colors and ways of life. Imagine then the surprise of the uninitiated faced with such a diversity of creatures all belonging to the same phylum!

Some mollusks likely to be encountered are:
— Chitons, with their overlapping plates which attach to rocks in the intertidal zone ...
— Giant clam shells, more than a meter in length, which are often used in the Pacific Islands as holy water fonts for christening babies ...
— Multicolored sea slugs with no shell at all, slowly browsing on rocks, sponges or coral ...
— Gastropods, including the venomous cone shells and the giant baler shells more than 40 cm long ...
— Bivalves of all shapes and sizes; some, like mussels, are firmly attached to the substrate while others, such as scallops, are capable of swimming rapidly through the water ...
— Cephalopods, the princes of the seas, the cuttlefish, squid and octopus with their remarkable ability to change the colors and patterns on their skin according to their moods or background ...
— Nautilus, strange and beautiful living fossils with their coiled compartmented shells of perfect symmetry.

All of these mollusks, and a great many more, may be seen at the same time by visitors to the Aquarium. The very brief table on page 157, which includes only the classes and orders represented in this book, allows the reader to be able to place most of the common mollusks in their correct slot in the proper scientific classification.

NUDIBRANCHS

Easily recognised by their exposed gills (*nudi* = naked, *branch* = gill), these animals are classified in the Order Opisthobranchiata of the Class Gastropoda. Families, genera and species show an astonishing diversity, as much in their general shape and color as in the details of their external structure and the complexity of their internal anatomy. It is almost impossible to draw a simple classic "plan" to cover all nudibranchs so we will restrict ourselves to showing the major characteristics.

1

2

3

1 *Platydoris cruenta* (upper face) nudibranch with a hard consistency. On the anterior side, to the right, the two rhinophores can be seen, and on the posterior side, two "bouquets" of gills.

2 The same individual. The under face shows the foot quite well, with the mantle largely overlapping it.

3 An *Antiopella sp.* on a *Chrysymenia* alga. A very small amount of surface contact with its support is enough to keep it secure.

4 The same individual, seen front on, showing the length of its rhinophores as in the previous illustration.

5 A close-up of a nudibranch gill "bouquet". These gills can retract at will and completely disappear in the general cavity.

Page 73: *Ceratosoma sp.* nudibranch.

4

5

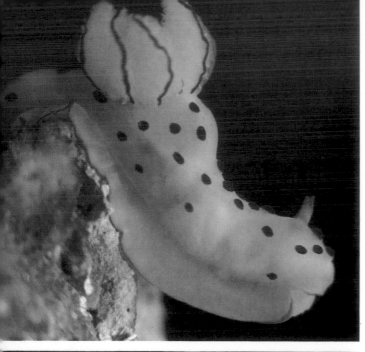

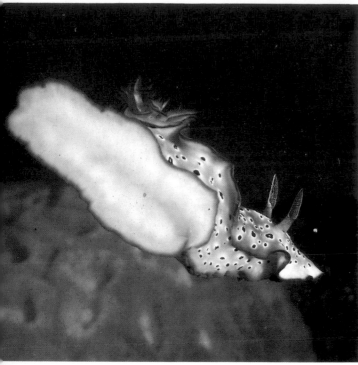

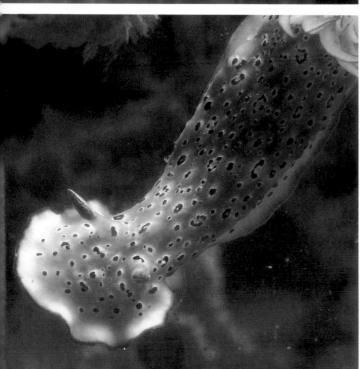

6 A *Gymnodoris coelonica* with such thin external tissue that several internal organs are visible.

7 A *Ceratosoma françoisi* (seen from a lower and upper side at the same time). Its large foot is stuck to the pane of a tank.

8 The same species showing the "head veil" whose rhythmic movements are so graceful.

9 An *Aeolidia sp.* nibbling at the polyps of a *Turbinaria turbinata* coral.

10 The same coral photographed 14 days later to show the extent of the damage caused.

11 A close-up of an affected area.

6

7

8

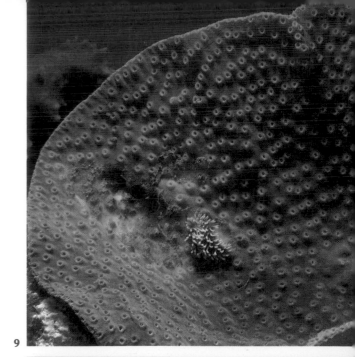

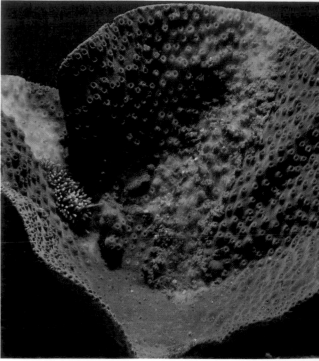

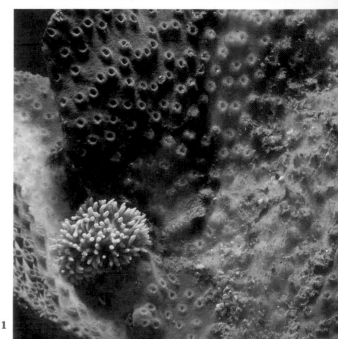

9

10

11

12 A *Hexabranchus imperialis*, the largest sea-slug (25 centimeters). Under the gill bouquets, to the right a symbiotic *Periclimenes* shrimp. See 42 to 50 also.

13 The egg masses of a *Hexabranchus imperialis*. Thousands of eggs are agglomerated to each other by mucus secreted by the animal.

14 *Dendrodoris communis*; perfect camouflage with the yellow sponge on which it feeds. Below and to the right, its whitish eggs in the form of a ribbon.

12

13 and 14

15 A *Phyllobranchus sp.* (*Cyerce?*) on the alga *Chlorodesmis.* When the animal is disturbed it sometimes adopts an arched back stance, tendrils very tight against each other and forming patterns.

16 The same individual with tendrils very separated.

17 The same individual on the move. The empty spaces caused by the loss of a few tendrils can be seen.

18 The same individual under the diaphanous eggs that it has just laid, forming a translucent disc.

The most obvious part of these organisms is the elongated foot of very variable length and width. Its adhesive power is so strong that it can hang on to the substrate very firmly, even though it makes only minor surface contact. The back can be smooth or rough or covered by protruberances (cirri) of different forms. The skin is sometimes so thin that one can see organs such as the liver, heart, genital glands and radula through it. *Gymnodoris coelonica* (**6**) illustrates this translucence.

In certain families, the sides of the foot extend to form a thin notum.[22] The underside of *Platydoris cruenta* (**2**) shows this clearly while the mantle of the violet and white *Ceratosoma francoisi* is less developed.[23] The rhythmical movement of the "head veil" — the frontal extension of the mantle — is one of the most graceful spectacles imaginable (**8**).

Nudibranchs receive tactile sensations by two types of tentacles of great sensitivity; the oral tentacles around the mouth and the rhinophores (**4**) on the head. The rhinophores, which look like horns, are more or less retractile and are lined with small lamellated layers. Their color varies according to the species and they may be single or multi-colored. The form of these organs, and the actual number of layers, determine their classification.

The range of sensitivities of the rhinophores, like some of the gills or branchiae we will be talking about later, is quite amazing. They react to light, to vibrations and, with a remarkable suddeness, to touch. But unlike the oral tentacles, they do not explore the ground. The multiple layers of the rhinophores act as chemo-receptors permitting them to distinguish chemical scents and also changes in the direction of water currents. I do not know whether the nudibranchs can actually see because the eyes are always internal.[24]

The nudibranchs also have hearing organs, the otocysts, which are capsules filled with liquid containing little calcareous bodies, the otoliths. They can have a single otolith but certain species have more than one hundred.

Nudibranchs breathe with external gills (**5**), usually situated on the posterior of the animal; these are called the acanthobranchs. The inferobranchs have these respiratory organs positioned between the foot and the mantle. The shape of the gills may be quite simple or vary in complexity to form an extraordinary profusion of branchings. It seems that the maximum number of divisions is reached among species of *Hexabranchus* which have six retractile groups (**12**). The gills are very sensitive and at the first signs of disturbance, can disappear instantaneously inside the pallial cavity. They usually quickly reappear and the unfolding of these delicate "bouquets" is always very elegant.

The beating heart is sometimes visible through their transparent skin, as I was able to see in *Aeolides*, and particularly in the beautiful *Antiopella* (**3** and **4**) where it beat at the rate of two per second. André Franc[25] said: "The density of the blood in marine species is close to that of sea water. It varies in the same way as the concentration of salts in the external medium."

Nudibranchs are mostly carnivorous, browsing on rocks, sponges, sea squirts, hydroids and bryozoans. Some live on the polyps of hard corals or nibble on some soft corals. Nevertheless, a small number of species are exclusively vegetarian, feeding on seaweeds. Like nearly all the terrestrial and marine gastropods, they scrape their feeding ground with the aid of a very sophisticated organ, the *radula*.[26] It is a resistant but flexible chitinous ribbon, on which rows of teeth are implanted, the number varying with the species. Some have up to 50 rows of teeth.[27]

With the aid of this rasping radula, the nudibranchs tear off nutritious elements which are carried along firstly into an oesophageal crop, then into the stomach and finally into the intestine which curves around the liver. Here, this curve usually lies beneath the base of the gill branches. Instead of being a compact mass, the liver may divide and the divisions can extend into the gill branches.

---

22   For some authors, the term *notum* is given to the single fold which extends more or less beyond the foot. For others, the definition of the word includes the whole mantle. Risbec calls it the *noteum*.

23   This species was identified for me by Jean Risbec himself. But a specimen recently sent to another specialist was identified as *Chromodoris vicina*.

24   Risbec, J. *Mollusques nudibranches de la Nouvelle-Calédonie*, Larousse, Paris, 1953.

25   Encyclopédie de la Pléiade, Zoologie, vol. I, Gallimard, 1963.

26   From the Latin *radula* meaning "scraper or rake". Photograph 102 shows the *radula* of the marine gastropod, *Cypraea tigris*.

27   The arrangement of these teeth, their form and number, are of great importance for the identification of nudibranchs.

19 A small white unidentified nudibranch which is mimicking the soft coral on which it is feeding (*Spongodes merleti*).

20 A couple of *Aplysia angasi*. These sea-slugs can escape from the view of a predator by ejecting purple liquid (protection cloud).

19

20

21 A large *Sebadoris nebulosa* nudibranch swimming horizontally.

22 *Melibe sp*. An extremely fragile nudibranch in one of its slow-motion postures.

21

22

81

Nudibranchs are hermaphrodite so that the one individual contains at the same time the vagina and the penis (armed with little hooks), the uterus and the spermatheca (a receptacle for sperm), plus all the reproductive gonads and glands.

The egg mass of the nudibranchs usually takes on a spiral form. Usually there are many whorls and it is rare to find only one. I am again illustrating the magnificent egg case of the *Hexabranchus* (**13**), though with a slightly different photograph to the one already published in *Carnaval sous la mer* on plate XXI which also showed a close-up of the rows of eggs covered in the protecting mucus. My underwater film *Carnaval sous la mer* highlighted the grace of these "marine roses" moving to the rhythm of the waves. Most of the egg masses of the nudibranchs are fixed to firm supports such as rocks, corals and sponges. Plate **19** Coelenterates shows the delicate lacework of *Aeolidia* feeding on the polyps of the coral *Goniopora*. The beautiful *Phyllobranchus* (alias *Cyerce*) is an exception in that it has attached its extremely thin, disk-shaped egg mass to the filamentous alga *Chlorodesmis* (**18**).

The number of eggs produced by nudibranchs can be considerable. After carefully dissecting some egg mass ribbons of *Hexabranchus*, I arrived at an estimation varying from 200 to 300,000 eggs, still quite a modest number compared to that of three million noted by P.H. Fisher for *Aplysia limacina*[28]. Under the microscope, and with weak magnification, one can see the young larva continually turning on itself in its gelatinous egg capsule. For the naturalist, the rotation of these thousands of "promises of life" is always a very moving spectacle. The embryonic life of nudibranchs is quite short, only six to eight days according to the species.

Each tiny larva is called a veliger and, after hatching, each has rows of quite long cilia which assures it a certain mobility. But this relatively weak means of propulsion is not enough to resist the currents which carry them along. And it is in the course of this dispersion that a large number of larvae fall prey to predators. Those that escape float for a few days and at this stage they usually possess a spiral shell. Little by little they grow heavy and descend towards the bottom. The shell is reabsorbed and the little slugs acquire their adult shape. In regard to the longevity of nudibranchs, the reader will learn later in the book why we do not have personal observations. P.H. Fisher and J. Risbec estimate that the Aeolidae only live for two months, other species from one to four months. Outside of the great slaughter of individuals at the larval stage, adult nudibranchs run few risks. They have, in fact, many assets to protect themselves against their predators. Most species spend the major part of their existence deep in the shelter of boulders and rocks under which they lay their egg masses.

Perfect camouflage

Other nudibranchs, which live and feed on the polyps of corals or sponges, are protected by a camouflage or mimicry that is sometimes so remarkable that they are unnoticed even by an experienced eye. This is the case in the perfect camouflage of *Notodoris citrina* (**23**) living on a sponge of the genus *Leucetta* which wouldn't be at all distinguishable from its nutritious support except for the two small rhinophores sticking out on its head. Another small nudibranch of less than two centimeters (I still have not identified it) which feeds on *Spongodes merleti* (**19**) is quite visible because I deliberately made it descend on the "trunk" of the soft coral so that its whiteness would stand out well on the pink background. But

23 *Notodoris citrina*. A remarkable example of camouflage with its foot support, the sponge *Leucetta*. Only the two very small rhinophores can be distinguished, top left.

23

---

28   The same author, explaining the fecundity of other mullusks — in particular certain oysters — suggests a figure of 60 million eggs for the *Ostrea virginica!*

24 to **29** *Melibe sp.* A few typical postures when swimming rapidly. **25** and **26** show the peribuccal opening in the form of a bell which enables it to attach like a suction-cup to algae and imprison micro-organisms on which it feeds. In **29**, the vigorous contortions of the animal, bringing its two extremities closer together for propulsion.

30 A tiny, transparent nudibranch (1·5 centimeters), (related to the *Bornella*?), looking more like an alga than an animal.

24

25

26

27

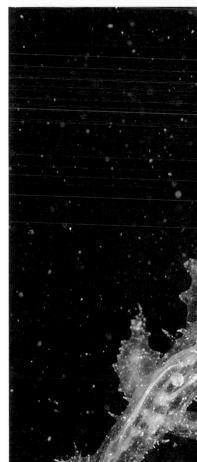

29

28

30

normally this sea slug keeps very close to clumps of white polyps. When the soft coral is quite swollen and all its polyps expanded (see Coelenterates **18**), it can only be distinguished with great difficulty, due to the combination of camouflage and mimicry.

Jean Risbec has already established that certain species belonging to the genus *Phyllidia* (**37**) gave off liquids "with a strong odor, indeed a stench or even worse" when they were disturbed. If, in the water, the acidity of these secretions is half as repulsive to their predators as their smell is to us, the sea slugs don't run much risk of being attacked or eaten.

Risbec has noted that the rare nudibranch *Kentrodoris pseudofusca* covers itself with a greenish mucus if it is disturbed.[29] He once observed it at the Rocher à la voile (a few hundred meters from the spot where we built the Noumea Aquarium) and we have seen another specimen there.

Besides producing repulsive substances, there are yet other methods of safeguard. Thus the Sea Hares (**20**) eject a jet of "ink" of a dark violet color which, without necessarily being toxic, is abundant enough to make them invisible. One finds the same device among octopus, cuttlefish, and man-made warships hiding behind thick smoke screens! Other methods of defense consist of either curling up in a ball (*Platydoris*) or dropping from their support and remaining in a state of perfect rigidity (*Aegirus*), recalling the behavior of the click beetles (Elaterids) and weevils (Curculionids) of the insect world. We will also find this technique of "playing dead" among certain crustacea such as the pretty little porcelain crabs *Leucosia* (Crustacea, **73**).

Certain nudibranchs show a remarkable aptitude for swimming freely. With a lot of large undulations of the whole body, and with their mantle completely spread out they can swim along for several minutes. The contortions of these great sea slugs, like *Hexabranchus* (**12**) which reach 25 centimeters, give the impression that at each movement their body changes form. One can imagine from the few postures shown here (**42** to **50**), the beauty of the movie film sequences that were taken of them — especially since we were able to film both *Hexabranchus imperialis*, the most brilliant in coloring, and a

---

29   Risbec, J. as before.

31 *Flabellina ornata.* A superb nudibranch which is only a few centimeters long and of which we have seen only one specimen in 20 years.

31

Hexabranchus flammulatus with more subdued shades. Our diver friend, Serge Bouron, who captured them was very surprised to find these two specimens of different species living side by side. The ballet danced by these two nudibranchs is one of the most graceful spectacles of the marine world. Less spectacular, because of the dull color, is the undulation of the large and rare nudibranch *Sebadoris nebulosa* (**21**) which swims most often in a horizontal direction.[30]

The famous *Phyllobranchus* sp.[31] (**15** to **18**) can protect itself by performing an extraordinary whirling motion. This slug rolls itself into a ball, spinning rapidly by the rhythmical beating of all its dorsal palettes. While this small sphere is continually rotating, it traces out a more or less elliptical path.

The movie sequences of this spectacle, which very few people have had the chance to see, are extremely difficult to take.

The presence of these palettes on *Phyllobranchus* and of similar multiple external appendages on other nudibranchs, provide yet another method of safety. When an enemy (a crab for example) begins to seize the slug, it simply breaks off its appendages by a mechanism of autotomy. Should the occasion arise, this voluntary amputation can be carried out at the expense of the foot which breaks off easily. The animal is able to regenerate the sacrificed part without difficulty.[32]

There finally remains one defense method of nature that is more elaborate than all the preceding ones. Certain species of nudibranchs feed on polyps of corals, hydroids and similar stinging creatures. They can absorb the cnidocysts,[33] or stinging cells with which the tentacles of these organisms are crammed. Great quantities of venomous cells thus accumulate in the intestinal loops of sea slugs. They do not suffer at all but certainly become highly toxic for predators.

---

30   The identification of this nudibranch is made with reserve because one of the specialists consulted determined it as a *Dendrodoris tuberculosa* from the photograph only. Perhaps it is quite simply a question of synonymy.

31   Identification J. Risbec, 1948. This nudibranch would now belong to the genus *Cyerce*.

32   For several hours these pretty "petals" continue to move quite curiously on the bottom.

33   Or nematocycsts (refer to Coelenterates).

32

33

34

32 *Halgerda sp*. The polyhedric form of this nudibranch seems to exist only in this genus. To the left, one of the two rhinophores, to the right and above, the gills looking like feathers.

33 *Chromodoris coi*, very rare and brought up from a depth of 40 meters. Part of the foot can be seen on the left.

34 An *Umbraculum indica* carrying a calcareous layer on top, probably the remains of a shell.

We know ourselves how severe the burns are from the slightest contact with a jellyfish or hydroid and we can easily imagine the reaction of a predator having inadvertently swallowed a nudibranch crammed full of stinging cells.

One day, we were very lucky to have the chance to see this for ourselves: The trevally fish of our largest tank are accustomed to swooping down in a frenzy of feeding on the live fry we give them. A voluntary assistant had forgotten that an *Aeolidia* had remained on the bottom of a bucket in which he had just been putting some small fish to be fed to these trevally. One of them (*Caranx sexfasciatus*, Fish, **72**) pounced on the venomous slug but spat it out again immediately. For several hours this unfortunate fish rubbed its fragile lips on the wall of the tank, on the rocks and on the sand, attempting to ease the pain.

I have referred to some nudibranchs living at the expense of certain species of hard corals whose polyps they eat. That is the case of the little *Aeolidia* in pictures **9** and **10**. The two photographs taken at 14 day intervals show the progression of destruction of this coral of the genus *Turbinaria*. Another, *Phestilla melanobranchus* (Coelenterates, **19**), had attacked the polyps of a *Goniopora lobata*. The photograph clearly shows, by the whiteness of the coral skeleton, how much of this coral has been "cleaned" of its living elements. We also see in close-up the graceful egg masses of this nudibranch. The corals of the genus *Tubastraea* sp. are also highly sought after as number **58** shows. These little sea slugs are not very common and the damage to corals over a long period of time is insignificant. It isn't these nibblings that will put the reefs in danger!

I have selected a few species that I wanted to illustrate here because of their strangeness, their beauty or simply because they are very rare. The scientists in general and the taxonomists in particular will be amazed that many of these specimens can only be designated by a name of genus or of family. I am the first to deplore it. The explanation of these gaps in our knowledge is very simple: in order that these nudibranchs survive longer, we place them in the large tanks whose concrete walls are lined with microflora and therefore by an abundant microfauna. These tanks are constantly supplied by an enormous quantity of clean sea-water. It is impossible to fit the overflow pipes with very fine meshed gratings

because they would be quickly clogged up by all the living and detrital elements washed through by the strong current. Gradually these small sea slugs accumulate at the level of the overflow pipes and disappear through the gratings. So they escape firstly being collected and preserved in formalin solution and secondly being examined by the scientists who classify them. And that is most regrettable in such a region like ours.[34]

The living lesson

But we cannot do everything! The Aquarium of Noumea is a private establishment which must offer the most remarkable organisms to satisfy the curiosity of visitors. But an aquarium is also a lesson in living things. Thanks to ours, thousands of schoolchildren have had their eyes and minds opened to a marine environment which was totally unknown to them. For nearly 20 years my wife and I have devoted a considerable amount of time so that they get the most from their outings. The majority of organisms which stock our tanks permanently are collected at depths that only a few experienced divers can reach.

Many international visitors, like the professors and students from the University of Hawaii, only came to Noumea because of our aquarium and to see as many specimens as possible from the astonishing and little known world of invertebrates. Nudibranchs take their deserved place in this world but, because they are so very small and are so well disguised, if we didn't point them out most visitors would not notice them.

It isn't always necessary to descend to great depths to find important subjects. Our great friend Bernard Conseil, who usually explores between 35 and 60 meters, one day found the extraordinary *Melibe* sp. represented here by numbers **22** to **29** in less than a meter of water. The postures of this sea slug are, as one can see, so funny that I had to take many photographs. When it contorts itself vigorously and rapidly, its body bends to such a point that its head touches its tail each time. Its method of movement is even

---

34 Of course we have thought of two methods which would avoid losing these nudibranch. But one would be too onerous and the other would necessitate an increase in labor which we cannot allow since the whole functioning of the Aquarium is carried out by only three people and our budget does not allow for an increase in staff.

35 A *Halgerda willeyi* with a hard consistency, seen on a dark background (see illustration 39 where the animal is crawling on its frosted glass support).

36 *Ceratosoma sp.* Head veil and rhinophores are to the left. On the posterior side the gills are totally retracted.

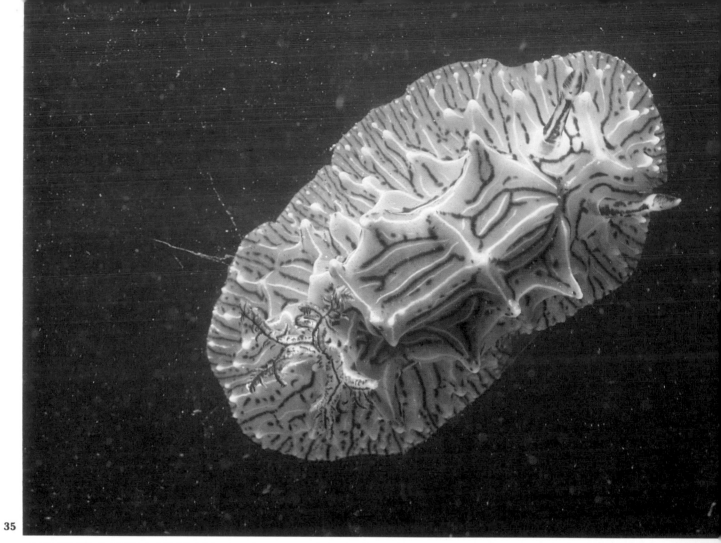

35

36

37 *Phyllidia sp.* The *Phyllidia* are of the same very hard external structure as the *Halgerda*.

38 A *Phyllidia ocellata*, quite a common species in New Caledonia.

37

38

more special, in fact, since this animal swims in reverse.

Another oddity is that the mouth of the *Melibe* is situated at the bottom of a sort of bell which is none other than a considerable extension of the frontal veil. This bell-like sac, which opens and closes at will, acts as a trap (**25**). I have seen it fully opened, acting as a suction-cup on algae or even on the glass of the tank. It would thus imprison micro-organisms and simply swallow them.

Jean Risbec[35] informs us that the *Melibe* does not have a rasping tongue (radula) and that is something quite exceptional for a nudibranch. The lengths of the two species that he studied were from four to five centimeters. Someone once brought me a relatively enormous specimen (more than 12 centimeters). Unfortunately, due to careless handling during transport, this strange nudibranch had lost most of its appendages by autotomy. The body, as well as the detached appendages, closely resembled some of the brown algae, *Dictyopteris* and *Sargassum*. The next day one of us went back to the same place in the hope of bringing back some complete specimens in a good state, but unfortunately we came back empty-handed.

We cannot say much about the pretty *Chromodoris coi* (**33**) brought up from 40 meters deep, or about the superb *Flabellina ornata* (**31**) of which we have only ever seen one specimen, or indeed about the *Halgerda* sp. (**32**) whose polyhedral shape is unusual among nudibranchs. As for the specimen illustrated by number **30**, brought up from 35 meters and which probably belongs to the genus *Bornella,* it only measured one and a half centimeters and looked more like a piece of seaweed than an animal.

One of the most unusual nudibranchs is the strange *Glaucus* (**51**). This marine organism, which is only about three centimeters long, swims near the surface of the open seas. It was only after strong storms that we happened to find some washed up on the shore amongst the banks of seaweed which had been torn free by the waves.

The most remarkable fact is that the *Glaucus* floats upside down, turning its blue underside towards the sky and its white topside towards the bottom. This is quite a remarkable example of protective adaptation because, up above there are the sea birds and, below it, a thousand potential sea predators.

In *Carnaval sous la mer* we were unable to resist illustrating this astonishing creature in two separate photographic techniques, one the conventional positive print, the other as a negative print thus bringing to one's imagination images like a bird or dragon or dancer.

The *Glaucus* also figures on the first issue of a series of postage stamps which used the rarities in the Aquarium tanks as philatelic subjects. And here I will digress a little to recall an amusing anecdote. In 1952 we were staying in Paris to select materials for building the Aquarium. Passing in front of an art gallery in Rue de Berri, my wife noticed a very large oil painting whose central motif was a *Glaucus* of proportionally immense dimensions! (**52**).

She admired this huge, but exact, representation of the little nudibranch of the high seas which was all the more amazing because, at that time, this sea slug had very rarely been illustrated, and then only in outline drawings in a few zoological books. Such a painting, which carried the signature of the famous Max Ernst, should have had its place in the entrance hall of the future Aquarium, so she asked the assistant the price. The sum was around one million francs at the time, and that explains why this desirable oil painting never came to the Noumea Aquarium.

"Could you tell me," my wife asked again, "what this painting represents?"

Although the personable assistant replied with confidence and assurance, we felt that she really had no idea of the answer. "But, Madame, it is a surrealist work!" So!!!

Today I am constantly reminded of fantastic photographs of real animals that could still pass for surrealist pictures. I think of the incredible mouth shapes of the blennies (Fish, **118**) and the patterns of the spider-crabs dressed in sponges or adorned with colored papers (Crustacea, **22** and **28**) or even the two beautiful "flying saucers" (Coelenterates, **83** and **84**). And why not, also, the *Pterocera lambis* in photograph **111**.

Again our friend Conseil had been diving at 25 meters and discovered two specimens of a nudibranch that we had never seen before. As a "retired" entomologist, they immediately reminded me of the beautiful caterpillars of certain *Bombyx* that I had once raised in

---

35   Risbec, J. as before.

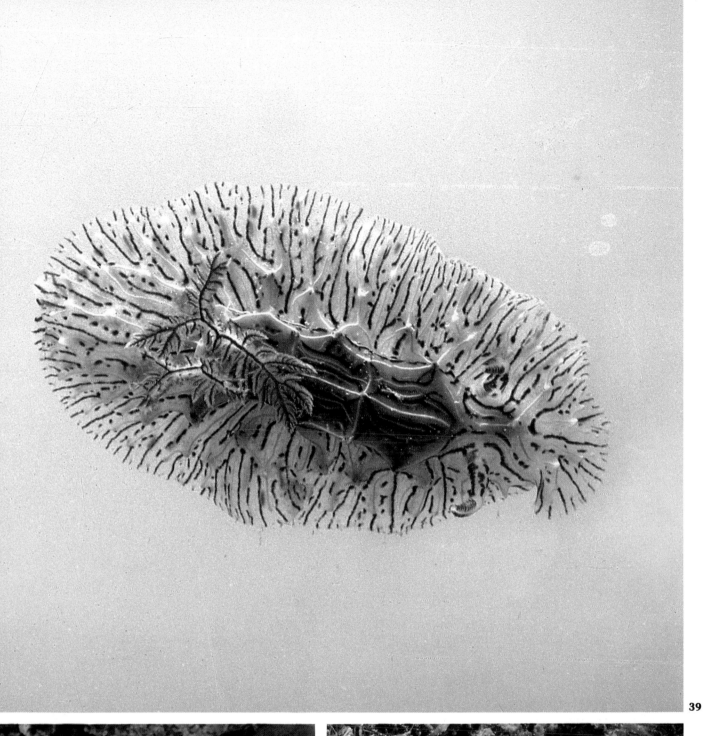

39 A *Halgerda willeyi* on its frosted glass support to show the translucence of the mantle. Very simple gill bouquet.

40 *Tritoniopsis alba.* Observe the multiple protuberances on the very ramified tips.

41 An undentified nudibranch. Diameter 1·5 centimeters: depth of origin, 35 meters.

40 and 41

91

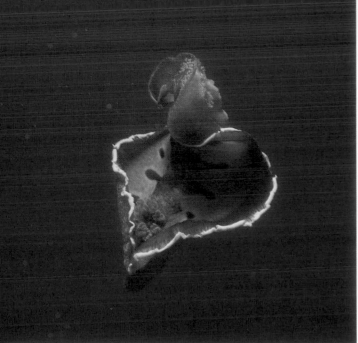

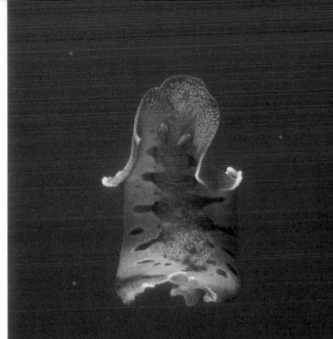

42 to **50** A ballet of nudibranchs. Some of the more remarkable postures of these superb sea-slugs as they swim. The two different species of *Hexabranchus* represented here (and which were found — quite surprisingly see text — side by side on a coral reef) are the *H. flammulatus*, recognizable in **42**, **43** (to the right), **44**, **45**, **46** (to the left), **48** and **49** (the one on the bottom) and the *H. imperialis*, the brightest in color, illustrated in **43** (to the left), **46** (to the right), **47**, **49** (the top one) and seen from close-up in number **50**. Given the rapidity of the movements carried out by the animal to propel itself, it is impossible to properly appreciate the elegance of most of the postures which can only be captured in photographs. Thanks to the quantity of shots taken (photographic and cinematographic), we have been lucky to capture the very graceful heart shape shown in figure **42**.

43   **46**

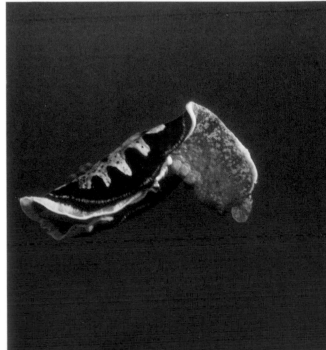

44   **47**

In **50**, one can clearly see one of the two rhinophores on top (the other partly hidden by the edge of the mantle), the gill systems and its multiple leaves on the bottom. The very large mantle is propelling from the bottom towards the surface. The normal length, completely extended, is 25 centimeters. In exceptional cases certain specimens can reach 35 centimeters.

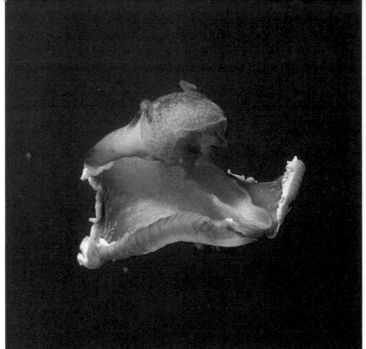

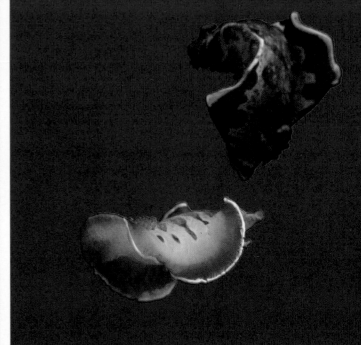

48 and 49

50

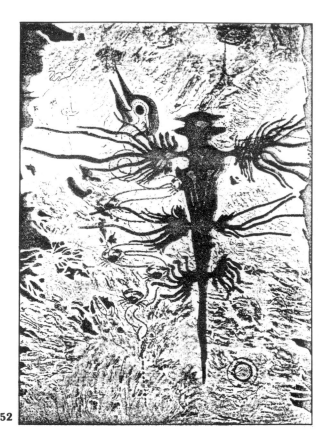

52

52 Facsimile of a work by Max Ernst (refer to anecdotal text).

I sacrificed and preserved those two beautiful sea slugs in order to send them to my young Australian colleague, Phillip Coleman who "knows a thing or two" on the subject of nudibranchs, even though he still denies this with modesty. He immediately replied that it was of the genus *Antiopella* and I quote him to show the public how difficult classifications in general can be, especially those of the nudibranchs.[37] "Your number 717 is an Arminidae, belonging to the genus *Antiopella*. This genus has been successively attributed to the families Antiopellidae, Janolidae, Proctonotidae and Zephyrinidae. It seems, furthermore, that one still hasn't come to a proper agreement as to which of these families it would be correct to attribute the genus *Antiopella*."

And later he added: "Recently the same species was caught (one specimen) at about 30 meters at Port Hacking[38] (near Sydney), which is very interesting. I am almost positive that it is a new species."

Phillip Coleman! What a very likeable person. He is very tall with a magnificent beard, reminding me of those wonderful illustrations of Ned Land in Jules Verne's 20,000 Leagues Under The Sea. And in his eyes there shines that beautiful light of those who are dedicated to their work. Judge for yourselves: his position in his father's printing-house was very comfortable but he was bored stiff. At the end of two years his passion for zoology took him to the Australian Museum in Sydney where he was already known for his passion for nudibranchs. He was initially taken on with the title of assistant-trainee, or something quite modest like that, at quite moderate pay. But he was happy, and he still is, because he is now part of the staff of that Museum. It really was a great pleasure to have him at the Aquarium for some time and it was so comforting to meet someone again whose

Madagascar. The comparison is even more remarkable since these two nudibranchs also lived on plants (an alga of the genus *Chrysymenia*). In fact, they didn't nibble the leaves themselves but ate the whitish bryozoans which grow on these seaweeds.

This species was so new and so beautiful that we took reels of movie film and several rolls of still shots as well. One of these (**3**) looks just like a caterpillar about to balance itself on the end of a branch. Through the thin skin of this nudibranch I could also see the heart beating. This was yet another striking analogy with the heartbeat of the chrysalis of the *Uranie* which is also easily visible by transmitted light under the microscope.[36] And my memory recalled the thousands of hearts of chrysalises examined during the years in my laboratory in the virgin forest of Madagascar. There it was the irregularities caused by thermal and electric treatments that interested me. With the sea slugs, however, it is the remarkable regularity of the heartbeat, at the rate of 70 pulses a minute, that is noteworthy (they do not need a pace-maker!). And I bitterly regretted that one couldn't have thousands of specimens of this species of nudibranch at one's disposal — as I had for caterpillars. What entrancing physiological observations would have been possible then with such material!

36   Catala, R. *Variations expérimentales de Chrysiridia madagascariensis*. Archives du Muséum, Paris, 1940, pl. III, fig. 9.
37   If taxonomists sometimes have problems determining correct names one should not expect too much from the non-specialist who still attributes a name which has become obsolete to a certain species, or even to a genus. It is therefore forgivable that I have sometimes confused the correct scientific names of some nudibranchs.
38   This is very remarkable because the temperature of the waters in the Sydney region is clearly lower than that of the New Caledonian waters. Port Hacking is 640 kilometers south of the first large coral formations of the Great Barrier Reef (Solitary Island).

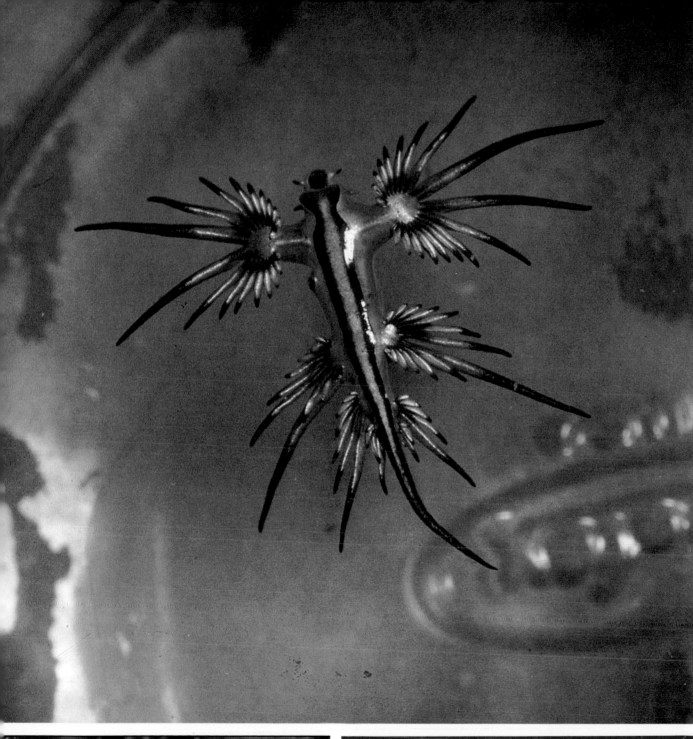

51 *Glaucus sp.* High seas nudibranchs which strong storms sometimes wash up on the shores along with bundles of algae floating on the surface.

53 A *Chromodoris quadricolor* photographed on an encrusting sponge, *Cliona schmidti*.

54 A *Phyllidia sp.* with very prominent sides and with a hard consistency like the *Halgerda*.

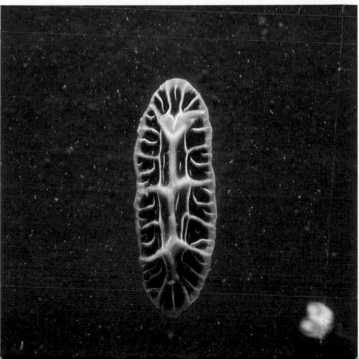

53 and 54

55

56

57

58

unselfishness was accompanied by dedication. He is quite consumed by his special studies of the radula. This hasn't prevented him from marrying and enjoying married life.

One has to sometimes regret only being able to either take the part of a man or woman (especially when one is an expert on nudibranchs) when recalling that the graceful sea slugs, being at the same time male and female, enjoy a great privilege. In fact, their "conjugation" (as an English lady, whom I shall mention elsewhere, would say) lasts for several hours without interruption. My marvellous friend, Pierre-Jean Vaillard, once reflected: "And you call them mere mollusks!" Professor P.H. Fisher, in his remarkable work on the life and habits of mollusks,[39] quotes: "After gathering together the animals couple, either in twos, or in groups of several individuals joined in a chain form. This last gregarious approach characterizes certain hermaphrodite gastropods (*Aplysia* **20**, *Lamellaria*) whose anatomy allows this loving link."

A quite remarkable Opisthobranch of the Umbraculidae family also exists in the tidal waters of New Caledonia, in very shallow depths. It seems rare because in 30 years we have only seen three specimens of this *Umbraculum indica* (vel *botanica*) represented by number **34**. This animal, shaped like a flattened cone, carries a curious calcareous layer on its back in the shape of concentric circles which is the shell or the remains of a shell. Joyce Allan, in her important work on Australian mollusks,[40] tells us that this shell is used as protection for the gills and other organs situated under this disc. It would be interesting to understand therefore why other species of the same genus do not possess this protective shield. The gills of these *Umbraculum* are placed only on the right hand side. There is the same unusual arrangement of gills on the superb mollusk *Pleurobranchus mamillatus*[41] (**63** to **68**), well named because the protuberances on its back look just like small breasts (**66**).

Because I took films and photographs of this superb creature night and day, my wife would say ironically: "Were you still with your mamilla?" This is an allusion to the fact that the same word

39   As before.
40   Allan, Joyce — *Australian Shells*. Georgian House, Melbourne, 1942.
41   From the Latin *mamilla* meaning breast.

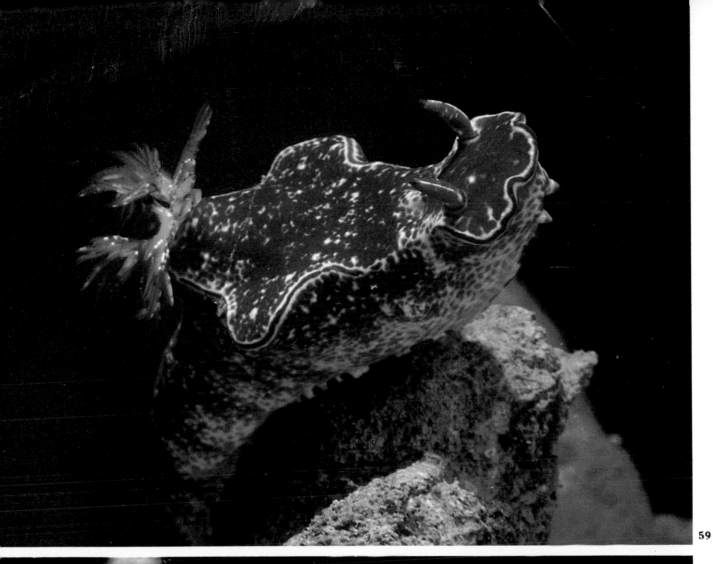

55 *Phyllidia sp.* In spite of the hardness of its skin, it can have varied forms.

56 A *Glossodoris sp.* on a *Chorodesmis* algae. Head veil, rhinophores and gills quite are quite distinct.

57 A *Phyllidia varicosa*, quite common in very shallow depths.

58 Two small *Phestilla sp.* devouring the polyps of a *Tubastraea* coral.

59 *Ceratosoma sp.* (or *Miamira?*). As well as the principal characteristics already shown in the preceding illustrations, this shows the importance of the foot.

60 A *Chromodoris sp.* on a deep-water sponge.

59

60

was used by the Latin poets as an expression of affection and it meant "my little sweetheart". This excessive photography was necessary because of the extreme difficulty in obtaining an exact reproduction of the beautiful violet color of the border of the mammary protuberances. It depended on the incidence of light and resembled the patterns that oil makes on water.

I am deeply indebted to Pierre Laboute, a deep water diver, naturalist and remarkable photographer of marine organisms in situ, who brought up this rare find from 35 meters and filmed some excellent sequences of it. Number **65** shows the animal on its back, which lets us see the external and internal faces of the mantle and the foot. Number **67**, a close-up of the head, emphasizes the two rhinophores and the cephalic veil. Photograph **68** features the unique gill formation. This *Pleurobranchus* began to lay eggs

from the third day and photograph **63** gives a good idea of the immaculate whiteness of its ribboned egg mass. Some scientists may be surprised that in this section I mention three remarkable organisms, namely *Hydatina physis* (**76**), *Bullina lineata* (**69**) and *Amplustrum amplustre* (**75**), but these three mollusks are, according to certain authors, a subdivision of Opisthobranchs even though they carry shells. However the shells are of an exceptional thinness and are extremely fragile.

And if you observe the considerably "undersized" shell on the animal — more particularly among the *Bullina* and *Amplustrum* — you realize that it cannot retract entirely into it. The only sure protection for these animals during the daytime is given by burrowing under a thin layer of sand or mud and only coming out at night.

61

61 and **62** *Aeolides*. Fully stretched out, about 10 centimeters. The flat-shaped tendrils remain stuck to the finger at the slightest touch.

63 A *Pleurobranchus mamillatus* and its immaculate ribbon of eggs.

64 A *Pleurobranchus mamillatus* in slow progress.

63

64

65 *Pleurobranchus mamillatus*. The animal is turned over, showing the two faces of the mantle and the foot.

66 *Pleurobranchus mamillatus*. A close-up of the mamillary protuberances.

65

66

67 *Pleurobranchus mamillatus*. Detail of the rhinophores, the small "hood" and "head veil".

68 *Pleurobranchus mamillatus*. A close-up of the only gill.

67

68

PROSOBRANCHS

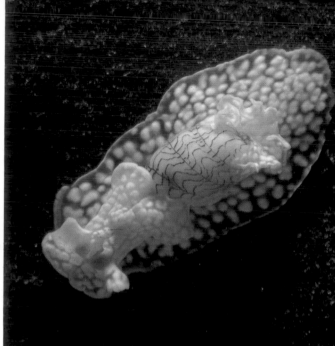

This is the group of gastropods called Prosobranchs,[42] more popularly known as marine shells. The extreme diversity of their shell shape and the multiple dissimilarities in the arrangement of their organs have led the experts to divide them in numerous orders, sub-orders, super-families, etc. Although this book is not a treatise on zoology, the Prosobranchs do have characteristics in common — the sexes are usually separate and are provided with a single shell which is generally spacious enough to shelter the whole animal. Many of them have a horny or calcareous lid called the operculum, situated on the upper side of the foot, near its posterior end. This operculum closes the aperture of the shell. As Professor Léon Bertin, my late lamented friend, wrote:[43] "When the animal is disturbed, it retires into the interior of its home and closes the door behind it. There is no need for a latch because the powerful muscles alone are sufficient to prevent anything from forcing the door."

It must also be noted that among certain families, such as the Cypraiedae (cowrie shells) and the very close family of Amphiperatidae[44] including *Ovula ovum* (**70**) and *Ovula costellata* (**71**), the mantle, which is an extension of the foot, can cover the whole shell at will. It is this mantle which actually creates the shell by secreting three calcareous layers of very different composition: an internal one (hypostracum) is the mother-of-pearl, an intermediate layer (ostracum) made up of prisms of crystalline limestone and an external one (periostracum) made of conchiolin. Finally the Prosobranchs eat either flesh or plant material, but some species are omnivorous and eat both.

All over the world there are such a great number of shell collectors that reference publications on shells make up an enormous bibliography. Many of these works, old and modern, are illustrated with beautiful color plates. I have in front of me one of the best among the

69

70

71

---

42   Because the gills are situated in front, while among the opistobranchs they are positioned towards the rear.

43   In *La Vie des Animaux*, Larousse, Paris.

44   Considering that they are such close relations, there is a great difference in the fact that during their juvenile stage cowrie shells have a twisted form and only become oval in shape at a more advanced age, whereas ovules are a definite oval from the start.

69 *Bullina lineata*. Like the *Amplustrum* (75) and the *Hydatina* (76), this bubble carries a very thin shell which is extremely fragile.

70 *Ovula ovum* (*Cypraeidae* cowrie shells). To the left, a shell which has been stripped of its retractile mantle (you can see the very important base of its foot). To the right, a shell re-coated.

71 *Ovula costellata*. The mantle covers nearly the whole shell. The foot, with a black border, is a considerable width.

72 *Natica sp.* about to bury itself in the sand (refer to *Carnaval sous la mer*, plate 31, the admirable "sand flowers" which are the eggs of gastropods).

73 A *Cassis cornuta* (helmet shell) moving about on the sand of one of the large tanks in the Aquarium. The weight of the empty shells can reach 4 kilograms.

74 A large specimen of the same species carrying out a last push to emerge from the sand.

72 and 73

74

more recent ones[45] and there is no need to be a shell collector to appreciate its real value. The photographer is undoubtedly a great artist. Having arranged each specimen in the most favorable position, sometimes alone and at other times in a group, he uses a clever technique — a discreetly reflective surface which molds the contours of these shells beautifully. There is the mark of talent and a very confident style. What would such a photographer have done if he had the living animal at his disposal as well as its shell? The foot, the mantle and the eyes of certain species have great pictorial impact. Nearly all books about marine gastropods only show the shell. In this book we have selected a few species that were satisfactory short or long term guests at the Aquarium because their diet was known to us and we were able to regularly provide it. Some are illustrated because of their beauty and others because of our knowledge from their behavior over a period of time.

The photograph of the *Natica* (**72**) was taken while the animal was burrowing in the sand and the one of the *Cassis cornuta* (**74**) was taken at the moment when this powerful helmet shell was exerting its last thrust to free itself. The weight of the *Cassis* shell alone can reach four kilograms. A specimen of this species has lived for several years in one of our large tanks where we feed it its natural food, *Protoreaster* (Echinoderms, **3**) which are common in our region. These large mollusks are predators of the sadly famous *Acanthaster planci*, the giant Crown-of-Thorns starfish so destructive to coral reefs.[46] I find it deplorable that these helmet shells are the object of indiscriminate collecting. Their increasing scarcity — indeed, in certain regions of the Pacific they have almost disappeared — has been one of the reasons for the mammoth proliferation and spread of the *Acanthaster*. One can say the same thing about another predatory mollusk of these same devastating starfish, the *Charonia tritonis* or conch (**92**).

Illustration **77** shows us the very pretty *Prionovolva hervieri* about to nibble on the beautiful deep-water soft coral *Spongodes merleti*. The photograph was taken in such a way that the mantle became visible. One will notice the similarity of its fine white protuberances and the texture of this soft coral.

There is the same imitation and harmony among two very close species[47] which also live at the expense of this species of *Spongodes*. The small (one centimeter) shell in illustration **78** clearly shows the white papillae on its back and fine purple streaks along its sides and on the foot. All these characteristics, as well as the violet color of the tentacles results in such perfect camouflage that one cannot distinguish these cowries from their source of nourishment at first glance.

The graceful *Phenacovolva* sp., which spend their life on gorgonian corals at 25 to 30 meters, are slightly bigger but more slender. The color of their mantle also gives them excellent camouflage. Number **82** shows us the same specimen totally covered by the mantle and in number **83** with its completely bare shell. I have also treated the beautiful *Cribraria* in photograph **87** in the same way. The two specimens of *Cypraea eburnea* and *Cypraea vitella* (**85** and **86**) are shown with the shell only partly covered. For the *Calpurnus verrucosus*, whose shell is uniformly white, it was interesting to photograph it when the mantle had covered it completely and its foot was widely spread out. One cannot help but be struck by the small spots of color which are almost replicas of the retracted polyps of the soft corals on which it is feeding (**84**).

Rostration in shells

Before leaving the cowrie shell family of Cypraeidae, it is necessary to show a few examples of abnormalities. In the living specimen of the famous *Cypraea stolida* (**88**), in addition to a little bit of its diaphanous mantle, one can see a large dark area on the shell. We also have the two *Stolida* in photographs **89** and **90** and a *Cribraria* (**91**), doubly aberrant because it is not only totally black (melanization) but it shows the beginning of a deformation called "rostration".

These remarkable shells belong to the very beautiful collection of my old friend Roger Lesage. Moreover, it is to him that I owe, among other discoveries, the following piece of information: "North of Thio (on the east coast of

45   Stix, H.M. and R. Tucker Abbott. Photographs by H. Landshoff. *Les Coquillages*. Seghers, Paris, 1969.
46   Refer to *Carnaval sous la mer*, p. 59, fig. 23.
47   The specific indentification of these two cowrie shells is doubtful. During an emergency emptying of tanks, because of a black tide in March 1974, a good number of invertebrates which had been killed by the fuel oil were sucked up by the pipes.

75 *Amplustrum amplustre.*
Because of the considerable
disproportion between the shell
and the animal mass, this species
obviously cannot shelter in its
shell. These types of gastropods
therefore remain under the sand
all day. The same is true for the
Bullina and the *Hydatina.*

76 *Hydatina physis.* To the
left, a red *Clathria* sponge. To the
right, a colony of botrylles (for
these *Protocordis,* see also
photograph 150).

75

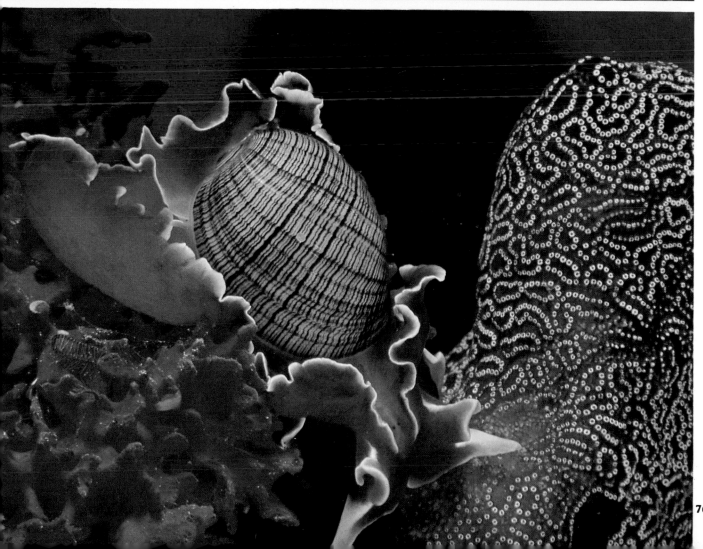

76

77

77 A *Prionovolva hervieri* on the *Spongodes merleti* soft-coral. This shows how much the fleshy "thorns" of the visible part of the mantle harmonize with whatever it attachs to.

78 *Prionovolva sp.* in mimicry with its soft-coral food source. Notice the fine streaks on the coat covering the whole shell and the lines decorating the foot.

79 *Prionovolva pudica.* Four specimens with the top one showing its siphon.

80 *Prionovolva hervieri.* Shell covered by mantle. The siphon is in complete prolapse.

81 The same species, with the shell largely uncovered.

82 A *Phenacovolva sp.* on a *Melithea ocracea* gorgonia with the shell totally covered. (Depth of origin, 30 meters).

83 The same species with its shell uncovered. The tapered elegance of this 3 centimeter shell is highlighted even more.

78

79

New Caledonia) and north of the Baie de Saint-Vincent (west coast), you will not find aberrant *C. stolida*." It seems that no expert has been able to discover the reason for these anomalies which affect other species of cowries as well. Joyce Allan tells us in her book on the Cypraeidae[48]: "They appear to have been attacked by some disease which has set up an arthritical condition; strangely enough, this is more apparent in adult specimens — juveniles appear normal. It is a complexity that occurs conspicuously in the Pacific regions. Many islands, in particular New Caledonia and some of the coral reefs and islands of the Great Barrier Reef and even along the mainland coast of Australia, exhibit this distortion of specimens, but is not confined to these only."

In admitting that the deformity is called "arthritism", we are little better informed on the conditions that cause the deformity. If there is such a disease, what is the causal factor? Another remark by Roger Lesage — whose knowledge of the New Caledonian marine habitats is as comprehensive as it is precise — is that these aberrant *C. stolida* are usually found in lagoon regions close to the mouths of rivers where much soil has been washed from the banks after heavy flooding of the river. Evidently this causes not only a great variation in the pH (acid) levels in the lagoon but considerable silt and organic deposits on the bottom. Lesage pointed out to me that he had found some specimens of aberrant *C. stolida* in muddy surroundings which were sometimes literally putrid.

The famous and late lamented American expert, Montague Cook, professor at the University of Hawaii, told us that such variations were caused by a parasite but he was unable to specify exactly what this parasite was. If this is the origin of these anomalies, it would explain the simultaneous presence in the same area of some aberrant specimens amongst others that were

48   Allan, Joyce. *Cowrie Shells of World Seas*. Georgian House, Melbourne, 1956, p. 3: "They appear to have been attacked by some disease which has set up an arthritical condition; strangely enough, this is more apparent in adult specimens — juveniles appear normal. It is a complexity that occurs conspicuously in the Pacific regions. Many islands, in particular New Caledonia and some of the corals reefs and islands of the Great Barrier Reef, and even along mainland coasts of Australia, exhibit this distortion of specimens, but it is not confined to those only."

80 a

81 a

84

84 *Calpurnus verrucosus.*
The white shell is totally covered
by the mantle whose spots, as
well as those of the extended foot
harmonize with the retracted polyp
calices which are the shell's food
source.

85 *Cypraea eburnea.* Fine
vermicular designs on the coat and
attractive fleshy protuberances.

86 A *Cypraea vitella* showing
the pilosity of its mantle.

87 *Cribraria cribraria.* The top
specimen has its shell completely
covered and the other is entirely
free.

88 *Cypraea stolida.* The shell
is partly melanized and the
diaphanous mantle can just be
seen on the right.

89 *Cypraea stolida.* An
aberrant specimen showing
rostration. Photo: G. Gaeta.
Collection: R. Lesage.

90 *Cypraea stolida crossei.*
Important melanization and very
pronounced rostration. Photo: G.
Gaeta. Collection: R. Lesage.

91 *Cribraria cribraria.* An
aberrant specimen. Total
melanization and the beginning of
rostration. Photo: G. Gaeta.
Collection: R. Lesage.

85

86

87

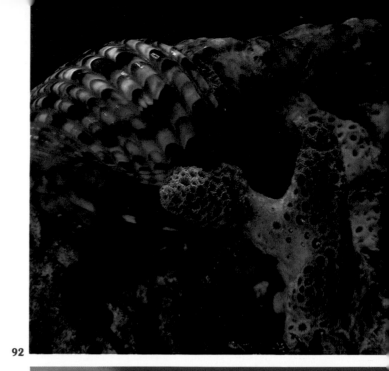

92 *Charonia tritonis* (conch). The usefulness of this gastropod as a predator of the dreadful *Acanthaster* starfish demands that it be protected.

93 *Trivirostra oriza.* This rare, tiny gastropod has very wide distribution and is also found in fossil form.

94 *Mitra sp.* (*episcopalis?*), showing proboscis (siphon), oral tentacle and foot.

92

88

93

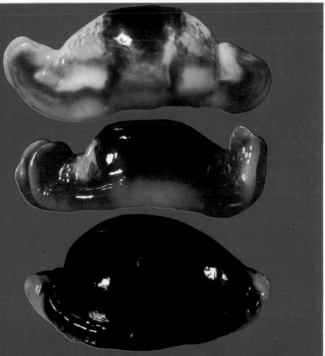

89, 90 and 91

94

absolutely normal. The discussion therefore remains open, but I think it will not be easy to clear up this small mystery because another great expert told me that the *Cypraea stolida*, aberrant and normal, has been the object of intensive collecting by those who make business out of them. As a result one hardly sees them now in the very localized habitats where they were to be found (Baie de Uié for example). One can only deplore this growing scarcity which deprives physiologists of such important experimental material. Research carried out by them would have perhaps led — at least in their studies of the phenomenon of melanization (*Cribraria*, **91**) — to attributing this to an alimentary cause.

There has always been a dogged belief that black forms of the *Cypraea stolida* and other species of cowrie shells (called "niger") are only found in New Caledonia and that it is the high percentage of mineral substances (chromium, nickel, iron, etc.) in the alluvial soil carried into the sea that causes these variations. But, according to Joyce Allan, their widespread occurrence and their ecological diversity tend to seriously weaken such a hypothesis. If it were simply the direct influence that these minerals had on the coloring of the gastropods in question, the percentage of anomalies on these shells would be much higher.

Rightly or wrongly, I am of the opinion that these variations of pigmentation are of a plant

95

origin. Quite a long time ago experimenters working on biological species from Europe obtained some intensely blackened butterflies. This was done without having recourse to thermal or electrical agents (as was the case for me with the *Urania* from Madagascar). Therefore I can imagine that one day a young morphologist will succeed in creating "black shells" at will by duplicating the natural conditions found in certain marine habitats of New Caledonia. The results would be very interesting, not only from the experimental point of view, but also the shell traders of the so-called "niger" species would see the exaggerated prices of such aberrations slump immediately.

One of the better known cowrie shells is the beautiful *Cypraea tigris*. Even though it is quite widespread, over the past ten years or so we have been seeing it less frequently (**102**).

Most authors stress the fact that cowrie shells are carnivorous. But the *C. tigris* adapts itself very well to an exclusively vegetarian diet. This is why we have kept some specimens of this species in a laboratory tank for several years, where they survived only on the thin coating of algae which grow spontaneously on the walls of the tank. In order to obtain such an interesting photograph as **102** I have, here and there, cleaned the glass of its layer of algae. One can clearly see the toothed rasp of the radula in the center of the mouth. We can see, from close-up, the suction-cup on the anterior part of the foot and the two cephalic tentacles on either side of the mouth. At the back there are numerous fleshy protuberances adorning the mantle, which can cover the shell completely.

The beauty of the shell of the cowrie *Talparia talpa* is particularly enhanced when partly covered by its dark mantle (**95**). I will end this very modest presentation of cowrie shells with the tiny *Trivirostra oriza* (**93**), described for the first time in 1810 by the great Lamarck. Slightly bigger than a small pea, its shell is pure white. On either side of a top crimping one can see very fine ribs stretching out from top to bottom. I wanted to take a picture showing more of its mantle, but it didn't want to cover itself anymore. I was only able to keep it for several hours since the young man who had kindly brought it to me was very anxious to have it back. Joyce Allen points out its extremely wide distribution through the Indo-

95 *Talparia talpa.*

96 An unidentified gastropod, 2 centimeters in length and from a depth of 22 meters.

97 *Rapa sp.* This shell resembles fossil forms.

98 The same shell showing the prominent, core-like, oval operculum and the crenated border at the foot.

96

97

98

Pacific and Australian regions up to Madagascar, and she also tells us that one can also find it in a fossil state.

And now here are two beautiful specimens of *Murex* (**99**) or Venus combs. This time the body of the animal has nothing especially graceful about it but our attention is drawn to the length and the importance of the foot. These *Murex* gave me quite an entertaining film sequence when the animal lifted itself upright on its strong foot. It makes the shell pivot slowly and one would say that it is like an underwater gun-turret turning into a shooting position. Illustration **100** shows that the thickness, length and color of the "horns" (cephalic tentacles) are equivalent to those of the thorns of the shell. We again see the power of the foot and the particular coloration in another two murex, the large *Chicoreus ramosus* (**101**) and *Burso buffa* (**109**).

Use of the operculum

I am also reminded of the even more astonishing strength in the foot of *Pterocera* and *Strombus*. In a very interesting note on these gastropods[49], Jean Risbec wrote: "The foot cannot simply crawl. Its flat sole is useless for crawling and it has a very elongate operculum. For this reason, therefore, the animal has been given the common name of Leaper (also given to other *Strombus*) and it progresses in great leaps after rising sharply on its foot."

If you place these large shellfish upside down they will always manage to get upright again. The extreme extension of the foot allows the curved operculum to "hook" into the ground with such efficiency that the animal re-establishes itself in only one movement. When the substratum is sand or mud, the point of this operculum plunges in like a ploughshare (**103**).

The representatives of the two genera of *Strombus* and *Pterocera* have eyes placed on long retractile stalks (**103** to **108**). Their keen vision is absolutely remarkable. I had many opportunities to confirm this when I did my utmost to take close-up photographs of these animals with their eyes fully extended. The only

---

49   Risbec, J. *De l'anatomie de trois Strombidés*, Annales du Musée de Marseille, vol. XXI, 1927.

hope of succeeding was by placing my camera at less than 50 centimeters from the subjects — but at a distance of five meters they could easily see me and retract their stalked eyes! I sat patiently with my eye fixed to my camera and finger ready on the shutter-release, waiting for an ocular peduncle to unfold. As the first inquisitive eye cautiously appeared it reminded me of a small puppet (107). My next simple movement to adjust the focus betrayed me and this resulted in an immediate retraction. We played this game of hide and seek for a long time and I wasted many photographs before I took some perfectly clear ones. It would take a long time to recount the many crafty ways I tried to make myself less visible.

With regards to the *Pterocera lambis*, Risbec summed it up: "Its eye is very perfect, the most perfect that you will find among the gastropods." Another expert, J.N. Prince, of the Department of Ophthalmology of the State University of Ohio, made a special anatomical-histological study on the eyes of the same *Pterocera*[50] and states: "The quality of the image is probably comparable to that of certain sharks and rays .... Among the invertebrates, and especially those with ordinary eyes, the eyes of the *P. lambis* can only be exceeded in keenness of sight by those of the cephalopods ... they are certainly comparable in performance to those of a large number of vertebrates."

One notices a small fleshy appendage with a very tapered point behind and to one side of the eyestalk (105). It seems that this organ is also peculiar to the *Strombus* and *Pterocera* among marine gastropods. For a long time I was unable to find any reference to it in any of the works in my possession and had quite often wondered what role it could have played. Since the animal moves by successive leaps, it probably was not used for making contact with objects. One might think that this appendage adds in some way to the keenness of sight. But the answer came from the work of J.N. Prince who called this little horn an "olfactory tentacle",[51] a description based on the

99 *Murex sp.* or Venus combs. The one on the right is raised on its vigorous foot.

100 A close-up of the same species to show the importance of the foot and the resemblance of the cephalic tentacles to the shell's thorns.

101 *Chicoreus ramosus* (or "watch-case") and its operculum.

102 *Cypraea tigris* (cowrie shell). In the center of the proboscis, the passage of the radula with its brilliant toothed rasp. Behind the two long cephalic tentacles, numerous fleshy protruberances decorate the mantle. A small area of the foot is stuck to the window pane.

100

101 and 102

---

50 Prince, J.N. *The molluscan eyestalk using as an example Pterocera lambis*. Ohio University, December 20, 1954.
51 The word "olfactory" should really be taken to mean gastronomic sensation since, as P.H. Fisher wrote: "one can only speak of olfactory among land animals".

103 *Strombus thersites*. The foot extended to the maximum to let the operculum "hook" in the sand to turn the shell upright again.

104 The same species showing the resemblance of the mottling on the peduncle eyestalks with that on the shell.

105 *Pterocera lambis.* The eyes at the end of long eyestalks and their sensorial appendage.

106 The same species placed vertically to show eyes, siphon, foot and operculum at the same time.

107 The same species again. The eyes cautiously appear, looking like small puppets.

108 Total elongation of the eyestalks of the same species.

109 *Burso buffa*. Showing the thickness and power of the foot.

109

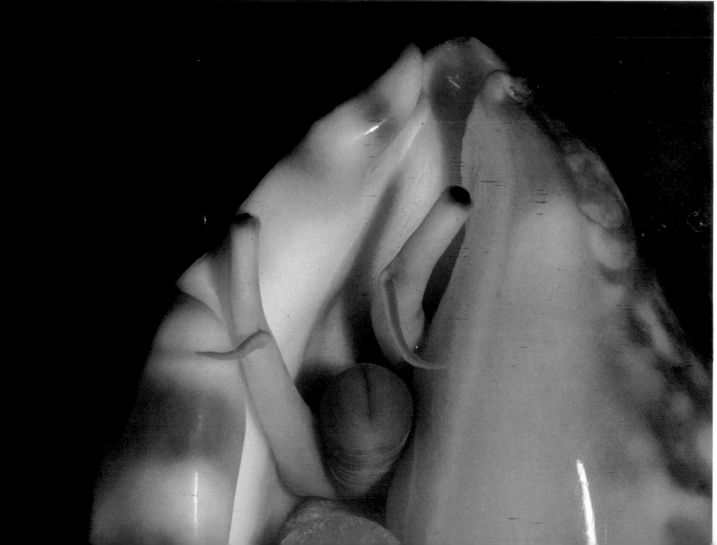

110 *Strombus thersites*. Eyestalks, "fuzzy" eyes and siphon

110

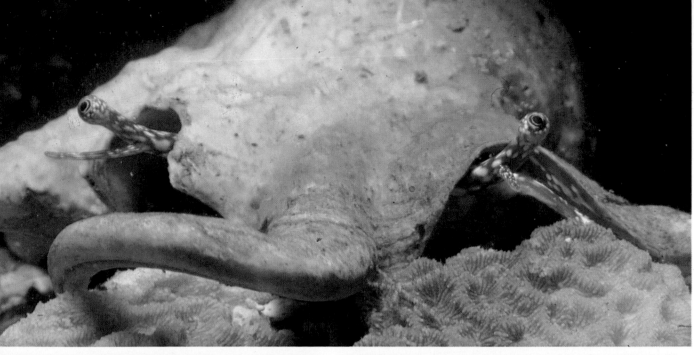

111 *Pterocera lambis*. Unusual photograph (refer to text).

112 *Conus sp.* (this is *merleti* for some, *moluccensis* for others).

113 *Linatella succincta*. The small siphon, top right, emerges from the enormous "head of hair" which is made up of foliations of the periostracum. Its foot is attached to the window pane.

114 The same gastropod seen in profile.

115 The same species on whose foliations a nudibranch has deposited its ribboned eggs at night.

111

112 and 113

114 and 115

117

organ's structure and its nerve connections, which suggest an acute sense of smell.

Careful reading of Prince's work also shows us that the eyestalk is pushed out by the pressure of blood (haemolymph) in a sinus situated in its center and running full length. The pressure of the blood is controlled by muscles which constrict or relax the sphincters.

Plate **105** shows *Pterocera lambis* in an obviously abnormal position. In nature, it always lies flat on the ground with its two ocular tentacles fully extended from its proboscis. Its very long foot and its pointed operculum, about which I spoke earlier, are also visible.

Illustration **110** is a partial view of the *Strombus thersites*[52] showing the extremity of its proboscis and its two ocular tentacles. The eyes are fuzzy in spite of all my photographic attempts to focus clearly on the impossible. Photograph **104** shows, in close-up, the considerably swollen mass of the foot and the proboscis quite free, and also illustrates the curious similarity that exists between the brown marbling of the eyestalks and those of the shell.

As for illustration **111**, I have only incorporated this amusing photograph for the pleasure of lovers of unusual images. While I was following the movements of this *Pterocera*, through the reflex lens of my camera, it suddenly looked as if it were an elephant or a buffalo. It was quite a sight ... so I took a shot just at the right time. It was like being on safari.[53]

Among many gastropods photographed at the Aquarium, I again choose to present the *Tonna perdix* (**116**) which shows the astonishing width of the foot and, on the flat sole (**117**), markings which must have given it its specific name of *perdix* (partridge). The immaculate whiteness of the foot and proboscis of the very pretty *Mitra* (*episcopalis*?) (**94**) is in complete contrast.

One couldn't speak of shells without referring to the famous cone shells which are avidly sought by collectors because of the remarkable beauty and variety of colors and designs. Cones are carnivorous, feeding either on mollusks or worms, and even small fish, which receive a terrible harpoon with a thrust of terrifying speed, when they pass too close.

In his "Catalogue on Shells"[54] J.D. Carthy writes: "Cones are probably at the summit of the evolution pyramid of the gastropods. They surely are when it comes to the specialization of their radula and the weapons that accompany them." In fact, certain species possess a barbed tooth acting like a dart which is connected to a large oesophageal gland secreting venom whose toxicity is sometimes fatal for man.

The most dangerous species is the *Conus geographus*, widespread throughout all the Indo-Pacific area. At the time of writing these lines (June 30th, 1975), a specimen of this species has just caused another fatal accident on the east coast of New Caledonia. In spite of her careful handling of the specimen, a young Tahitian girl (8 years old) was stung and died one and a half hours later. The venom of the animals — a powerful neurotoxin — acts, as one can see, very rapidly. Many other species of cones are dangerous, but not fatal, like the *Conus textile*. Their sting results in tingling sensations or numbness and impaired vision.[55] It is better to be wary of all cones, because species that generally don't have a bad reputation can, in certain seasons, prove to be more toxic than at other times (one suspects such "seasonal" toxicity among other mollusks like the octopus for example).

I have not illustrated the above cone shells, because they have been in all the works on mollusks, but I will illustrate a small cone (5 cm) about which collectors don't quite seem to be in agreement (**112**). For some it is regarded as an extremely rare shell which they named *Conus merleti* after our late friend Yves Merlet. For others, it is only a variety of a relatively common species: *Conus moluccensis*.

One day I was watching our two beautiful "mermaids", Martine and Brigitte, preparing their reef-collecting equipment, thinking: 'They will certainly put some worthwhile specimens into our

---

52   I do not know why the specialist who first described it (Gray) chose to associate this name with a character from Juvénal known for its ugliness and deformity, because this species *thersites* is very beautiful, even for a non-collector.

53   This is the *Elephanto bubalus* Catala!

54   *Panorama des Invertébrés*. vol V. Bordas, Paris/Montréal.

55   Joyce Allan quotes cases of death which happened on Australia's Great Barrier Reef.

116 A *Tonna perdix* showing the astonishing width of its foot.

117 The same species turned over to show the sole of its foot.

116

117

119

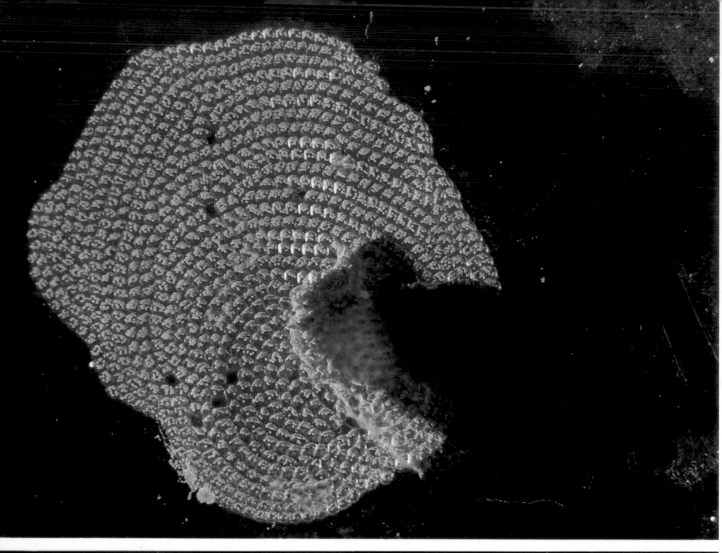

118 A gastropod, *Ergalatax recurrens*, has just spawned and one can admire the remarkable regularity of its produce.

119 Another, a *Vitularia miliaris*, in the act of spawning. On top of the gelatinous capsules enclosing the eggs, the small black disc marks the thinnest area through which the larvae will emerge.

120 A *Janthina violacea* and its floating spawn which keeps it on the surface.

121 A *Gyrenium gyrenium* depositing its eggs on the pane of a tank.

122 A close-up of a few egg capsules, each containing about 200 eggs.

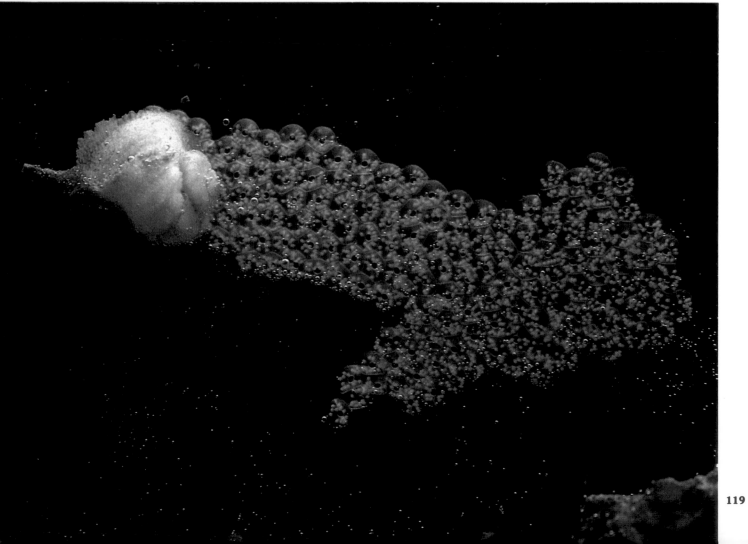

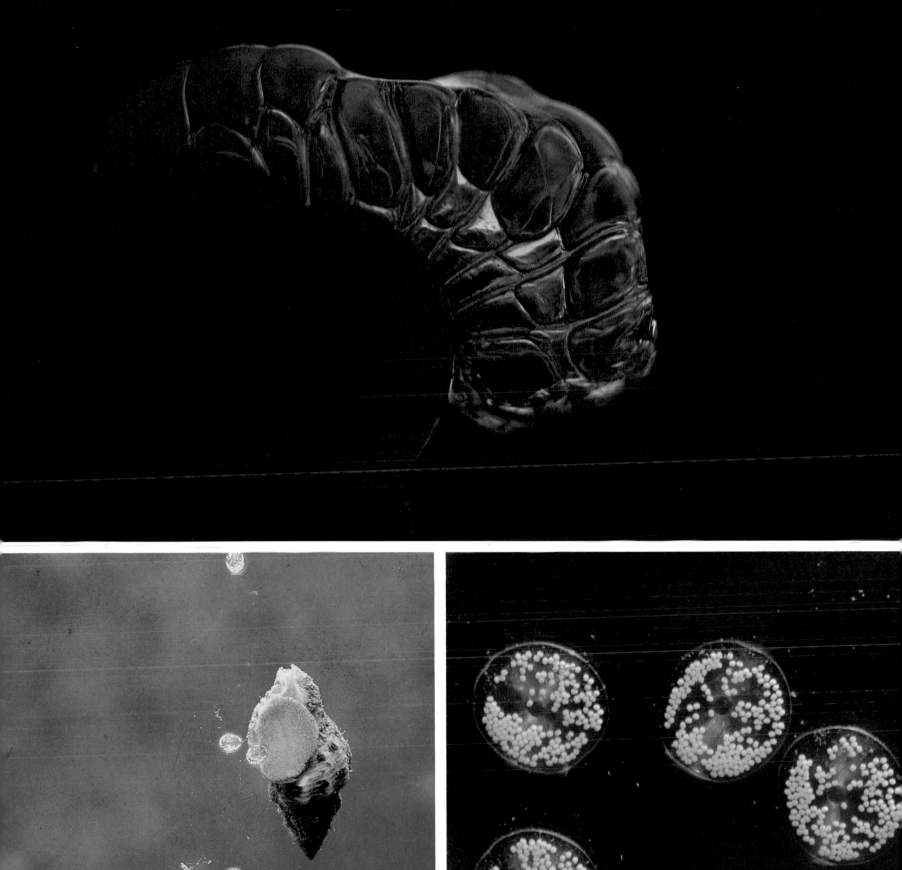

laboratory tanks by tonight.' After many years they have acquired wide knowledge of life on the coral reefs and know whether something is worth collecting. I asked: "Why do you take so much collecting equipment?" to which they replied with wry laughter: "We are going to do some reef-prospecting along the hard, raised, coralline algal rim of the reef".

At the end of the day, dead-tired, shivering and overjoyed, they said: "We bring you many good and beautiful things and especially a young *Glyphisodon xanthonotus*" (Fish, **91**), and added nonchalantly: "We also collected a hippy". This is the name they have given a shellfish that is always covered by an astonishing head of hair. We have never seen such a proliferation of a brown alga on another substrate, fixed or mobile. What were the reasons for this?

One day I decided to send a specimen to my friends at the Australian Museum. Elizabeth Pope, who was the Acting Director, and Phillip Coleman examined it with Winston Ponder. They soon replied to me: "If you had thought of looking at these algae under your microscope, you would have immediately seen that they are not algae because there is no cellular structure. In all probability we are looking at a very particular type of periostracum. This specimen (*Linatella succincta*) belongs to the same group as the hairy oyster borer *Monoplex*. Phillip also added: "We do not have any other specimen which would enable us to carry out a comparison, but many Cymatids have a hairy periostracum. If that is what it is, again, it is a magnificent specimen."

Photographs **113** and **114** show these curious foliations of the external calcareous layer of the shell and the magnitude that such a "mop of hair" can occupy. This is certainly not the reason that gives this *Linatella* its specific name of *succincta*!

Plate **115** is quite unusual in the sense that the egg mass (like a rosette) evidently doesn't belong to the shellfish, but to a sea slug that has laid it during the night on this unusual support.

123 *Mimmachlamis subgloriosa*. As with scallop shells, *Chlamys* have two rows of spherical organs which are sensitive to light. The true base color of these blue "eyes" is red (see photograph 126). Innumerable papillae. In our tepid New Caledonian waters, the external face of the valves (test) of the *Chlamys* is always covered by a more or less thick bed of different sponges.

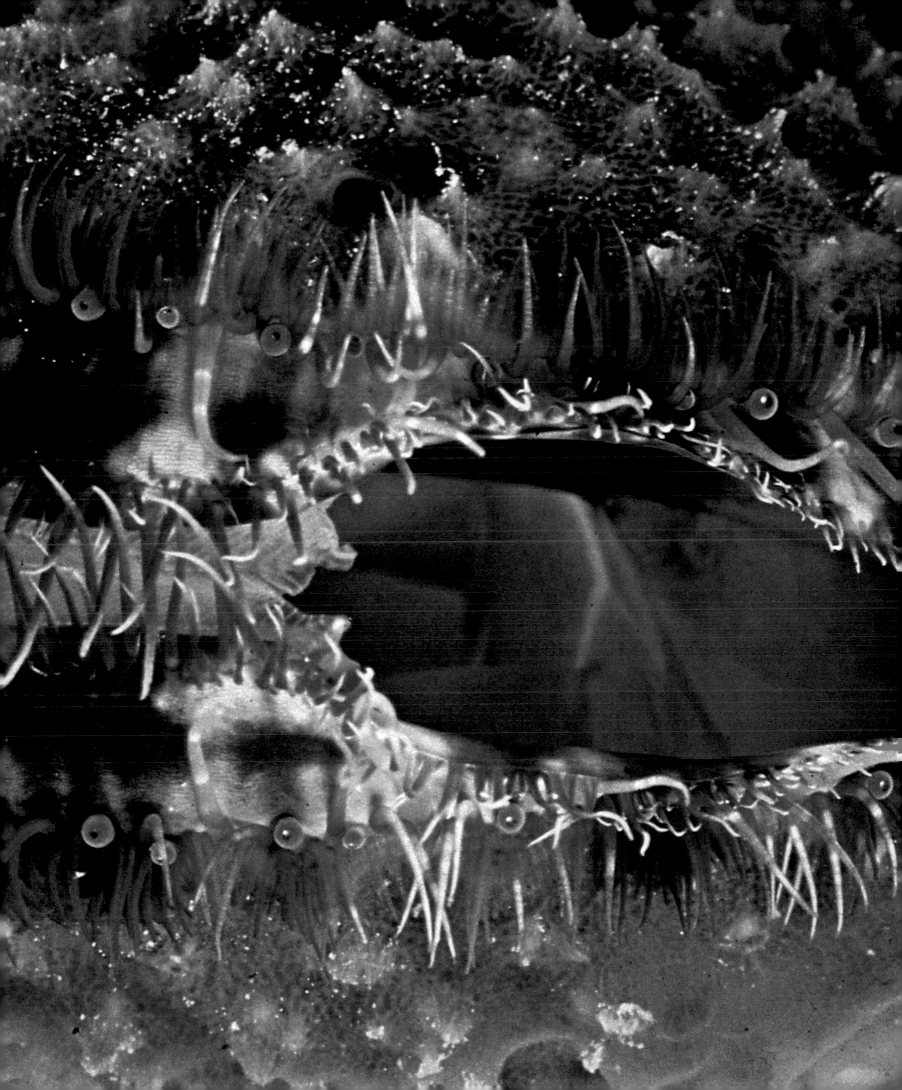

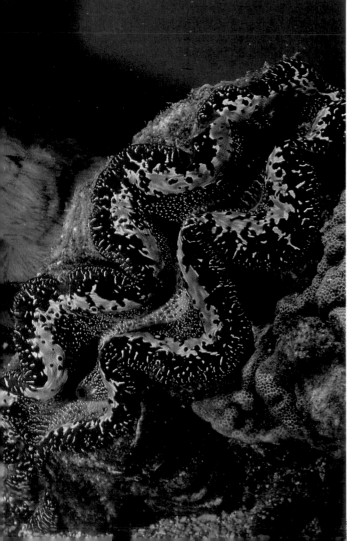

LAMELLIBRANCHS

Having dealt with the Gastropods, and the univalve Prosobranchs, we now come to the class of Bivalvia or Lamellibranchs. Strictly aquatic, the majority of these mollusks live in the sea.[56] They are represented by a considerable number of species ranging from tiny to giants, like certain specimens of *Tridacna* whose length can reach 1.2 meters and weight a quarter of a ton.

The two valves of the shell of lamellibranchs are often joined by interlocking teeth in the grooves forming the hinge (**131**).[57] At the level of this hinge, an elastic ligament permits the valves to open while two adductor muscles contract to make the valves close. One of the most typical examples is given by the oyster *Ostrea* (*Lopha*) *cristagalli* (**132**).

Many lamellibranchs attach themselves to whichever support suits them by many fibers which form a byssus, secreted by a special gland situated at the base of the foot. Examples of bivalves with byssus are mussels, the wing shell (*Pinna*), the *Chlamys* (**134**) and the superb *Ctenoides* about which I will speak later (**140**). This very strong bundle of fibers can be cast off voluntarily by the animal when it wants to move. Sending new fibers a little in front of it, it hauls itself along on them and progresses like this by small successive steps. Unlike the mollusks that I spoke about before, lamellibranchs do not have a radula, but have a mouth bordered on either side by a pair of expanding flaps called palps. The shell is progressively thickened from the inside by the two lobes of the mantle which respectively secrete the two valves. They are formed, like the shells of other gastropods already studied, by an external layer (periostracum), a prismatic layer (ostracum) and a mother-of-pearl layer (hypostracum).

Among bivalves such as the *Pecten* (scallops or Coquilles Saint-Jacques), the *Chlamys*, and the *Spondylus*, the mantle border is amply provided with papillae of remarkable sensitivity. I

56   There are about 5,000 living species and 10,000 fossil species.
57   A small example showing the diversity of structure in closely-related mollusks: the flat oyster (*Ostrea edulis*) possesses a hinge whereas in the Portuguese oyster (*Gryphaea angulata*) this is absent.

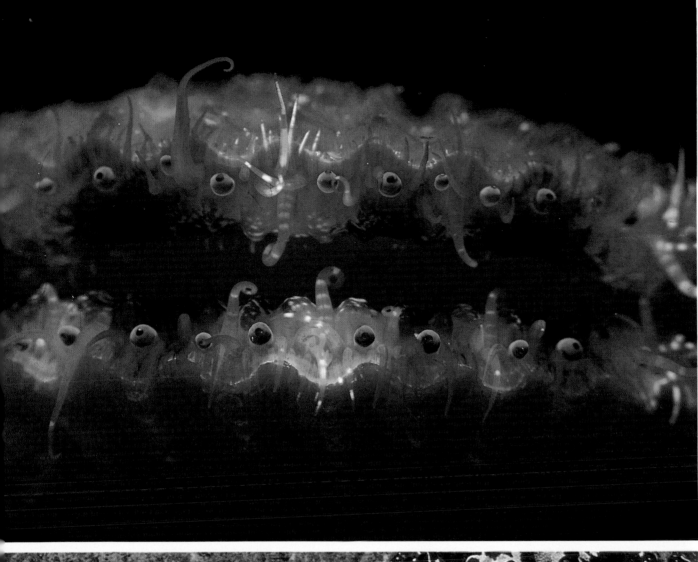

124 and **126** A *Chlamys
vexillum* clearly showing the
bottoms of the red "eyes" and the
diverse lengths of the papillae
(tentacles).

125 and **127** A *Tridacna sp.*
(giant clam) and a close-up of the
flesh which owes its often superb
coloring to the presence of
microscopic algae (zooxanthelles).

126

127

128

129

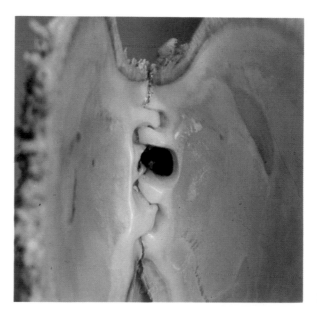

131

was a little bewildered because, in his remarkable work on mollusks[58], André Franc pointed out (p. 1026) that among lamellibranchs the tentacles are absent but the caption of figure 3 (lamellibranchs) says: "the border of the mantle shows the eyes and the tentacles" and, finally (p. 1086): "the olfactory center would essentially comprise, among the lamellibranchs, the border of the mantle, the tentacles, the siphons".

Although the tentacles are very short and similar in length in the *Spondylus varius* (**133**), they are of very variable sizes on the same individual in *Chlamys* (**126**). As for those of the *Ctenoides*, represented here (**140**), they become so long that they end up resembling tentacles of certain coelenterates such as those of the cerianthids (Coelenterates, **44**). Numerous eyes are spaced between these papilla-tentacles and, under certain light conditions, they are of such an intense brilliance that it masks their real color. However, if a slight movement of the mantle transfers them to a position where this iridescence is removed, then these small spherical gems offer us a marvellous spectacle. Even though I have found some very pretty ones, I consider the few pictures that I took of them to be poor in comparison to reality. Under a microscope these little pearls of color sharply contrast in overwhelming beauty with the modest shades of the mantle. Photograph **124** shows the blue eyes and the abundance of papillae while number **129**

58   In Zoologie vol. I. Encyclopédie de la Pléiade, Gallimard, Paris, 1963.

128   A *Spondylus sp.* spontaneously fixed on one of the partition walls of the Aquarium's decantation basin.

129   *Chlamys vexillum*. The gills can be distinguished between the valves.

130   A *Chlamys vexillum* whose two valves are covered by two different species of sponges.

131   Type of hinge on two valves of a lamellibranch (here, a *Spondylus varius*).

132   *Lopha cristagalli* ("cockscomb" oyster). Better than any other lamellibranch, this shows the tight interlocking of the valves.

133   *Spondylus varius*. A large deep-water bivalve (35 meters).

134   *Chlamys vexillum*. To the right, the silvery filaments of the byssus made during the previous night.

135   The same *Spondylus* from close-up. To the right, the "eyes" and the papillae which border them.

132 and

134 and

130

shows us a part of the gills or branchiae between the two valves. In the waters of the lagoon of New Caledonia two species, *Chlamys vexillum* and *Mimmachlamys subgloriosa*, are quite abundant at depths between 20 and 25 meters. These are usually covered by sponges of different species (**130**) and quite often some botryllids have grown on these sponges or directly on the shell.[59]

Photograph **148** shows us a *Chlamys* bivalve covered by groups of *Botrylloides* sp. which were beginning to migrate onto the clumps of algae also growing on this bivalve. Picture **147** is a close-up of them. It was also on a *Chlamys* that a colony from another species of botryllid (not identified) came to attach itself. This is shown by photograph **150**. Finally, the very pretty picture **146** gives us the chance to admire some tiny yellow sea squirts which look just like small amphora jars lined up against each other. Each sea squirt shows the two entrance and exit openings for the water and, deep down, the throat which is pierced by gill slits in the form of a grill.

Experts are of the opinion that, despite the high development of their eyes, *Spondylus, Chlamys, Pecten*, etc., are not able to form actual images but can clearly detect variations in light intensity. Indeed I have readily observed that some *Chlamys*, of which we always have many specimens in the Aquarium, immediately close their valves at the slightest variation of light — as, for example, when one of us passes in front of the glass panes of the tanks. I was often intrigued by the fact that certain individual *Chlamys* had eyes of different sizes (**126**), while among other specimens all the eyes are of an identical size.

The name lamellibranch was given to these bivalves because of the layout of the partitions or lamellae of their gills. These (**139**) divide the pallial cavity in two. Each of these partitions is made up of a double sheet whose internal edges are joined together while the external edges are joined to the mantle. These partitions play a double role of oxygenation and filtering food. The vibratile filaments, with which they are so abundantly provided, move continuously to create a continual water current circulating from

59   These organisms belong to the same phylum of *Provertebrates* of which *Carnaval sous la mer* showed a giant species *Polycarpa aurata* — figs. 1 and 2 of the color plate XXIII and fig. 36.

136

137

138

136 *Ctenoïdes sp*. Completely closed.

137 *Ctenoïdes sp*. The beginning of the separation of the valves, with a few tentacles or papillae appearing (see text).

138 *Ctenoïdes sp*. Valves quite open and papillae extended.

139 *Ctenoïdes sp*. Segments of the gills quite visible.

140 *Ctenoïdes sp*. A little below the summit the perforation of a boring mollusk can be seen.

139

140

the inhaling chamber to the exhaling chamber. The quantity of water that the lamellibranchs force through their valves evidently varies with the species. According to certain authors, it is in the order of 20 to 30 liters an hour for some oysters. The epithelium of the gills and of the mantle can take up oxygen from the seawater and also expell its blood impurities and thus complete all the respiratory requirements.

After food elements have been filtered out, the remainder is covered in mucus secreted by the gills and violently ejected. Photograph **144** shows the little balls of slimy conglomerate that our beautiful deep-water *Ctenoides* rejected by frequent contractions of its valves. This happened during the days of a storm when water arriving into our tanks was loaded with an excess of sediment. I will have more to say about this rare bivalve. The food elements that are filtered out are protozoa, diatoms and other planktonic organisms floating in the water.

One couldn't speak about the nutrition of these mollusks without noting the quite strange mechanism and function of an organ in the stomach, called the crystalline style, which can reach a length of many tens of centimeters among the large bivalves such as the giant clam (*Tridacna* **125** and **127**). This translucent crystalline finger can rotate rapidly to mix the mucus and food elements. These are forced against the lining of the stomachal region called the "*bouclier gastrique*" and, once broken up, are moved into the digestive diverticulum. Apart from the mechanical role played by this style, it also serves

a chemical function. In effect, the organic matter of which it is made dissolves in the stomach.

G. Ranson tells us[60]: "The enzyme that it liberates (an amylase) transforms the starch and the glycogen into easily assimilated, reducing sugars." This crystalline style thus suffers a loss of considerable substance but is constantly reforming. According to D. Barnes,[61] this regeneration can occur twice in 24 hours among certain species of bivalves when their food intake coincides with the two returns of the tide.

Based on the anatomy of lamellibranchs, they can be divided into three orders — the Protobranchs, which include the primitive forms such as the *Neotrigonia* on the Australian coasts, the Filibranchs (mussels, oysters, wing shell, scallops, Coquille St-Jacques etc.) and the Eulamellibranchs (giant clams, clams, teredos, etc).

I will spare the reader a description of all the other organs of digestion, excretion, reproduction etc., so those who wish to know more about the anatomy of bivalves will have to consult one of the works listed in the Bibliography of this book. However, I will add a small paragraph on the swimming ability of certain species of bivalves, particularly the *Chlamys* which is common here. Their movement is carried out by the sudden opening and closing of their valves. Water is violently ejected on each side of the hinge and this makes the animal move with its valves forward. When several *Chlamys* have been grouped together in a tank, it is always an amazing sight to see one of these mollusks, then another, "fly away", twirl and fall to the bottom. If you want to increase the spectacle and provoke a general "stampede", all you have to do is place a starfish in the tank, a great enemy of these bivalves. Then you can watch a bizarre dance with all the little castanets fleeing from danger.

Two diver friends explored a region rich in giant sea squirts[62] at a depth of 25 meters and noticed in the blue distance something which they took to be a cerianthid (Coelenterates, **44**). They

141

60   Ranson, G. *La vie des huîtres*. Histoire Naturelle Nouvelle Revue Française. Gallimard, 1943.
61   Barnes, Robert. *Invertebrate Zoology*. W.B. Saunders Company, Philadelphia, 1968.
62   Referring to the superb, yet so strange, *Polycarpa aurata* shown in color in figs. 1 and 2 of plate XXIII, *Carnaval sous la mer*.

141 *Lima lima*, a very common small bivalve, usually hidden under stones.

142 *Ctenoïdes sp*. Suspended by its long and thin byssus.

143 *Ctenoïdes sp*. Placed on a glass plate (see text).

144 *Ctenoïdes sp*. Little balls of slimy agglomeration. One of them (above the shell) has just been ejected.

145 *Ctenoïdes sp*. As in 144, the foot is extended and it is exploring the ground.

146 The *Chlamys* often carry colonies of sea-squirts on one of their valves. Some sea-squirts look like jars and on the inside the "grill-like" pharynx can be distinguished.

147 and **148** Groups of *Botrylloïdes sp*: here you can see the whole colony fixed on the shell of a *Chlamys* bivalve, as well as on a species of alga.

149 and **150** Two other species of *Botrylloïdes* also growing on *Chlamys*.

146

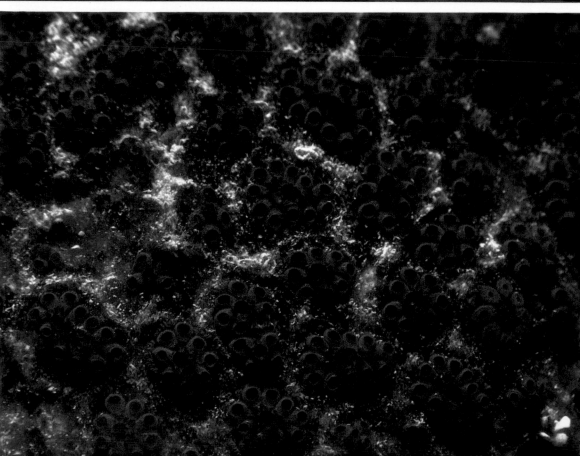

147

132

paid little attention since the Aquarium already had plenty. "However," my friend Conseil told me, "we were in a rocky area and I suspected it must have been something else because the cerianthids are always on sandy, muddy bottoms. So we swam back and ... we bring you the object."

I thought it was a joke because I didn't find anything especially attractive about this closed, modest bivalve (*Ctenoides,* **136**). But Conseil said to me: "No, it isn't a joke, as you will realize when it has opened its valves."

As soon as it was installed calmly in one of the laboratory tanks, the exceptional beauty of its long papillae or tentacles was revealed (illustration **140**). Each morning I would find it in a different place in the tank, attached by its fine byssus which it would reconstitute after its nocturnal movements. However, as it was always "moored" to one of the rocks right down at the bottom of the tank, I was very frustrated in trying to take good photographs. I therefore put it on a glass sheet half way up the tank and during the night it would attach its byssus "cable" to the pane of the tank; then, with infinite care, I would take away its glass support, but often its weight alone was enough to break the mooring threads and I would have to start all over again. The game was worth it because certain photographs show us the branchiae, the foot and the very fine byssus (**142**).

This ctenoid lived for several months but a lengthy storm from the west took this poor mollusk's life because of the necessity for prolonged filtering of the sediment in the circulating water system. An oyster, or another bivalve which normally lives in muddy surroundings, would certainly have had more chance of surviving than this ctenoid which comes from a depth where the effects of storms are very rarely felt. This precious bivalve (of which we have never found other specimens) had previously brushed with death. One of its valves had suffered an attack from some drilling animal, probably another mollusk. The perpetrator of this incident had drilled many holes (**140**) and it must have in turn been disturbed by another predator, just at the moment when it was going to penetrate the body. This boring through of the shell must have taken place shortly before its capture because I could not make out the beginnings of any attempt to repair these perforations.

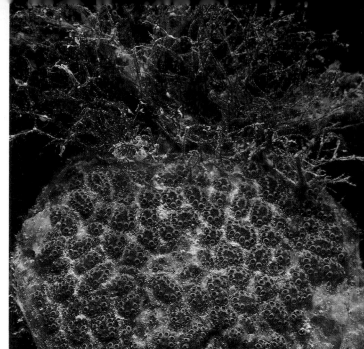

148

149

150

CEPHALOPODS

All Cephalopods live in a marine environment. Their habitats range from the clear coastal waters, where we see them swimming near the surface, to the darkness of the ocean depths. Their size varies from 15 millimeters in length, as is the case for a tiny little cuttlefish of the genus *Idiosepius*, to the 17 meters of the ghostly *Architeuthis*, which are at the moment the largest known invertebrates. I say "at the moment", because there is nothing to stop us from believing that the legendary Kraken really exists.

The more-specialized mollusks feature in the Dibranch subdivision (octopus, cuttlefish and squid). They are noted as much because of the perfection of certain organs as for their intelligence, coming from a nervous system with a remarkable concentration in the head. Because of the size of this nervous mass in the head, it can be considered a true brain. The tanks of Aquarium of Noumea have contained cuttlefish, squid and octopus for 20 years.

Cuttlefish

The species that we have observed for a long time is commonly called the cuttle-bone (**183**). Some scientists have given me the identification *Sepia latimana*, others *Solitosepia liliana*, and others still have replied that they couldn't decide. In Joyce Allan's work, *Australian Shells*, color plate 44 shows a *Solitosepia plangon* which closely resembles ours. I am therefore happy with the generic name *Solitosepia* because it is really its behavior that matters most. I will add that, as susceptible as it is to the most subtle excitations, it never went pale or blushed red at hearing itself being called *Solitosepia* rather than *Sepia*! The photographs allow me to dispense with tedious descriptions of its external morphology. However, it should be noted that the front part of the animal has a crown with eight short oral arms to which are added two extensible and prehensile tentacles, visible only during the extremely brief time when they stretch out to catch distant prey (**161**). For a body measuring only 23 centimeters, a young cuttlefish, about which I will have more to say later, had prehensile tentacles that were 22 centimeters long!

The arms have suction-cups strengthened with firm circular edges, as is also the situation for the two extensible tentacles whose blade-like shape increases their adhesive power. Anything captured by them is brought to the short arms which quickly push it into contact with the terrible parrot beak. These powerful beaks grind and tear prey to pieces while the radula exercises its function as a rasp. It only takes a few minutes for a fish or crab to be sighted, captured and swallowed.

The eyes of the cuttlefish, squid and octopus, are of great specialization. They are made up of a cornea, iris, crystalline lens, retina, ganglion and optic nerve, vitreous humor, etc., which clearly compare with the components of the eyes of vertebrates. The statocysts (organs of balance) are situated on both sides of the brain. The shell or cuttle-bone of the cuttlefish is internal and in the *Solitosepia* occupies a considerable space under the dorsal skin. The buoyancy of the animal is assured by this cuttle-bone and by the almost continuous undulations of the lateral fins bordering the posterior part of the animal. This fin, which is in fact a thin expansion of the mantle, acts both as a stabilizer and as a rudder. Moreover, it also plays a role of slow propulsion when the animal moves forwards. Rapid backward propulsion, however, takes place by the contraction of the mantle muscles which force water back through the funnel (**153** and **171**). The animal therefore moves by jet propulsion, as do squid, octopus and the nautilus about which we will talk later.

The skin of cuttlefish and other cephalopods is provided with a myriad of small starry cells called chromatophores. These cells react to the visual or emotive excitations of the animal by expansion or contraction of color. Some general colors will persist all the time, colors necessary for perfect camouflage with the surrounding environment, while others are fleeting and only appear when there is fear or anger or in the course of movements associated with capturing prey.

The overall range of colors is remarkable because certain chromatophores react by expanding their pigments while other color cells are simultaneously concentrating theirs. To the multiple combinations that are thus possible there must be added the shimmering effects of

151 A sleepy *Solitosepia* cuttlefish with its "eyelids" closed. It is lying in contact with the ground.

152 *Solitosepia* cuttlefish awake and freed from the bottom.

153 *Solitosepia* cuttlefish in a state of defence or anger, caused here by a stick which has been plunged into the tank.

151

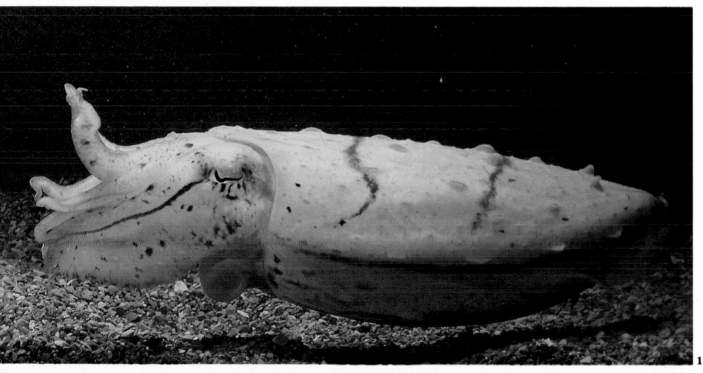

152

153

135

154 *Solitosepia* cuttlefish with arms crossed, but attentive and slightly worried.

155 *Solitosepia* cuttlefish in mid-waters. Its light color matches the sandy bottom.

156 *Solitosepia* cuttlefish. Having allowed itself to be diverted to a rocky bottom, its pigmentation has darkened.

154

155

156

iridescence, due to another type of cells, the iridocytes, which have the ability to reflect light.

I have listed below the most frequent activities of the *Solitosepia*, the pigmentations that correspond to them and also the texture of the skin.

151 - Sleepy with "eyelids" closed. It is on bare ground. Contrary to the European cuttlefish, (*Sepia officinalis*), it never buries itself. Notice the remarkable camouflage to match the sand it is on. It is a uniform shade.

152 - Awake, it has immediately freed itself from the bottom. Two dorsal stripes appear in brown on a cream background, and a stripe goes from the eye to the extremity of each arm. These arms are slightly erected.

154 - Arms crossed, but attentive and slightly worried.

157 - Arms erect, it is a sign that it is alert, but among tamed *Solitosepia* this also means that it is waiting for food. The protuberances jut out strongly.

158 - A close-up of the arms showing very fine pigmentation.

153 - In a state of defence or anger.

155 - Underwater calm. Its yellow shade matches the sand in the background.

156 - Having been diverted to a rocky background, the animal's pigmentation has immediately darkened.

159 - It has just noticed prey. The prehensile tentacles shoot out only to retract immediately, its "shot" not having any chance of reaching the target.

160 - Sometimes, when the prey is small in size and close to the suction-cups, the protuberances do not jut out and the skin remains perfectly smooth.

162 - "Aiming up". **163** "Aiming down".

164 - Out of hundreds of photographs, this is the only one that allows us to distinguish the two tentacles separated from each other. One can notice the curvature of blades carrying the suction-cups.

157

157 *Solitosepia* cuttlefish alert with its arms erect.

158 *Solitosepia* cuttlefish. A close-up of the oral arms and the fine granulations of their chromatophores.

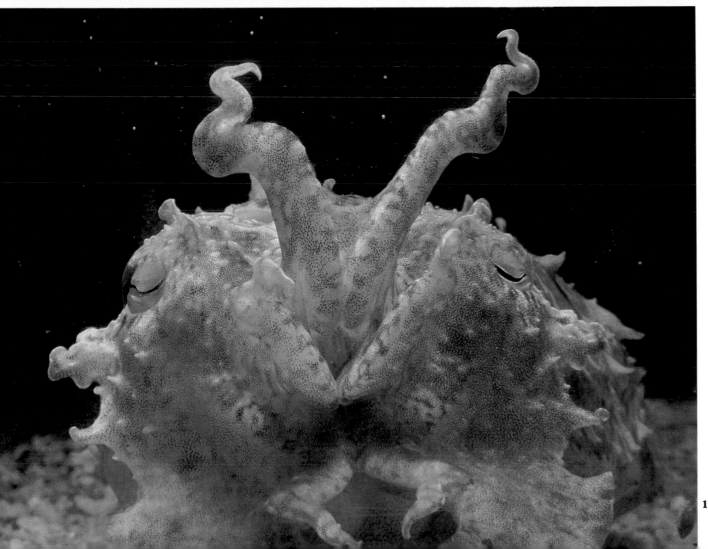

158

165 - An adult *Solitosepia* that has just caught a big mullet which is being solidly held by the powerful grasp of its arms. The anterior half of the fish has already been dealt with. At this stage its head has already been crushed by the beak. One immediately notices the contrast in intensity of the brown spots — a coloring that always appears as soon as large prey has been captured.

172 and **173** - Characteristic pictures of moments of libido.

174 - The beginnings of mating. Initial caresses. The male (white) puts its arms on the head of the female (extremely dark).

175 - Mating.

The eggs of cuttlefish (or "sea grapes") are laid by preference between the branches of coral or at their base (**168**). Illustrations **161** and **164** require a little explanation. The thrust of the tentacles and their return to bring the prey back to the mouth is extremely rapid. The reflexes of a photographer are not quick enough, from far away, to press the shutter-release at the precise moment. Therefore, not to miss the impact, many shots were taken either a little too early or a little too late, and we had to take many in order to get the correct one. It is evident, in similar cases, that it is necessary to film at great speed, but even the most sophisticated material is not able to resolve all the problems, whether biological or technical.

For nearly 20 years of this aquarium's life, we have seen sea organisms go through our tanks that belong to just about all the classification groupings of animals. The strangeness or peculiarity of their behavior, undeniable acts of intelligence among some, skilfulness among others, and the superb visual value of most of them have greatly satisfied our wonder and biological curiosity. But our constant concern and care for them was because of our scientific or aesthetic interest. In other words, emotional sentiments didn't necessarily interfere.

A favorite cuttlefish

Nevertheless, certain specimens in the Aquarium were very dear to us and became our favorites. Which animal lover would sneer at the affection given to a faithful dog whose beautiful gaze often expresses so much and whose attachment can be so moving? Therefore we will admit (even though many persist in being amazed) that a real sentiment can exist on our part for marine organisms. My wife was the one who took care of their well-being each day of these 20 years, fed them, watched them, looked after them and she knew when all her tanks were in perfect equilibrium, but also worried if one of the older residents was going through a bad period. This digression is because of one little cuttlefish, with which I lived so intimately for many months and which held such an important place in my daily life.

I could dedicate a book just to the subject of this cuttlefish, but I will limit myself to some observations about its food preferences. It is well known, of course, that cuttlefish and squid are only interested in living prey. The minute whitebait (*Lebistes*), although naturally living in fresh water and swampy areas or estuaries, and sometimes even putrid waters (where cuttlefish have never been able to venture), were always a feast for this cuttlefish. The estuarine *Tilapia*[63] which, in nature, remain quite close to the banks, were appreciated by it for only a few weeks. When I deliberately stopped feeding it mullet (*Mugil*) for 48 hours, the cuttlefish would scorn the few *Tilapia* moving around within easy reach. Another time it found some whitefish (*Gerres*), more to its liking than the mullet but it lost interest after several days. From time to time we would catch young trevally (*Caranx sexfasciatus*) and *Trachinotus blochi* in our throw nets and, of all these fish that featured on the "menu", it was the small trevally that were always preferred.

But there is another category of prey that cuttlefish are very fond of: crabs. I wanted to see just where the gluttony of our little resident led to

---

63   A fish imported into New Caledonia about 20 years ago. I have an unfavorable opinion of the person who took the initiative for this introduction, remembering the astonishing proliferation of a species that was closely related to it in Madagascar (*Paratilapia pollenni*). *Tilapia* has now invaded rivers, streams, lakes and marshlands in New Caledonia. One can even see them in areas of the bank where the water of certain marshlands overflows. We kept some in our sea-water tanks for many months. They remained in good health but never reproduced.

159 *Solitosepia* cuttlefish which has just noticed prey. The prehensile tentacles shoot out only to retract immediately when the "shot" has little chance of success.

160 *Solitosepia* cuttlefish. Sometimes, when the prey that has been lined up is quite close and small, skin protuberances do not form.

161 *Solitosepia* cuttlefish in the act of capturing. Seen from the side, the two tentacles seem to be one, looking like a chameleon's tongue that is totally extended.

and I put a fiddler crab (Uca[64]) in its tank, which immediately put itself on the defensive. Its large red nipper, which was very menacing, didn't frighten our cuttlefish at all and it sprang at it without hesitation, wrapped its prehensile tentacles around it and swallowed. The crushing of the crab with its parrot's beak was quite laborious and, during the whole time, the large nipper and the long stalked eyes hadn't yet been crushed. What a peculiar sight this was — like some strange animal resembling both a mollusk and a crustacean at the same time ... enough to give the specialist nightmares! On film this is very intriguing.

One day I invited a few friends to come and watch this spectacle which was always captivating because of the precision of its "shooting arms" and the changing color patterns that follow. Having taken care not to feed it before — I wanted to be certain of a perfect demonstration and one that could be repeated several times — I gave it the whitebait, knowing that it would never refuse them. My friends and I kept at an appropriate distance from the tank so as not to frighten the "star" and I also asked them not to make any sudden movements for fear of upsetting it. But, despite all these precautions, this animal refrained from lashing out. My guests had come for nothing! But they had barely moved away when, in front of me, watching it alone now and from close up, the little cuttlefish was lashing out at will.

Of course I will not go as far as to say that it recognized the different faces of my friends (and yet!), but could it distinguish different silhouettes?[65]

I had established a regular program for longterm observations of this precious specimen but it unfortunately died and there was no chance that we would ever find another young individual of the same species.

At that age, they still have quite a lot of things to learn but even more to teach us! I do not want to speak too much about taming these very gifted animals. They do not need to be tamed to rapidly learn certain habits on their own. That little cuttlefish only squirted its ink once, when it was first transported from the collecting bucket into the laboratory tank. A few days later, I dipped in a large glass bowl to transfer it into the special outdoor tank I use for taking photographs. It squirted some water in my face. The next day it

was much quieter and, a few days later, I only had to push it with my finger to make it go into the bowl.

This little cuttlefish which, in front of strangers didn't want to lash out at its prey, would not hesitate in capturing them even when my hands were plunged in the tank to replace some coral only 60 centimeters away. Several times it would clutch a finger but without ever biting. I believe that it was doing it for fun!

Another observation deserves to be highlighted. I said that cuttlefish have great need of very well oxygenated, very abundant and perfectly clear sea-water. The accidental loss of large specimens in the Aquarium was nearly always a result of rough seas, when the wind from the west creates such huge waves that they raise the muddy sands off the bottom. Therefore the quantity of sediments arriving in our tanks is fatal for these cephalopods.

This was always our greatest problem with our little resident. To endeavor to give it some chance of survival when one of these nasty winds from the west sprang up, we decided to transfer it to a tank without sand on the bottom. The storm lasted two days and nights and during this period of dirty water our cuttlefish remained propped in a corner of the tank and did not stop blowing with its siphon. The mud was deposited in front of it, thus creating a continually clean 180° field. It was thanks to this continual "sweeping" that it came out victorious after such a long trial.[66]

The large specimens of the same species in our tanks died after only one night in such conditions, and they had never behaved like this. Sweeping at the sand level would have been completely ineffectual. That is probably why they would always remain in midwater. We could not transfer them into tanks without sand since this

64 Anglo-Saxons have given Uca the name "fiddler crabs" because of the bow-like movement of one of the nippers which is disproportionately large among the males. (Crustacea, 74).
65 The American physiologist, Arthur Martin, from the University of Washington, Seattle, told me that he and his associates had often observed that octopuses could distinguish one person from another . My old friend, Jean Painlevé, quoted several examples of this as well.
66 During all this time, it did not make one single attempt to capture a few small fish that we had put in on the off chance, as if it intuitively knew that the slightest movement of its body could be fatal.

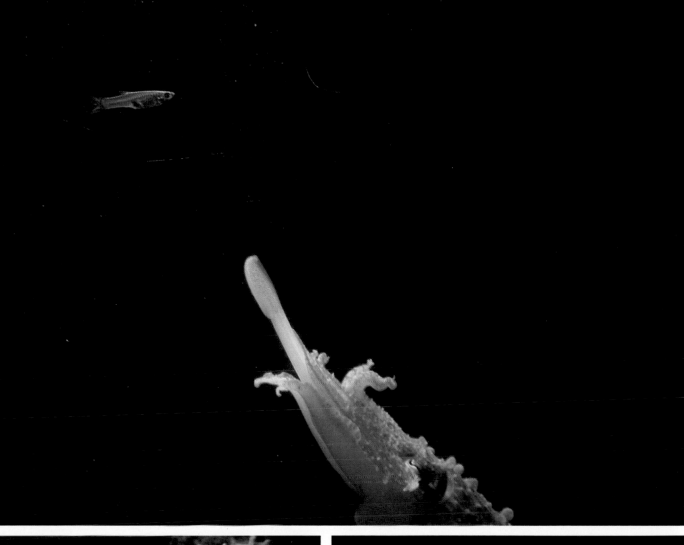

162 *Solitosepia sp.* Aiming upwards for a *Lebistes* (whitebait).

163 *Solitosepia sp.* Pointing down, still perfectly aimed.

164 *Solitosepia sp.* Quite separated from each other, the tentacles capture a small prey. Notice the prehension curvature of the blades carrying the suction cups.

162

163 and 164

141

165 *Solitosepia sp*. A big mullet has just been caught. Large brown spots always appear when good-sized prey are caught.

166 *Solitosepia sp*. A "white fish" (*Gerres sp*.), inhibited, remains stationary in front of the cuttlefish. It would have had all the time in the world to flee.

167 *Solitosepia sp*. showing curiosity. The very open eye observes attentively.

165

166

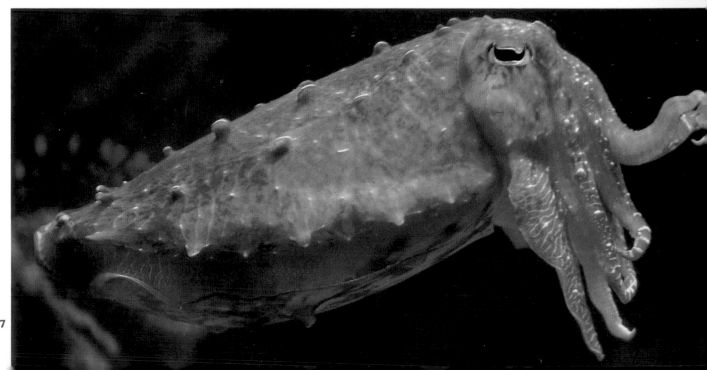

167

168 *Solitosepia sp.* with its spherical eggs (sea grapes) laid at the base of a branching coral.

169 *Solitosepia sp.* What does one make of that strange tumor in front of the eye (see anecdotal text)?

170 *Solitosepia sp.* A large crab (*Scylla serrata*) being crushed by the cuttlefish's beak: a few legs are still showing but they will soon be consumed.

would have forced them to submit to inevitable trauma during their violent struggles. It is logical to think that at sea, when bad weather occurs, they move towards coastal areas and generally reach zones where the water is more protected.

Let's come back to our little *Solitosepia*. If it had a notion that a desired prey could not be captured at the first attempt, it would refrain from lashing out. Its prehensile tentacles would sometimes make a half-hearted attempt, but then one would only see them coming out one or two centimeters and retracting immediately. A cuttlefish uses its tentacles intelligently. It moves slowly and skilfully into a more favorable position until it finds itself at a perfectly calculated distance so as not to miss. However, there are times when it does not succeed in its attempt to capture the prey. This is not because of the inaccuracy of its lashing tentacles — I have never seen the slightest mistake — but because its suction-cups have slipped off the scales of the fish. I have often wondered if an adhesive mucus wasn't used as well, to supplement the suction-cups with their thousands of tiny teeth.

A frequent observation of ours might help this hypothesis. One day our cuttlefish was again resting on an empty stomach. Instead of giving it a good sized mullet, I gave it some tiny whitebait which immediately scattered in the tank. Waking up, it took quite a time to organise its arms. It also changed colors immediately, its skin bristled with small protuberances, a pair of short arms came out and the cephalic arch appeared. It then "aimed at" a small fish and accurately caught it. A simple cocktail snack! At that moment I put in a mullet. With its usual approach precautions, it headed in its direction, shot, and this time the mullet was perfectly hooked. Despite its vigorous contortions, the mullet was taken to the short arms which imprisoned it. I tried some more experiments and they always ended in the same way.

A saliva coating

Another time our young cuttlefish was resting in its dormant position and had nothing to eat for 24 hours. Through one of the openings used on the lid of the tank, I very slowly put in a mullet of convenient size. Despite appearing sleepy, it had already seen the vibrations caused by the fins of the fish. But this prey, arriving unexpectedly and

168

169

170

so close, surprises it. Being hungry, it reacts too quickly. It pivots and is in a position to strike in less than five seconds. The lightning shooting of the tentacles is felt in full by the fish but it escapes. Now such a slip would not happen if the cuttlefish had taken its time to get ready. "Get ready for what?" you might ask. Not being able to see exactly what goes on inside, I will restrict myself to guessing that, in the space between the root of the short arms and the eyes, the skin arches up, in the same way as when the animal is crushing and tearing apart prey in its jaws. Therefore one can postulate that our cuttlefish coats the suction-cup on the tentacle blades with saliva. One knows, in fact, that these cephalopods possess salivary glands discharging in the head region. The experts have told us that this saliva is toxic but one cannot see how its venomous action can be utilized by the tentacles when they are out. In other words, this saliva wouldn't have venomous effects on the prey until it had been passed to the mouth by the short arms. But nobody has suggested that this saliva has adhesive properties.

On the subject of mullet offered as food to our cuttlefish, I must mention some strange behavior. Anyone having caught live mullet from a fish-pond of sea-water must appreciate their astonishing ability to avoid the landing net. And as every good throw-net fisherman knows only too well, it takes a lot of guile to successfully cover a shoal of these fish, so quick are they to react.

I have just put one of them into the tank where our young cuttlefish is dozing. The mullet has many places to shelter thanks to algae, rocks and corals behind which the cuttlefish would undoubtedly never be able to reach. Now, we are witnessing this astonishing scene. If there had been no cuttlefish in the tank the mullet would not

have stopped swimming about, but now he remains there, facing it, completely fixed as if hypnotized. Only the fins quiver. In these conditions, the cuttlefish could quite easily reach prey which literally seems to be offering itself, and the poor fish has all the time to get out of its reach. Many of us have also noticed this complete inhibition[67] among white fish like the *Leignathes* or the *Gerres* (**166**).

We had the chance to observe a mating of the *Solitosepia* in one of the Aquarium's large tanks. The partners faced one another, their 16 arms endlessly tangling and untangling. Such voluptuous caresses lasted for several hours. The continuous elegant undulations of the mantle's iridescent fringe adds to the infinite grace of this tandem of love. This is a beautiful spectacle, perhaps the most magnificent that marine organisms can provide, and unfortunately none of my photographs have been able to do justice to it (**173** to **175**). A little before night the couple separate and by dawn the female is ready to lay. The eggs slide out on the two extensible tentacles, at intervals of a few minutes, and are fixed between the branches of an *Acropora* coral (**168**). After the eggs are laid, it blows non-stop on these large "white grapes" with its swivelling siphon so that no impurity can attach to them.

The male only rarely participates in this activity, but is very intent in watching over the area where the eggs are laid. The eggs are very fragile and there are many potential predators. The most feared are crabs who can make a very quick meal of them. But no matter how quick they are, their chances are much reduced by the watchful male.

The days passed and we waited impatiently for hatching. Alas, a violent westerly wind sprang up which blew for a very long time, with the fatal consequences that have already been mentioned.

One morning we noticed that our cuttlefish had a swelling like a tumor in front of one eye (**169**). I say like because a tumor obviously doesn't form in one night. Perhaps it was a parasite, but the cuttlefish wouldn't allow its flesh to be penetrated by a parasite of this size. In the following days — and this lasted for more than

171

67 This is also observed when mullet are placed in the tank of the stonefish. But then the conditions are different. If a mullet stops still, it is because it has just witnessed one of its fellow creatures being swallowed. It gives it something to think about!

171 *Solitosepia sp*. The cuttlefish has just orientated its siphon, laterally, in order to pivot.

172 *Solitosepia sp*. The vertical white bands stand out — the first sign of sexual excitement.

173 *Solitosepia sp*. Superb coloration accompanying the state of intense libido.

172

173

174 *Solitosepia sp*. The very pale male caresses his partner.

175 *Solitosepia sp*. The couple's position during mating.

174

175

two weeks — the tumor persisted but, fortunately for the animal's eye, it did not grow. It had been agreed that we would immediately dissect the tissues of its head the day this *Solitosepia* died to discover the nature of this puzzling tumor.

Some time later we had a second cuttlefish brought to us, but we alway hesitate to place two animals together which are not acquainted with each other because, even if they are of a different sex, one never knows the reactions that the new arrival will cause. It may either be fury, with jets of ink that do not actually lead to a battle to the death, or it may be curiosity by feeling or caressing the eventual possible companion or the adversary.

On this occasion the arrival of the new cuttlefish gave rise to a reaction of fear. Our "patient with a tumor" made such a hurried lurch — like an aeroplane carrying out a barrel-roll — that a large bubble of air escaped from it and the tumour disappeared!

It was only then that we realized the origin of this puzzle. Our cuttlefish must have sat for a long time near one of the powerful aerated water ducts supplying its tank. It must have had, as my doctor friend, Philippe Couzigou, would laughingly say, "a subcutaneous air embolism".

Squid

When our Aquarium was started we captured shoals of about 30 young squid close to the shore in less than two meters of water. Their size scarcely reached 20 centimeters. They were placed in a long, 10,000 liter tank, and their eagerness in immediately trying to capture the little live sardines gave us the impression that they were going to survive very nicely. But after about only 30 hours they would die.

After several attempts we gave up, thinking that the fact of being captives explained these quick deaths. This is where we were wrong. Much later we learned that it was all to do with the water. Although it was continually running, the flow rate wasn't rapid enough. There were many fragile organisms that we were not able to preserve in the early days because the flow was less than 400,000 liters a day. These organisms would have behaved admirably if there had been a daily flow of more than one million liters in all of our set-up.

The same conclusion could be made about the newly-born squid that would not survive more than 30 to 36 hours. But at least their brief lives allowed us to make a few interesting observations. Photograph **178** shows the laying of squid eggs brought up from 25 meters. These clusters of eggs were fixed to a sponge. For most of them hatching stretched out over two days. As soon as the babies had emerged from their eggs, they quickly ejected the contents of their ink pockets and these expulsions were carried out at intervals of about ten minutes for a few hours. In their first two to three days, they swam in a succession of vertical jumps broken by periods of rest.

Watching these tiny creatures (only a few millimeters long) attaching themselves suddenly by their back to the panes of the tank, I was very surprised that they left not the slightest trace of adhesive substance on the window pane, especially after remaining so tightly stuck to it for several minutes. A large magnifying-glass revealed that their attachment was all done in a mechanical manner. A small indentation would form at a given point on their dorsal skin and this little indentation would act as a suction-cup. This was exactly like the rubber suction-cups on toy arrows that we used to shoot at targets from small spring-operated guns as children. Photograph **179** allows us to see this little suction-cup.

However, we still had to wait for nearly 20 years for the opportunity to finally see two squid, with respective sizes of 45 and 30 centimeters, moving around our large tanks at the Aquarium. They had been captured at sea by our friend Elie Lechanteur, a professional fisherman who, like many of his colleagues, was always eager to bring us valuable specimens.

Cuttlefish, apart from the moment when they are capturing prey, are always placid and often remain quite stationary. Squid, however, are perpetually active night and day, with their slender bodies making them look extremely graceful. Their swimming movement is very rapid and can be just as efficient backwards as forwards, thanks to continual undulations by the sides of the mantle, and by water jetted out of the siphon. The two oral arms that are furthest from the major axis of the animal, almost constantly carry out a scissor-movement (**182**) which can lead one to think that it is playing a feeding role. These lateral

176

177

178

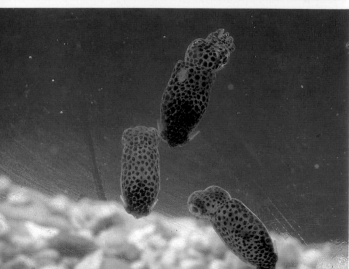

179

beatings, combined with the undulations of the mantle, remind us of a bird's flight.

Like the cuttlefish, the skin of the squid is abundantly provided with chromatophores which gives them remarkable color variations. However, in the species considered here[68], the scale of colors is reduced and is less widespread over the body. In return we get rich rewards in the metallic reflections from bronze to silver and through tones of old gold, copper or tin, and, in some instances, shades of sky-blue on the edges of the fins and arms.

One of the most delicate shades appears as night falls, when the fine membrane of the undulating fringe become opaline with a milky edge. The squid's large, superbly brilliant eyes take on an incomparable brightness if we shine a torch at them during the night.

The capture of living fish by the squid is less spectacular than that of the cuttlefish because the action of the prehensile tentacles is even more rapid. However, we can observe what is going on internally because of the body's translucence and the fact that the internal bone of the cuttlefish is only a simple, transparent, cartilaginous feather (**183**).

A *Tilapia* fish has just been firmly captured by the squid's eight arms. It struggles vigorously, but for no more than 30 seconds, because the parrot-like beak has just taken a large section out of the back of its head.[69] The arms make it pivot slowly and the bites are taken along as it rotates, so soon the head is completely separated from the body, falling to the bottom. This first

176 and **177** Squid (*Loligo* or *Sepioteuthis*). The variation of coloring under the influence of emotional states can be instantaneous.

178 Squid eggs in individual chambers in thick, but translucent, gelatinous sheaths.

179 Three baby squid have just been born. The one on top quite clearly shows its small suction cup by which it fixed itself on the tank's pane for a moment of rest.

---

68   I do not know the exact identification and I am not at all keen to know what names scientists will ascribe to it. Their preparation in formalin is achieved rapidly. If it isn't a *Loligo*, perhaps it is a *Sepioteuthis*? I have read, and heard it said, that squid cannot survive more than one or two days in captivity. At the time of writing, the largest has been with us for two months and the other for 53 days. We had to place a fine net against the three concrete sides of the tank to avoid these superb "guests" wearing out their rear ends on the rough walls, because we all know that squid, like cuttlefish, nearly always move backwards! The largest of the two squid had already worn away quite a bit of itself before we installed the net.
69   Sometimes this moment is longer and stretches out to two or even three minutes if the prey hasn't initially been seized in the best positions and, above all, if it is very large. At the beginning we were quite amazed that one of these squid didn't hesitate to seize fish more than half its own size.

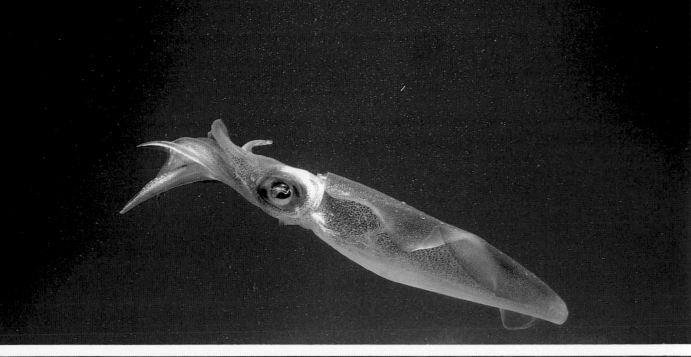

180 Squid. From front to rear: the suction cups of one of the oral arms; the eye, with its perfect structure; the undulating border of the mantle; the fine granulation of the chromatophores.

181 The slenderness of these two squid, which are like long, continuously active spindles.

182 Squid. The two oral arms which open out the most usually display a scissors-like movement.

180

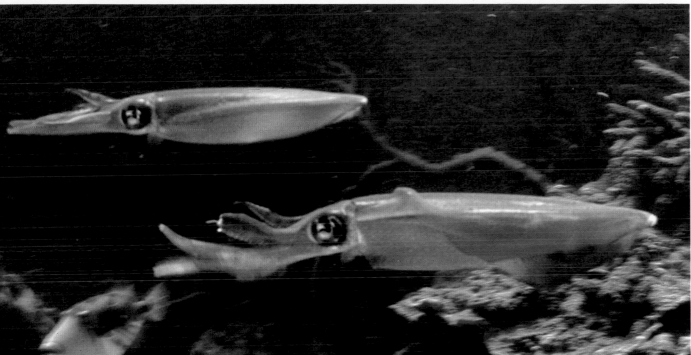

181

182

149

183

operation doesn't take longer than ten minutes. The second operation consists of opening up the abdomen to get rid of the viscera which the squid will not eat.

During all this time, the scales of the fish have been scraped off in large numbers and, finally, all that is left are succulent fillets. The digestion is remarkably rapid and the squid can begin another feast in a short time. It is also quite interesting to note that if we put in several mullet that are not too big our squid will lash out time after time. The first mullet will be fed into the mouth directly while another, sometimes even two, will be firmly held by the free arms and will be brought to the beak once the way is clear.

This voracity brings me to mention some of the battles we saw between two squid for the same food. The intrusion of the arms of one into the middle of the arms of another to steal prey, already securely caught, is so violent that one is surprised that armed with so many suction-cups and teeth, the arms are not ripped off. One can imagine what a terrifying spectacle it would be seeing two giant squid in the great deep fighting this sort of battle.

Octopus

I will not dwell too long on octopus, having already written a lot about them in *Carnaval sous la mer*, particularly our games with these very intelligent animals and the reciprocal amusement

we had from them. Because of the intimacy created between them and us, any fear of being bitten by their terrible beak disappeared. What was to happen many years later on the Great Barrier Reef in Australia showed that I had been too much of an optimist on the subject of safety with octopus.

At least one of the species is deadly, that is the Blue-ringed *Octopus (Hapalochlaena) maculosus*.[70] No larger than a hand span, its background color is brown, ringed with large yellowish bands and superb violet/blue designs which enlarge when the animal is excited. These iridescent spots take varied shapes on the eight arms: some eights, some sevens, some circles.

In 1967, a young man accompanied by two friends was exploring in the low-tide pools on an Australian reef at a place called Camp Cove. Attracted by the beauty of this little octopus, he captured it and let it crawl up his arm. It bit him. Only a few moments later the first signs of trouble showed (similar to those seen after bites from dangerous cones) — neurotoxic effects, muscular paralysis, breathing problems etc. Despite all the expert attention received very early at the nearby medical center, this robust young man died in less than one and a half hours.

Our great friends from the Australian Museum wrote to us: "This deadly little octopus is not so rare on the Great Barrier Reef but it has never been spotted in New Caledonia and it is possible that it doesn't exist there. Furthermore, you have been exploring your reefs for many years now ... but it is still to be feared that other species like the ones with which you play are toxic at certain times of the year. Conclusion: be careful."

A few months after this, three professional fishermen from Noumea, whose love of the Aquarium often inspires them to bring us rare specimens, told us that they had recently spent a long time trying to capture an extraordinary little octopus which they had never seen before. The description that they gave was comparable to that of an *Octopus maculosus*, so we put them to a small test. The first volume of *Poisonous and Venomous Marine Animals* by Bruce Halstead[71] is

---

70 Commonly called the Blue-ringed Octopus by English-speaking people.
71 United States Government Printing Office, Washington D.C., 1965.

illustrated with superb color plates which feature numerous species of octopus. We asked our friends to look at them very carefully. At each new page they said: "No, no resemblance", or "Not at all". One of them added: "Ours had such brilliant circles just like the fluorescence of your deep-water corals." Then, in unison, they cried out: "There it is!" It was only then that I showed them the press articles from Australia and the black and white illustrations with them. "My dear friends," I said, "you have perhaps been very fortunate to escape."

Providing they had not been bitten, we would have liked them to have been able to bring the creature to us. We now know that it exists in New Caledonia, but fortunately must be very rare.

Nautilus

The first pearly nautilus that lived in the Aquarium was captured by Gervolino and Leconte in the lagoon of Noumea, at a depth of less than four meters and in the middle of the day It was on the 15th of May, 1958 — a memorable date for us! This capture was destined to create immense interest in the scientific world and the living conditions offered to invertebrates by our aquarium installations was to provide a healthy environment for the nautilus for a long time. The maximum lifespan was seven months and I will mention later why this time can be considered a record. At that time we could not have imagined how maintaining such cephalods alive would lead to remarkable future research.

This first live pearly nautilus was a great curiosity and gave us an opportunity to take numerous photographs, some of which appeared in *Carnaval sous la mer*[72] and were also a godsend for many authors. One of them was also the subject of a new stamp which was a great success.

But I was to discover, many years later — and here is another lesson in humility — that a photograph of a living nautilus had already been taken long ago. It was of a *Nautilus pompilius* taken in 1895 which is featured in black and white in the masterly study by Arthur Willey.[73] His specimen had been photographed in an archipelago situated between New Guinea and the Solomons. Even better, the same work shows a photograph of two eggs of a *Nautilus*

macromphalus credited to M. Grant of the University of Sydney and as clear as the one illustrated in this book (**186**).

However, I still have the privilege of being the first person to be able to obtain an X-ray of a living nautilus[74] and also to shoot several movie films which were shown in public theaters from 1959. In 1961 they were shown at the Pacific Scientific Congress at Honolulu and, finally, in the documentary on *Carnaval sous la mer* which came out in 1964 and which had some very original sequences.

Even though there is an extensive bibliography on the nautilus, it is still useful to mention some essential data on this mollusk which is, in many respects, so precious. Every visitor to Noumea has seen the empty shells of the nautilus which end up on the small islands of the lagoon, or on the shelves in souvenir shops as curios. But if one cuts through this shell, which is a regular spiral rolled up on the same level, one will notice that it is divided in the interior by numerous cells formed by transverse partitions (or septa). These are concave towards the front and the animal manufactures new septa behind him as he grows. It then comes to live in the last large exterior chamber. All these partitions are crossed in the middle by an opening corresponding to the passage of the siphon. The nautilus swims by jet reaction against the surrounding water. This principle of jet propulsion is also found among octopus, cuttlefish and squid. But the external lobes of the siphon form a tube which has the ability to turn laterally and helps the animal change direction. Thus the nautilus often jets itself backwards. However, this does not prevent it from moving forwards, even though it is much slower, especially when it is looking for food.

Unlike other cephalopods, the nautilus does not possess an ink-sac. It is classified in the Cephalopods Tetrabranchia as the nautilus possesses four gills and two pairs of kidneys.

Some of its numerous tentacles have a tactile role, some a feeding role and others are prehensile. The people who feed nautilus in the

---

72   Catala, R. *Carnaval sous la mer*, color plate XXIII, fig. 3 and fig. 26 and 27, Sicard, Paris, 1964.

73   Willey, Arthur. *Contribution to the Natural History of Pearly Nautilus*, Cambridge University Press, 1902.

74   Catala, R. *Carnaval sous la mer*, color plate XXIII, fig. 3 and fig. 26 and 27, Sicard, Paris, 1964.

Aquarium know exactly which group of tentacles will grasp a crab's nipper or a piece of fish. Photograph **185** clearly shows the tentacles, the siphon (or funnel) and the large eye which is attached by a stalk and endowed with easy mobility. In structure it is much simpler than other cephalopods I have written about. If you live with the nautilus for several years you realize that they are short-sighted. Nevertheless, these eyes are sensitive to certain rays and, it seems, to red light especially. I could not show the beak in a photograph but it came up remarkably well in an X-ray which is shown on page 69 of *Carnaval sous la mer.*

The nautilus is to mollusks what the coelacanth is to fish: a "living fossil". In fact, the ancestral forms of all nautilus appeared in the Cambrian Era and reached their peak in the Silurian Era (360 million years ago). The survival of these mollusks over the ages is quite a remarkable feat because, after having lived in the most ancient seas of the globe, the nautilus have survived to our times without variation. In the Silurian Era, nautiloid cephalopods were represented by hundreds of species as proven by numerous fossil forms. These days there are only about half-a-dozen species in existence, spread out in the Indian Ocean and the Indo-Pacific area. The one that frequents New Caledonian waters is the *Nautilus macromphalus.*

The Aquarium was able to show these nautilus every year, but only between the end of May and early November. For the following five months the sea-water temperature is too high (more than 27°C) and these mollusks are not be able to stand this for a long time. It would therefore be unwise, just for the sake of showing these nautilus year round, to risk such precious lives.

At sea the situation is completely different because these cephalopods swim to the surface during the night and retreat to the depths at the first light of day where the water is sufficiently low in temperature for them to be comfortable. But sometimes individuals are caught unawares and fishermen then find them in the lagoon of a barrier reef. These few imprudent ones are sometimes brought to us by people wanting to do us a favor, but they only survive for a few days in our tanks because the depth is no more than one and a half meters. Rather than wasting them, these rare specimens are scientifically prepared

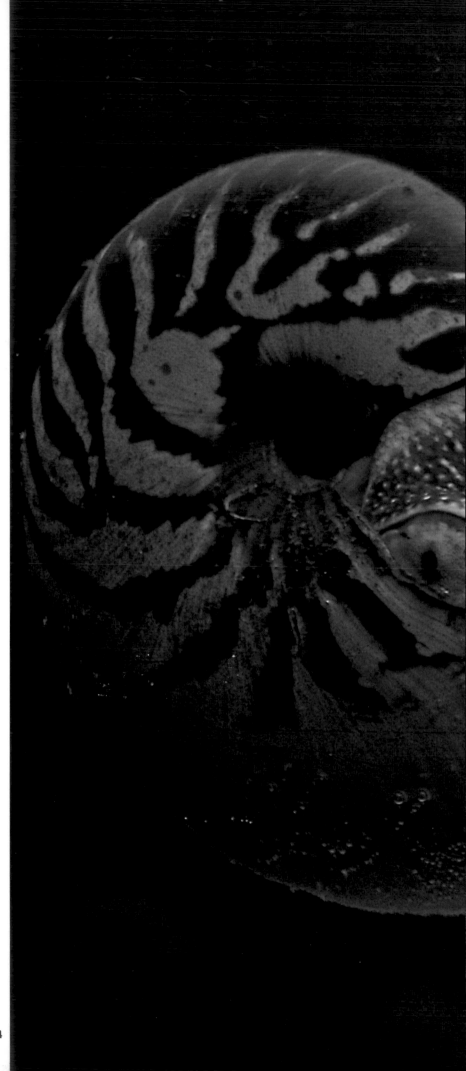

184

184 Two nautili (*Nautilus macromphalus*) join together (refer to real coupling in the text). One tentacle alone, fixed to the window pane, is sufficient to hold the pair in place.

185 Nautilus in motion. Notice the propulsion "nozzle" (swivelling siphon) under the tentacles.

186 Nautilus egg capsules. The egg itself can be distinguished through the sheath (a very thick but translucent wadding).

185

186

and sent to laboratories where they are always appreciated by anatomists who very rarely have these cephalopods at their disposal. It would be possible to keep these nautilus in the aquarium for a very long time if we had sufficient finances to maintain them in temperatures that suit them. Perhaps if we were able to recreate the pressure conditions of several hundred meters we might even get their eggs to hatch. From an embryological point of view this would be of great interest.

The nautilus that lived in the Aquarium during the favorable season laid eggs each year but there were never any successful hatchings (**186**). We thought that this was because there was insufficient pressure which prevented the full development of the eggs. The opinion of Arthur Martin[75] is that the temperature is too high for normal spermatic activity to take place. Whatever the reason, we believe that these eggs were fertile because they came from nautilus that had remained coupled together for long hours (**184**).

The layings usually take place at a rate of two eggs every ten days. Arthur Martin believes that complete egg development takes about eight months. The mere fact of seeing all these cephalopods' tentacles intermingled does not necessarily imply that there is a true mating. Photograph **184** illustrates a real mating. Not only did the female lay eggs, but a dissection made after the death of this couple proved quite conclusively that it had not just been a "homosexual exercise".

Professor Arthur Martin, of the University of Washington in Seattle, stayed here several times to carry out his physiological works on these cephalopods and gave us a great deal of information that went well beyond just simple knowledge of these mollusks. This was because his research and studies on the growth of the shell were also related to blood circulation and kidney functions.

It was interesting to follow the rhythms of electro-cardiograms which were picked up by the microsensors that he placed in an artery. At the same time, small vials were attached to the shell which collected the kidney excretions through catheters. Even though they are very fine and of a very supple plastic material, these catheters require a very delicate operating technique so as not to damage the thin walls of the ureters. It would be improper to divulge the conclusions

that Arthur Martin arrived at, because the results of his research have not yet been entirely published. I will therefore restrict myself to relating some observations by my wife on the growth of their shell during the course of 16 weeks (the 9th of July until the 22nd of October).

A juvenile specimen weighing 610 grams the day after its arrival at the Aquarium on the 9th of July, weighed 692 grams on the 22nd of October and its shell growth was 13 millimeters. Another juvenile specimen increased in weight from 582 to 687 grams in the same period of time and its shell increased in size 11 millimeters. However, a third specimen observed over the same time period, and considered to be an adult because it weighed 892 grams, did not increase in weight or shell size. In general, specimens that already weigh more than 800 grams on arrival remain basically the same, like the last example quoted.

Starting from the end of October, the specimens lose their appetite as the temperature begins to rise above 26°C. At this time of starvation, buoyancy problems appear. The animals slowly begin to lose the ability to dive down and they remain on the surface — even sticking out of the water. It is possible that the influence of heat causes an excessive expansion of gases contained in the chambers, which would explain this very abnormal behavior. If one attaches light ballast, weighing from one to two grams, the animal is uncomfortable and will not stop trying to swim to the top, continuing to do so to the point of exhaustion.

On the other hand, an individual in which we had to cut a little "window" in its shell at the level of the fourth chamber as an experiment, remained on the bottom without apparent inconvenience. It continued to feed normally and did not lose any weight.

Since weight and shell growth increases quickest in juveniles, one can only regret how rarely these smaller specimens are captured. The smallest specimen we had living in the Aquarium measured only seven centimeters in diameter and weighed 280 grams. Unfortunately, because it

75   Martin, W. Arthur and Catala Stucki I, *The Growth Rate and Reproductive Behavior of Nautilus macromphalus*. Department of Zoology, University of Washington, Seattle and Aquarium of Noumea, New Caledonia and Peter D. Ward, University of Columbus, Ohio.

was captured late in the nautilus "fishing season", it lived too short a time to allow us any proper observations. We only had the satisfaction of filming it for long periods, swimming in the company of adult specimens. At this young age it is entirely covered by reddish-brown transverse bands (**187**), while among the adults these "flakes of fire" are absent on all the anterior part which remains white. Tiny nautilus found in the stomachs of fish, and whose diameter was no more than 15 millimeters were, like the individual shown here, completely colored.

In a chapter of *Carnaval sous la mer*, I made a statement about the poor mental aptitudes of nautilus. I still maintain that by comparison with the other cephalopods (octopus, squid and above all, cuttlefish) the nautilus is less intelligent. However, after having observed these strange survivors from the past for about 20 years, I can say that even if they do not show great cerebral

capacity for initiative, their "character" varies considerably from one individual to the next, regardless of the sex of the animal.

During physiological research carried out in our laboratory by Professor Arthur Martin, special traps dragged from depths of 30 to 40 meters would also procure many dozen nautilus for us. As soon as they arrived at the Aquarium, my wife would take charge of their installation and care. So many times I have heard her say, "They are all in good health, but three are difficult and two are going to give me trouble". For some emotionally disturbed individuals she would have to go back to the Aquarium each night at awkward hours to see whether they would finally eat and could be tempted by one food rather than another. In other words, the nautilus have to be treated like pampered livestock and it is nearly always necessary to bend to their characters and individual tastes and needs.

187

187 Four empty *Nautilus macromphalus* shells show that the reddish-brown bands occupy different areas according to the animal's age.

Mollusks

This table, of the classes and orders of subjects depicted in this book, gives the reader a quick reference to the classification group of the organisms described.

Class	Order	Type		
Amphineura	Placophora	Chiton	no 188	page 157
Gastropoda	Prosobranchiata	Cypraea	no 102	page 112
		Pterocera	no 105	page 115
		Gyrenium	no 121	page 120
		Murex	no 99	page 112
	Opisthobranchiata (Nudibranchs or sea-slugs)	Chromodoris	no 53	page 95
		Halgerda	no 39	page 91
		Hexabranchus	no 12	page 77
		Phyllidia	no 37	page 89
Bivalvia or Lamellibranchia	Pseudolamellibranchiata	Chlamys	no 146	page 132
		Ctenoides	no 136	page 129
		Pinna	no 34	page 27
		Spondyla	no 128	page 126
		Tridacna	no 125	page 125
Cephalopoda (page 134)	Dibranchiata (Decapods)	Solitosepia	no 151	page 135
		Loligo	no 176	page 148
	Tetrabranchiata	Nautilus	no 184	page 152

188

188 Chiton (Placophore), generally living in intertidal zone.

Crustaceans

The class Crustacea belongs to the Arthropoda or Articulata — the same branch as the immense world of Insects. Because of the curious analogies between the nervous systems of the Arthropoda and the Annelida (segmented worms), some zoologists believe that the former were derived from the latter. Whatever the reality, the Arthropoda — and therefore crustacea — already existed about 500 million years ago at least, as is evidenced by fossil forms found in the Cambrian rocks (the Palaeozic Period).

Some authors have estimated the number of species of crustacea actually living today at about 25,000. Others estimate the total at about 30,000 (of which 4,000 are crabs). However, as science is often discovering new species, these differences in estimates will soon narrow.

The great majority of crustacea are marine. There are, however, some that thrive in brackish waters while others can live in fresh water; such is the case of amphibious fiddler crabs of the genus *Uca* (**74**). Some have adapted themselves to an exclusively terrestrial existence, as you find with the tree-climbing coconut crabs (*Birgus*). We generally think of crustacea as being fast-moving like crabs, so it is very difficult to accept that some spend their whole existence firmly fixed to a stable support that their mobile larvae have settled on. This is the case for barnacles belonging to the quite strange group called Cirripedes. They live on piles, on wrecks and on many floating objects such as pieces of timber, bottles, coconuts or buoys, as photograph **79** shows (*Lepas*). Because of their bivalve shells they were originally thought to belong to the mollusks. The body is secured by a long stalk.

While the sexes are separated among most of the crustacea, one group of barnacles, the stalked barnacles, are hermaphrodites but are able to cross-fertilize. Since these very gregarious organisms form dense communities of individuals pressed against each other cross-fertilization is quite easily achieved. The long whips (cirri) that project from the bivalve shells are in fact six pairs of modified legs which constantly expand and retract through the shell opening, creating a current of water which is indispensable for their nutrition and respiration. It must be mentioned that some, such as the *Paralepas*, live as endo parasites on other very mobile crustacea as we have seen from numerous colonies on rock lobsters.

Another group of the cirripedes are sessile barnacles which do not have stalks and attach directly to rocks. Finally, a third group of cirripedes are internally parasitic in other crustacea. The classic example is the *Sacculina* whose strange system of internal tendrils gradually invades the organs of its host — usually a swimming crab.

The table given at the end of the chapter (page **206**), only mentions the orders relating to the genera or species studied and featured in the present work.

As their name suggests, crustacea (from the Latin *crusta*, meaning crust) have a shell which is hardened by calcium carbonate. It is made up of three parts: head, thorax and abdomen. The first two can be joined into one and this is called cephalothorax. The abdomen, which is of considerable importance for the rock lobster, is reduced in crabs to a small triangular flap pressed back and fitted into a depression in the sternum. Photographs **5**, **14**, **62** show the large tail fans of mantis shrimps. These powerful organs are also found among many other crustacea: rock lobsters, true lobsters, shrimps, prawns, slipper lobsters, etc. The enlarged blades on the last tail segment allow the animal to flip backwards with great vigor.

In the higher crustacea (Malacostraca) like those which I have just mentioned, each body segment possesses one pair of appendages which, in the cephalothoracic region, is modified to form the sensory organs (antennae, antennules), the prehensile organs (claws), and the masticatory organs (jaws, mandibles). The appendages of the thoracic and abdominal segments are generally locomotory organs, but these are sometimes modified as swimming or copulatory organs. The abdominal appendages of the female are to support eggs during incubation.

Photographs **4** and **7** show the antennary scales of mantis shrimps. When these stomatopods swim, their two little wings beat rapidly and act as forward stabilizers or rudders. The magnificent *Odontodactylus scyllarus* (**3**), which has been in our tanks for many years, performs this act for us every evening.

Situated at the base of the antennule is a special organ for balance in the decapoda crustacea, the statocyst. It is a liquid-filled vesicle containing minute grains of sand (the statoliths). The experts have discovered that this little pouch

1 *Odontodactylus scyllarus.* This superb mantis is especially active during the night. Robust, rapid, agile but fierce.

2 *Odontodactylus scyllarus.* Rest position on its back. To the far right, its stalked eyes. Very fine antennae, powerful jaws, large antennae scales.

3 An *Odontodactylus scyllarus* facing directly to camera. It has just come out of its cavern. Notice how the eye differs from that in the next illustration.

Page 159: Close-up of the *Ranina serrata* crab's claw.

is lined with bristles to which nerve fibers are connected. Whatever the movements of the animal, these statocysts monitor its state of equilibrium. Photograph **4** shows the stalked eyes of the mantis shrimp, which among other crustacea are situated on the edge of the shell, as is the case with the slipper lobster (**75**).

STOMATOPODA

The Stomatopoda consist of a large number of mantis shrimps including the genera *Squilla, Lysiosquilla, Pseudosquilla, Harpiosquilla, Gonodactylus, Ondontodactylus...* and I am still forgetting some! Certain species remain buried in the sand all day long and sometimes only the head comes out of the burrow opening like this *Lysiosquilla maculata* (**10**). The stalked eyes have a considerable field of vision: certain authors (L. and M. Milne) estimate 200° for *Squilla mantis*. The large pair of jaws is often camouflaged under an extremely thin layer of sand, but this does not hinder the sudden triggering movement of those dangerous prehensile arms. Just let prey come within its reach, and that will be the end of it, cut in two.

Other mantis shrimps dig deep galleries, but more often they enlarge existing cavities amongst rocks or corals and make safe retreats out of them. Probably to add even more protection, some transport stones and pebbles which they either heap up or scatter around the approaches of the entrances and exits. These shelters are sometimes actual labyrinths. I envy young naturalists with the time to discover all that one can still learn from these mantis shrimps, whether from their behavior or from their anatomy. On the latter I am thinking particularly of their eyes. Remarkable studies have already been made by research workers such as L. and M. Milne's *Scanning movements of the stalked compound eyes in crustaceans of the order Stomatopoda,* University of New Hampshire, Durham (U.S.A.), and at the Lerner Marine Laboratory, Bimini, Bahamas (British West Indies, 1961). I hope that these specialists will be able to carry out the same studies on the eyes of *Odontodactylus scyllarus* which seem even more complicated than those of other mantis shrimps. Some sequences in my film *Carnaval sous la mer* show close-ups of the strange eye surface reflections of this species. According to the position of the eye, dots and

3

4 An *Odontodactylus scyllarus* in profile. Three small dashes appear from the bottom of the eye. The articulation of its folded claw gives a good idea of its power.

5 *Odontodactylus scyllarus* "seated", the animal shows off its superb tail fan (*Telson*). The eyes can be seen above.

6 *Odontodactylus scyllarus*. A close-up of some of the blades of the tail fan.

4

5 and 6

7 *Odontodactylus scyllarus.* The arms apply all their force to lift stone after stone.

8 *Odontodactylus scyllarus.* The stone has just rolled over. It will be pushed still further to be brought into contact with the previous ones collected.

9 *Odontodactylus scyllarus.* A *Cribraria cribraria* whose shell had already been seriously damaged by this mantis shrimp. The gastropod's mantle will gradually be restored.

7

8

9

dashes can either appear or disappear. Photograph **4** shows this clearly.

Certain species of mantis shrimps display a definite aptitude to learn and remember. What an excellent area of investigation this would be for observers! Another rewarding research project would be the diurnal and nocturnal behavior of these stomatopods.

The silence of night always draws me to work late at the Aquarium. The continual sound of the torrent of sea-water which pours from the overflow pipes of all the tanks is such an integral part of our existence that we are no longer conscious of it, and so for us the background noise does not blank out other sounds.

I can therefore easily make out the clicking nippers of the little shrimps *Alpheus strenuus*, so well named by English-speaking people "pistol prawn" or "snapping shrimp". From my office, about fifteen meters from one of the laboratory's large tanks, I also hear the "toc-toc toc" made by the superb mantis shrimp *Odontodactylus Scyllarus* when, by violently snapping its powerful arms, it strikes at the most diverse array of objects. With continual and repeated strikes at a precise point it succeeds in splitting bivalve shells to feed on their very succulent flesh. It does the same to the beautiful, thick-shelled cockscomb oysters *Lopha cristagalli* (Mollusks, **132**) and also to gastropod shells like the solid *Cribraria cribraria*: photograph **9** shows a damaged area which was already quite broken when we came to rescue it from being subjected to this frenzied hammering. However, the mantle that covers it will gradually repair the damage.

This mantis shrimp seems to be a compulsive destroyer. It will break the thin edges of a calcareous rock or coral into pieces. If it was deliberately searching for the small crab *Hapalocarcinus marsupialis*, that lives in the shelter of galleries that it hollows out in the *Acropora*, one could understand its eagerness to hammer away. But there is nothing to consume amongst the lamellae of a *Merulina* coral or the thin discs of a *Pachyseris*. Nevertheless it persisted in breaking these corals into small pieces. The window panes of the Aquarium tank are also a victim of this need to destroy.

If it attacked the window pane at the back, one could think that it was guided by instinct to excavate an even deeper gallery under the layer of sand. In fact, one night it succeeded in cracking it. If the supply of water hadn't been sufficient, it would have found itself high and dry the next morning. What we cannot understand is why it would want to attack a vertical pane of glass. Perhaps the size of this tank ($0{,}90 \times 0{,}45 \times 0{,}40$ m) was too small. This thought had come to me and it led me to conduct some small experiments. I placed a dividing pane of glass in the center of the tank, placing it so that on one side there was enough space to allow this animal easy access from one compartment to the other. It investigated it immediately and showed such remarkable topographical memory that it used this passage without hesitation and without ever bumping into it, both day and night.

One day, I adjusted the glass pane in such a way that the passage was moved from right to left. After having struck against it several times, the mantis shrimp quickly found how to get through. From then it became accustomed to this new route. One night, however, it attacked this dividing window pane, not on the side, which may have made us think that it wanted to make the already sufficiently large passage bigger, but right in the middle, a few centimeters above the bottom of the sand. In a few hours it had damaged it considerably. I then took another smaller glass pane ($0{,}33 \times 0{,}40 \times 0{,}40$ m) and placed it parallel to the two longest sides of the

10 A *Lysiosquilla maculata* almost completely out of its burrow, but only for a moment.

11 *Harpyosquilla sp.* A close-up to show the golden eyes (which are fluorescent under ultra-voilet light) and the transparency of the antennary scales.

10

11

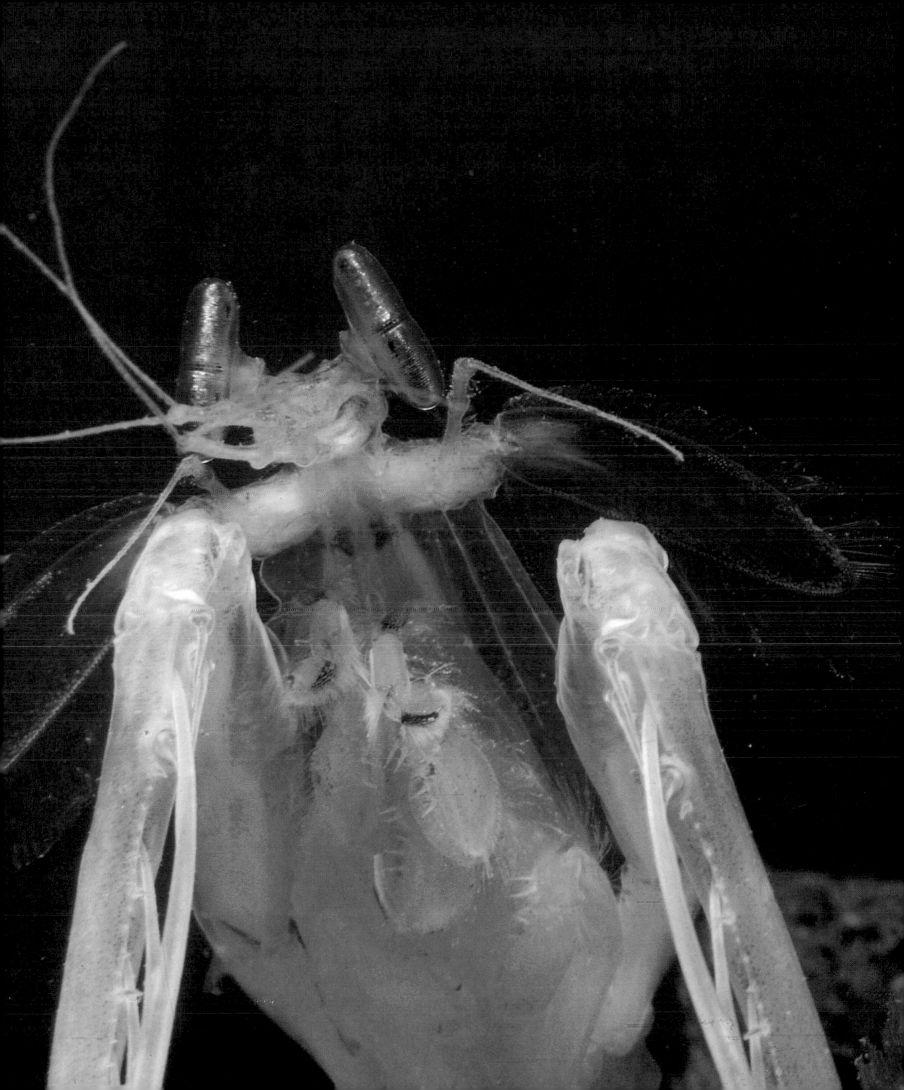

12 *Harpiosquilla sp.* A close-up of the head illustrating the resemblance of the arms to those of the praying mantis.

13 *Harpiosquilla sp.* The claws of a praying mantis (Photo: J. Carayon).

12

tank. Driven into the sand and well wedged with a few stones, this transparent sheet no longer inconvenienced the comings and goings of the mantis shrimp and it didn't worry about it.

Biologists who have had a chance to observe the admirable suppleness of the *Odontodactylus* will not be surprised to learn that our lodger would amuse itself several times a day by using this false obstacle for steeple-chase demonstrations. At first it was only interested in the wedging rocks which it tried to move in order to rearrange its galleries, but they were too heavy. So, instead of exerting itself in vain, it went to look for some stones from the far end of the tank and rolled them up to the rocks. In photograph **7** it is about to lift a stone and in number **8** it has just pushed it up against those already positioned. The determination and effort is quite evident. I was able to film some very good sequences of the pile it made by rolling the stones into place. These sequences give an excellent idea of the force and tenacity of mantis shrimps.

Weeks passed, and then one evening the small glass pane was the object of its strange destructive desire again. In the circumstances it wasn't difficult for the *Odontodactylus* to break the thin glass; it wasn't much more substantial than a photographic plate.

Why do mantis shrimps have this eagerness to smash everything? Perhaps it could be simply to maintain the strength in their terrible arms — but how is one to know? (In some ways it may be similar to the habit of cats sharpening their claws on the bark of a tree). A simple snap on a human finger by one of these cruel arms is a very painful experience.

Other biologists have already mentioned the ability that certain mantis shrimps have to *learn* and *remember*. Lorus J. and Margery Milne have written: "Some stomatopods... may well prove to be the arthropods capable of a high degree of learning, perhaps comparable to that of cephalopod mollusks."

Our *Odontodactylus* created other problems for us when we tried to photograph its curious behavior during the night. At night any attempt to focus is doomed to failure because the mere light of a single match is enough to make the subject scuttle into its gallery.[76] Therefore, at dusk, I would focus my lens on a given point where I knew the mantis shrimp would come out of its tunnel. An extremely feeble lamp (definitely not enough light

for focusing) only just allowed me to see the animal. A remote control triggered the flash. At each flash the mantis shrimp would very hastily re-enter its tunnel, but by then the photo had already been taken. A month later many rolls of developed film were returned from France and there were some magnificent behavioral shots. But unfortunately they were just a few millimeters away from being sharp. In several months I took over 500 shots of this mantis shrimp alone. Fortunately I managed to get some particular behavioral shots which are typical of it shown here in numbers **2**, **3**, **4**, and **5**.

Thankfully the movements and behavior of all mantis shrimps are not as difficult to photograph. This is the case with the very beautiful *Harpyosquilla* (**14**) which, in plain daylight and without any inhibitions, goes for a stroll, sits, takes it easy and spends a lot of time on

13

its meticulous toilette. Photograph **12** highlights the astonishing resemblance of the head and jaws to those of the praying mantis. Photograph **13**, sent to us by J. Carayon from the Paris Museum, shows the insect for comparison. The scientific name of *Squilla mantis*, given to another species, makes clear reference to the praying mantis insect and the common name of "mantis shrimp" combines the two.

It must also be pointed out that its golden eyes, already very beautiful in natural light, unexpectedly revealed a superb silver-green fluorescence when subjected to ultra-violet rays. It was the first time that I had seen the eyes of a crustacean react to such irradiation. We had the same surprise when we noticed that the eyes of certain boxfish (*Ostracion cubicus* — Fish, **134**) also reacted to the ultra-violet rays at the same wavelength of 3,650 angströms.

---

76 The juveniles — which often live close to one another — have less fierce behavior and show greater ambulatory activity. In general they also seem to be less disturbed by light.

14 *Harpyosquilla sp.* Soated, in full daylight, and seen front on. It does its "toilette" in this position.

15 A *Harpyosquilla sp.* in profile. Pretty, pearly reflections from its claws.

14

15

CRABS WHICH DISGUISE THEMSELVES

The *Oxyryncha* or spider crabs of the Maiidae[77] family are very strange creatures. Endowed with an extraordinary talent for disguise, they use living plants and animals taken from their immediate surroundings to help them with their artifice. The different techniques of camouflage were the object of numerous early observations and experiments, the greater majority carried out on species from European coasts.

Fairly deep dives (20–30 meters) carried out for our Aquarium in regions of the lagoon which are rich in algae, sponges, gorgonians and other colonial animals, would sometimes provide us with two species of spider crabs which are particularly skilful in rigging themselves out in the most unusual gear.

The first of these crabs (16) belongs to the *Picrocerus*. It well deserves its specific name *armatus*, which refers to the two long rostral horns arming its head, as well as other sharp spikes on the shell. Moreover, these sharp, long spikes make it look larger. The second species is a *Camposcia* (22) whose species name, *retusa*, means that it is blunt, and without sharp spikes. These two small etymological details have deliberately been given to serve as descriptive help in identification.

In spite of the differences in the general appearance of these two, and quite often in their behavior, I didn't think it necessary to devote a separate section for each one since their methods of disguise are so similar. Therefore, as we go along, I will draw your attention to certain facts that are common to both and others which differentiate them.

Of the two, *Composcia retusa* is the most "disguised" and for experimental purposes the most attractive. This is not only because of its speed when working, but also because of its ability to acquire the maximum amount of trimmings in the minimum amount of time. Even in nature enough is never enough! The tiniest of space left free is always an opportunity to add more. Photograph **22** is a typical example of this. The brown sponges have ended up by forming "sleeves" around the claws: they would have had to be attached when very small, several months before. On the other hand, the red ones are more recent additions.

Photograph **23** shows us what a *Camposcia* would look like in the morning if it were completely stripped naked and placed in a tank where it had not had time to choose its costume. It took a large number of small stems from a clump of whitish algae, (*Cheilosporum spectabile*), which it attached all over its body. It is the object on the left of the photograph. You have to know what to look for!

Here is an interesting minor observation: instead of taking all the fragments from the same place, this interesting animal collects oddments from further afield as well as from the main clump, even if it means moving out into the open a little. Such disguise can also be carried out in plain daylight, making it easier for our observations. While one of the nippers of the crab firmly holds the base of the large algae, the other cuts off medium-sized pieces. It trims them according to the required size and gives the pieces a round or oval shape, bringing each to the mouth and turning it regularly between its jaws. The edges are chewed sufficiently to readily hook under the curled bristles with which the crab's shell and legs are abundantly provided. It is quite evident that the animal knows in advance the exact place on its body where it is going to attach the pieces of algae, because hesitation is very rare. In other words, it does not place them in a haphazard manner. The hooking operation does not take place in one single movement. The nipper rubs the piece of alga on the hooked bristles several times, then, when it has succeeded in hooking it, it tugs at the piece of alga two or three times to assure itself that it is firmly attached. All of this is carried out with great application and extreme dexterity.

Let us now compare the materials used for disguise selected by a *Picrocerus*; pieces of animal organisms such as soft corals or gorgonians or other coelenterates are chosen rather than plant material.

With short but strong strokes, one of the nippers rakes a defined area where the fragment

---

77   Some authors write *Majidae* for the family and *Maja* for the genus. Without wanting to quibble for the sake of it, I think that it would have been more logical to keep the spelling *Maia* which Pline already used to designate certain crabs and, perhaps correctly, the spider-crabs. (I know why it is debatable!).

16 A *Picrocerus armatus* (spider crab) with its "original" disguise: a large yellow sponge and living fragments of a gorgonia.

17 *Picrocerus armatus*. A nipper, just at the moment when it is fixing on a piece of black soft coral.

18 *Picrocerus armatus*. Disguised with an extremely venomous coelenterate (*Lytocarpus*). A few small *Apogon* fish pass by with indifference.

19 *Picrocerus armatus*. In such a jumble of disguise, the animal is difficult to distinguish unless it is moving.

20 *Picrocerus armatus*. At the front of its rostrum, *Haliclona* sponge. Behind it, all erect, a soft-coral. The nipper controls the angle at which the sponge fragments are attached.

21 *Picrocerus armatus*. The same specimen as that in 19 seen from front on. It is "plumed" with the bottle-green sponge *Megalopastas*.

22 *Camposcia retusa* as it was found at a depth of 25 meters, completely covered in sponges. The two little antennae can be seen between its anterior legs.

23 *Camposcia retusa*. It is to the left of the photograph, camouflaged in sprigs of the white alga, *Cheilosporum*, a specimen of which is growing on the right.

24 *Camposcia retusa*. To the right, disguised with the polyps of a *Polythao sp.* which it has taken from the colony to the left. Only its two nippers can be clearly seen.

23

173

25 *Camposcia retusa.* Apart from a few pieces of dead coral, we completely stripped its abundant disguise and provided it with strips of colored paper.

26 *Camposcia retusa.* It has begun to cut up the paper. What choices is it still going to make?

25

26

27 *Camposcia retusa*. The text explains that it is facility which guides its solutions.

28 *Camposcia retusa*. "Ready for the ball". Only the shell and the base of the legs are not camouflaged.

27

28

29

32

30

29 *Camposcia retusa.* A new disguise. Here it only had three colors at its disposal.

30 *Camposcia retusa.* When the paper became frayed and faded, the spider crab was put into another tank with an abundance of sponges, gorgonians and other coelenterates with which it completely covered itself.

31 *Camposcia retusa.* Another disguise with fragments of a *Siphonochalina* sponge taken from a *Chlamys* lamellibranch shell (plus a few pieces of tinfoil. Also see 31a).

32 *Hoplophrys ogillvyi.* On a *Spongodes merleti* soft-coral on which this crab feeds. Complete camouflage.

33 *Hoplophrys ogillvyi.* The crab had to be pushed to the side to be seen.

31

33

is to be attached. It is a little like a craftsman measuring off a piece of metal to be soldered. While one claw is holding the soft coral firmly, the other cuts out a piece with remarkable precision. It takes it to the mouth. This time it doesn't really chew but takes small bites and, above all, adds a good impregnation of adhesive saliva. This living fragment is immediately pushed onto the chosen place with the crab's claw exerting firm but soft pressure for a moment. I tried many times to attach some fragments of soft corals, carefully cut with fine scissors and impregnated with different adhesives, on the shell of *Picrocerus* and *Camposcia*. Sometimes my pieces held in place for a while but decayed in a few hours, whereas the planting carried out by these crabs had an almost total success rate.

In his remarkable book, *Contribution à l'étude du comportement vis-à-vis d'objets chez les Majidae* (Masson, Paris 1968), Alfred Bürgi summarizes some of the early studies carried out on these crabs:

"In his detailed description of normal behavior, Aurivillius (1889) insists on the fact that the spider crabs rub all objects amongst the appendages surrounding the mouth before attaching them on their shell. He discovered that these appendages contain some specific glands and concluded that they produced a secretion which facilitated fixing foreign objects on the shell."

There is quite an interesting study to be made here to discover what there is in the saliva that prevents the pieces that have been attached from rotting.

Isn't it interesting and admirable that these objects of disguise not only remain alive, but continue to grow, and that the little soft coral polyps and the gorgonians still open out or retract to the same rhythm as the parent colony?

Another interesting example is the excellent disguise acquired by a *Camposcia* (**24**) which has taken a few polyps from a colony of *Palythoa* (a coelenterate from the Zoantharia order). Except for one of the nippers, which is slightly visible between the colony and the polyps already fixed on the crab, it would be very difficult to distinguish it.

Photograph **18** shows us the *Picrocerus* crab which has chosen a quantity of stems from an extremely venomous coelenterate of the genus *Lytocarpus* (Plumularidae). The crabs show complete indifference to these hydrozoans which

cause a burning itch if we handle them without taking precautions and also cause much harm to any fish which happens to rub against them by accident.

Unlike the *Camposcia*, the *Picrocerus* is happy enough to be lightly dressed. In photograph **17** the major elements of disguise are limited to a piece of pink sponge and a vertical branch of soft coral stuck on its long rostrum. The small pieces of sponge fixed on the legs decrease in size from their "base" to the "tips of the toes". Someone remarked: "What a sense of aesthetics!" This remark is amusing but too anthropomorphic. The practical advantage to disguise is likely to be a matter of equilibrium! In fact, it seems logical that the basal joint of the leg, which is large and strong, should receive the heavier piece of sponge and the slender terminal joint receive the lighter piece.

A completely different arrangement — and one that at first seems contradictory — is made by *Picrocerus* which sometimes attaches as much, if not more, to the extremity of its legs as to their base (**21**). But in this case it is because it is using certain extremely thin and lightweight algae. With this choice of clothing the spider crab can dress-up in any way it fancies.

The *Picrocerus* in number **16** was photographed as soon as it had been captured at a depth of 25 meters. Among other elements of disguise it is wearing a large yellow sponge. From its position on the two large rostral horns, the sponge must originally have been attached while still quite small and thereafter gradually gained its considerable importance. This spider crab lived for many months in a large tank of the Aquarium. On many occasions we observed one of the nippers busily scraping around its eyes and mouth. The animal was "shaving" where the invading sponge was becoming annoying. It was almost sacrilegious to disturb its magnificent disguise but we did venture to conduct some harmless experiments. This spider crab was moved into a very large tank with a colorful assemblage of algae and sponges. Would it "undress" and replace its precious covering with any of the "garments" it could have easily procured in this new environment? It did nothing! On certain days one could see it slowly strolling about in front of, and on top of, very red sponges (*Clathria*) or in the proximity of corals with green flesh (*Cataiaphyllia*) (**16**). So that species did not fit into the theory of complete camouflage by matching the colors of the surroundings — "synchromatic chromotropism" (Minkiewiez, quoted by Alfred Bürgi[78]). In the specific case of the *Picrocerus armatus*, a final understanding of its disguises is not possible. Except, of course, if one believes these disguises are a means of camouflage to protect itself from predators such as the cuttlefish and octopus.

The *Camposcia retusa*, on the other hand, hastens to completely or partially "undress" to adapt itself to the new environment in which it has just been placed. However, there were exceptions. When the disguise (**22**) was entirely made up of sponges which were so thick that there was no room for anything else, and their development around the legs had formed complete sleeves, the animal did not attempt to undress. I think it would have been a long and testing job to pull out all those sensitive and hooked bristles.

If I had known about the works of Bürgi at the time, I probably would have stopped my experiments because my conclusions were very similar to his. However, I would not have been able to take many amusing photographs. For his experiments on the European spider-crab *Maia squinado*, Bürgi used different colored thread in his "dressing" experiments.

For our experiments into colors chosen by the tropical *Camposcia retusa*, we used different colored paper stuck onto sheets of cardboard (**25**). With the help of a pair of fine tweezers, a young assistant gently removed all the living organisms clothing the animal at the time of its capture. It was a very thorough and careful job which needed to be undertaken with caution so as not to upset the animal and, above all, to prevent it from spontaneously throwing off a nipper or a leg. I could hear the "surgeon" saying: "Come on! Keep still. It's not the end of the world to have a few hairs pulled out!" (I do not know how she would have reacted if the roles had been reversed!) When the naked spider-crab was finally prepared (**25**) she said: "And now, madam, go and get dressed."

The *Camposcia* went into a sulk for a few hours in a corner of the tank. But as total nudity was intolerable, and it could find no living organisms with its nipper, it initially made do with some small debris of dead coral skeletons and hooked on a few with great difficulty, as we can see in **25**. On its way, it contacted a cardboard sheet. Immediately it managed to scrape off a small piece of paper, then another and behaved in the same way it had done with the fine algae. It always had a freedom of choice of colors and, among many examples that were photographed, this is how its disguise ended up (**28**). We took it in shifts to watch the whole process and see what order it chose to do things in. I once observed its relentless attempts to loosen the edge of the paper. I amused myself by helping it loosen a nearby piece of paper with the tip of my fingernail. One of the nippers touched the paper I had loosened and it began to work on it immediately. From this, and many repeats of the experiment, I was soon convinced that it wasn't the color that mattered but the ease with which it could pick up the paper.

From then on we operated in another way. Abandoning our system of panels, we let the cardboard soak for a long time in a sink. Then the colored papers were spread over the bottom of the tank, in equal quantities, and mixed as much as possible.

After many observations I reached the same conclusions as Bürgi: there is no choice of colors. Someone said to me: "Well, how come all the colored papers are so well spread over the animal's body?" I think the explanation is very simple. It never hooks the pieces on one next to the other, but scatters them over its body. The first piece of paper might be fixed on the base of a leg, the second on another leg, the third on the shell and so on. Little by little it fills up all the spaces that are still bare as it moves from area to area, where different colored sponges (or paper) are present.

Moreover, when the dressing operation takes place in the middle of the night we assume that the spider-crab cannot see a thing; yet in the morning the colors show the same diversity of distribution.

There is, however, one very curious exception to be made. Black paper is avoided. When the range of colors is quite extensive (six or seven different ones), it is always the black that interests the *Camposcia* least. This was even the case when we only put two colors at its disposal. The black was hardly ever attached. Finally, if it only had black with which to cover itself, the small

---

78   As before.

34 *Xenocarcinus depressus.* The female, left, has extended its rostrum with a fragment of the gorgonian, *Melithea ocracea.* To its right, the small male.

35 *Xenocarcinus depressus.* In all likelihood, a specimen of the same species but with a different color, matching with that of the gorgonian.

34

35

pieces of paper were a little more scattered. But I still wonder what that means to the crab. I will now summarize some observations relating to the photographs of these two crabs.

Picrocerus

16 — Apart from the yellow sponge (*Dendrilla*) attached to the two rostral horns, we can see a few "twigs" of the animal colony which have not opened out. Under the very fleshy green coral (*Catalaphyllia plicata* Wells) there is a small pale red gorgonian and, next to it, a few arms of a red feather star. *Picrocerus*, *Camposcia* or other spider crabs never use complete or half-sized echinoderms, a fact which will not surprise the experts.

17 — A nipper is about to attach a fragment of black soft coral, seen in front of the crab. The red *Clathria* sponge is totally disregarded during the whole period of disguise.

18 — The animal is disguised here with coelenterates of the Plumularidae family and of the *Lytocarpus* genus. The spider-crab doesn't care about their stinging characteristics.

19 — The bottle green sponge which covers the rostrum is a species of the genus *Megalopastas*. The pink elements of disguise were cut from an alga that was extremely thin. A few fragments of yellow sponge (*Dendrilla*) complete this incredible jumble in which the crab itself is no longer distinguishable.

20 — This *Picrocerus* was entirely stripped of its disguise when it was captured and dressed itself with sponges (on the front of its rostrum and on the legs) and with an erect soft coral that one can see behind the sponges. The nipper is about to fix the last fragments of sponge on the legs.

21 — This front view shows the surprising lightness of the fragments. They are more numerous on the extremity of the legs than at the base but, because they are light, there is no chance of overbalancing.

Camposcia

22 — When captured at a depth of 25 meters, it was completely covered in sponges. One can distinguish the two small antennae just between the two anterior legs.

28 — If, at this stage of dressing, parts of the legs or shell are not yet covered, it can draw on living organisms to finish off its costume and sometimes it immediately gets rid of all its pieces of paper, leaving only one or two fragments (**30**).

29 — However, if the "paper disguise" has been fully completed, the animal has a tendency not to change anything and will conserve it for as long as possible. Living pieces of organisms (sponges, soft corals, gorgonians etc.) will only be used as the paper deteriorates.

31 and **31a** — The crab, installed in a tank where it had only been supplied with tinfoil, is about to complete its disguise with pieces of sponge which most often cover bivalves of the genus *Chlamys*. This bivalve, which is usually extremely sensitive, remains half-open, not showing any fear of the crab's nippers. How does it know that first of all *Camposcia* have extremely light movements, and that secondly, they do not like the flesh of *Chlamys*?

A quite astonishing spider crab called *Xenocarcinus depressus* (**34**), was brought up from a depth of 35 meters at the same time as the gorgonian *Melithea ocracea*. The female on the left of the photograph had cut off a piece of this gorgonian and fixed it on the point of its rostrum.

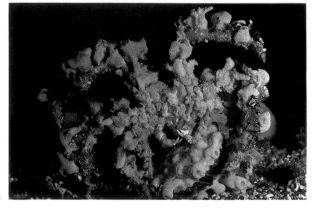

31a

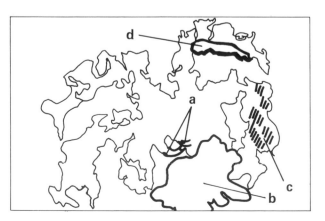

a — nippers taking fragments
    of sponges
b — bivalve and its sponges
c — tinfoil paper
d — area not yet covered

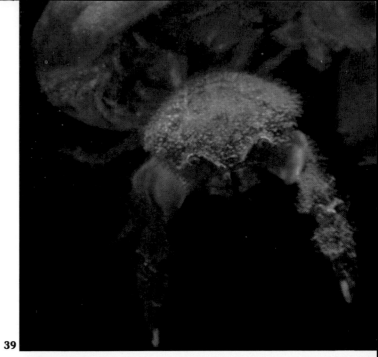

36

39

37

40

36 *Dromia sp*. The camouflage most often utilized by this crab is a sponge in which its shell becomes embedded.

37 *Dromia sp*. Without this protection, it would be easy prey for predators such as the cephalopods (octopuses and cuttlefish above all).

38 *Dromia sp*. This sponge crab "prefers" a *Spongodes merleti*. On top of it is a small *Prionovolva* cowrie shell which uses this soft-coral as a foot support.

39 *Dromia sp*. The sponge isn't fixed, but simply held by the crab's posterior legs.

40 *Dromia sp*. Having had its sponge taken away by us, the sponge-crab "retrieves" it again by reversing.

41 *Dromia sp*... and restores it: quite hard work if the sponge is very cumbersome or heavy.

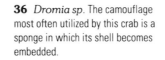

38

41

42

43

44

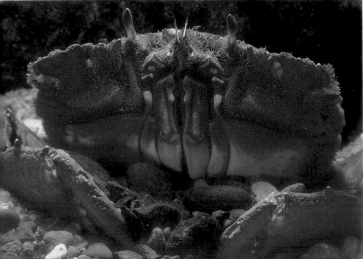

45

During the whole time that we kept it alive, it did not add another bit of gorgonian! And the small male, one can see to the right, never took the slightest fragment from it. Besides, was there any need to do so? Here one can speak of mimicry and camouflage without fear of being contradicted.

Our friend from the Museum, Danièle Guinot, to whom I am indebted for the identification of this crab (and that of many others), wrote to me: "This *Xenocarcinus* is certainly very variable and the identification for this type is not quite precise." It is a fact that other specimens found on purple or purplish-blue gorgonians had taken on the same color (**35**).

However, I think that it is impossible to find a more beautiful example of camouflaging than the disguise of that other spider crab, *Hoplophrys* sp. (**32**). Its pinkish-white color and its numerous thorns allow it to be absolutely hidden amongst the beautiful soft coral *Spongodes merleti* on which it lives permanently. To make it visible in a photograph (**33**), I had to push it to the edge of its support with the help of a stick. This was hard work as these animals really hold on to their substratum.

Sponge crabs (Dromidae) are another group whose art of camouflage has been equally well known for a long time. Massive and completely rounded, they do not behave in the same manner as the *Picrocerus* and the *Camposcia*. The sponge crabs usually carry only a single very large piece of sponge over the back (**36**). Even though these sponge crabs do not separate themselves from their disguise, even for a brief moment, they do not fix it to any hooked bristles, but simply hold onto it with the help of their last pair of legs. Thus they stroll about with a slightly staggering gait, hidden under their large protective umbrella.

In the very remarkable work on the arthropoda[79] by Madame D. Guinot we read: "When the sponge crab doesn't have a sponge or another animal to hide under, it takes hold of anything. In the aquarium at Concarneau there once was a captive crab which, for lack of anything better, had put on a small overcoat appliqued with the arms of Brittany."

79   Guinot, D. *Les arthropodes. Encyclopédie des animaux dans la nature. Panorama du Monde Animal.* Hachette, 1968–1974.

42 *Dromia sp.* On alert, these two sponge-crabs will immediately lower their heads and flatten themselves completely under their respective sponges.

43 *Dromia sp.* Deprived of sponges, a sponge-crab rapidly cuts a piece of cardboard and puts it over its head.

44 *Calvactea tumida.* This crab, which is completely round, lives in a nest made in the trunk of a *Spongodes* soft-coral.

45 *Ranina serrata.* A large crab which is most often buried under the sand from which only its telescopic eyes emerge.

46 *Macrophthalmus telescopicus* with astonishingly long eyestalks. The male is the brighter in color.

47 *Galathea elegans.* "Long live the free crab". In fact it gets used to being separated from its crinoid for a while (see the chapter on Echinoderms).

46

47

A few years ago, on a festive day, a happy group of children wearing masks happened to come through a courtyard in the Aquarium where I was filming a very large sponge crab strolling about with its sponge on its back. One of the children, who was very intrigued, asked: "If I gave it my mask, do you think it would cover itself with it?" "Why don't you try and we will soon find out! But wait until I take off its sponge." That gave me the opportunity to film a sequence that proved to be very comical for the audience because the mask was quite frightening.

In our large tanks containing superb deepwater sponges, sponge crabs have sometimes cut off large thin pieces, for example, the *Haliclona* (Sponges, **18**) and the *Acanthella* (Sponges, **42**). In this case, the large sheets resembled a canopy rather than a hat. When some laboratory crabs were deprived of sponges they cut pieces of cardboard (**43**). However, crabs caught in areas where sponges are in abundance almost always have their shells thickly covered by a massive sponge, as shown by photograph **36**. They have not bored a hollow into the sponge, but the latter, because it has been constantly pressed to the shell, ends up taking its form. As it grew the sponge has ended up muffling the crab so well that it manages to hide it completely, thus protecting it from the covetous desire of potential predators. Photograph **42** (the individual to the right) shows us a typical example of this remarkable camouflage.

If we separate a crab from its sponge, leaving the sponge nearby, it has two ways to put its "hat" on again, according to the position of the headgear. It will either replace its "hat" over its shell like someone crowning himself, or it will reverse backwards (**40**) and snuggle itself into the hollow using its sharp back legs. Getting upright again is sometimes very laborious if the sponge is bulky and heavy (**41**).

It is difficult to write about the "activity" of sponge crabs because they don't travel very far and lead a very calm, easy life. They take their time about everything they do; there is never any great haste except for their innate reflex to hide. When I am about ten meters from the tank I can distinguish it quite easily under its large hat. But when I am no more than two meters away it will see me and suddenly lower its head, thus rocking the sponge forward to hide.

If it is approached by any animal in the tank, whether it be a starfish, a rock lobster or a crab, it no longer relies on the rocking movement to conceal itself. It quite simply flattens itself close to the bottom and remains inside its sponge for the required time. I noticed one many times crouching under a sponge covering one of its fellow sponge crabs and staying there for many hours without realising there was another being underneath.

This leads me to write about another curious association of one animal sitting on top of another (**38**). A sponge crab was found at a depth of 20 meters, covered with a beautiful, healthy *Spongodes*. The protuberance at the top is a very pretty little cowry-shell, *Prinovolva hervieri*, about which I wrote in the chapter on Mollusks. One can see it here, its white foot spread over its nutritious support and also its mantle covering the shell.

Certain crabs do not resort to disguise to shelter from predators; they prefer to find refuge inside other animal organisms. This is why we see a *Calvactaea tumida* (**44**) installed in a little nest in the trunk of a *Spongodes merleti*. In this particular case, I imagine that the animal hollowed out its chamber when it was small and that the notch grew larger as it grew in it.

The superb feather stars (*Echinoderms*, **73**) also give protection to numerous other species of crustacea, such as shrimps and crabs, especially the small but very amusing *Galathea elegans* (**47**). After initial shyness they become very friendly in captivity. Deprived of their feather star, they find a hollow in a rock to run to in case of emergency. However, they gradually become accustomed to the presence of the person feeding them. They do not take long to figure out the reason for the intrusion!

Other crabs take refuge by burying themselves in the sand. The *Ranina* (**45**) and the *Calappa* (**49**) are two examples of this. Only the telescopic eyes come out, ready to disappear back under the shell at the slightest warning. The large nippers of the *Calappa* mold themselves so closely to the body that the whole animal sometimes resembles a small box. The species which is represented here, the *Calappa calappa* (**49** and **50**), is not rare in other regions of the Pacific, but it is the only specimen that I have seen in New Caledonia. Thanks to Niki Lafontaine, who brought me one from a faraway reef, some

48

49

50

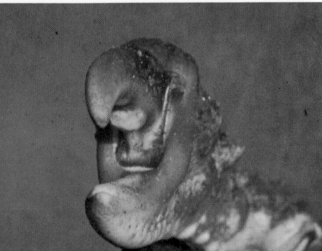

51

48 *Ranina serrata.* A close-up of a nipper looking like a toucan's beak.

49 *Calappa calappa* (dorsal side). Like the *Ranina*, it remains buried in the sand all day. Telescopic eyes.

50 *Calappa calappa* (ventral side). Everything is comfortably kept in this "little box".

51 *Parthenope horrida.* A close-up of a nipper of this large crab which is very well know for its mimicry.

excellent and very amusing film sequences were taken of this pretty crab. I always thought that one could handle *Calappa* without fearing their powerful nippers, because they usually keep them tightly pressed against their bodies. But one day when one of them was obviously in a bad mood it caught hold of my finger. What a grip they have. Their pincers don't let go so I had to resort to the only thing possible to make the muscles slacken: force a pin in the crab's claw joint. A crab that I will always be wary of is the *Parthenope horrida*: a detailed close-up of her nipper (**51**) explains my caution.

Having written about crabs with telescopic eyes, I must mention the *Macrophthalmus telescopicus* (**46**) whose eyestalks are of such an extraordinary length. For quite a long time we kept a couple of these very curious crabs to observe — the male with his beautiful violet colors and the much duller female. I always thought that the stalk carrying the eyes was perfectly rigid, until the day I noticed that it had a lot of flexibility, allowing the eye to look "underneath". This was a sequence I would have liked to have filmed, but there was no time to wait for it, because this curving happens very rarely.

Other crabs have quite a well known way to protect themselves from exterior dangers. These are the hermit crabs which live permanently inside empty gastropod shells. They are forced to change their home as they grow. However, being very vulnerable without this protection, they do not leave their old habitation until they have accurately measured up a more spacious shell and also tried it out. *Dardanus megistos* (**69**) is long-lived and well represented at the Aquarium. Certain specimens have been here for more than twelve years. Illustration XXII in *Carnaval sous la mer* shows one of them about to proceed with this delicate operation. Having lived in a small glass jar for a long time, he had begun to feel a little claustrophobic. We watched him methodically exploring the inside of a new jar and the width of its neck. Only when its measurements satisfied him did he leave his old container and back into the new one. Of course he was perfectly protected there, but quite visible. The container didn't matter.

Hermit crabs use the most unexpected abodes, even in nature. In 1952, on a mission in the Gilbert Islands, my wife and I had just pegged

52 *Periclimenes sp.* shrimps walking around the gills of an echinoderm.

53 *Periclimenes sp.* moving around here on a *Miamira* nudibranch, close to its magnificent gill bouquet.

52

53

down our tent on the the small island of Betio, close to Tarawa, a name that's synonymous with the American tragedy in the reconquest of the Pacific Islands from the Japanese. During the night, we could hear an unusual clicking accompanied by metallic tinkling. This mysterious concert forced us out of our tent and we saw a very comical sight on the moonlit sand. There were about one hundred spent cartridge shells crossing each other, knocking against each other and climbing over one another. These were the small Bernard hermit crabs which had chosen man's version of a shell as fitting homes. During the day we had not noticed them because the sand's very high temperature would have forced them to regroup in some shady spot or even in the water. Their metallic shells would no doubt have made things too hot for comfort under the equatorial sun!

Certain hermit crabs cover their shells with sea anemones which are more or less venomous (*Adamsia* sp.) to give them added protection. These sea anemones open out and retract their tentacles as they would on a fixed support. Photograph **70** shows us a hermit crab that Mme de Saint-Laurent, from the Paris Museum, has identified as *Dardanus pedunculatus*. The largest anemone, in the form of a ball, is attached on the right and another's tentacles hang between the legs. It looks very Scottish with its "bagpipes", "sporran" and "kilt"! Some small dead fish were put into the tank and the hermit crab, after having taken its share, offered some to the sea anemones which swallowed them slowly. One couldn't be a more generous commensal (**72**).

We cannot leave the crabs without showing (**77**) the pretty little *Zebrida* (which is not so unusual in the New Hebrides as some had believed from its name. *Zebrida* simply means that it is adorned with stripes, not that it comes from Africa). This *Zebrida adamsii* wouldn't need its designs for camouflage or mimicry: its extraordinarily rapid movement alone would allow it to escape from predators. I do not remember seeing any of the more nimble crustacea disappear as suddenly behind a coral or rock. What a time I had trying to take photographs of it. The specimen shown here was brought up by chance from a depth of 35 meters with a fluorescent coral.

However, there was no difficulty in taking a picture of the *Zozimus aeneus* (**76**) which spends its days under the shelter of a rock and only comes out at night. Even then it doesn't go too far. This superb species was captured at a depth of 25 meters by our friend Bernard Conseil and was identified by Mme Danièle Guinot. She pointed out to us that it was a rare crab whose flesh contains a poisonous toxin called saxitoxin according to Dr. Y. Mashimoto.

The great majority of the Aquarium's crustacea behave just as they would in their original surroundings at night. This is the case for the butterfly lobster or slipper lobster (**75**) which goes for a walk only at night. During the day these "sea cicadas" live in the shelter of small reef caves and most often cling to the ceiling. It is their best method of protection. Looking at their progress on sand, some people think that they resemble some strange prehistoric animal, others think that they resemble a tank that is advancing slowly and relentlessly. In reality they are quite inoffensive creatures who unfortunately have an excellent and well-earned reputation among gourmets.

SHRIMPS

Some crustacea escape their predators because their colors and designs harmonize with those of certain mollusks. This is the case with two small shrimps *Periclimenes aesopius*[80] and *P. imperator* which live permanently on sea-slugs, the first on the beautiful large *Hexabranchus imperialis*, the second on the *Hexabranchus flammulatus*. Photograph **56** shows a couple of these *Periclimenes*. The posterior part of the male is concealed under the gills of the slug. The female is completely exposed and one might think at first glance that it is too exposed on the red background, but closer observation shows some elongated yellow spots very close to it. These could roughly resemble a shrimp. The many observations made on the living shrimp are most interesting. While the slug is resting, its guests hide under the branches of its gill tufts or in a marginal fold of the mantle. When it moves on the ocean floor or swims vigorously (Mollusks, **50**), the shrimps can go from a yellow area to a red

---

80 Having been given two different identifications for the *Periclimenes* featured in plate 58, I have some doubt about the value of the specific name *aesopius*.

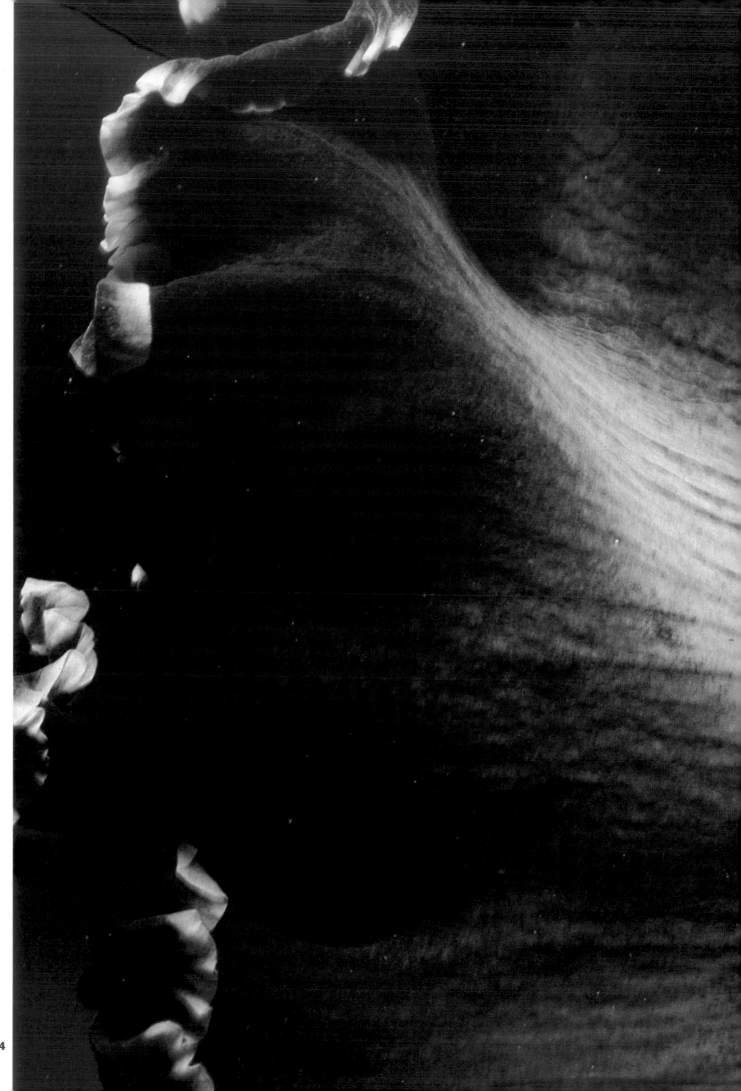

54 *Periclimenes sp.*
(*Aesopius?*) moving around on
the mantle of the largest of the
nudibranchs (*I lexabranchus
imperialis*).

54

area without being recognized because the rapid contortions of the slug constantly blend the colors. Photograph **57** reveals one of the most remarkable cases of combined camouflage and mimicry. Apart from the general base color of these shrimps, so similar to the hue of the slug, the numerous small clear spots are faithfully matched too. Only the nippers have a purplish-blue coloring — just like the color one finds in the many small lines adorning the gill tufts.

Photograph **55** highlights the remarkable diversity of colors and designs in this large mollusk, and the multiple color combinations, which explain why the *Periclimenes* can sometimes be difficult to spot. Moreover, their small size in relation to their support surface offers these shrimps a vast field for movement (**54**). But destiny has put on some other nudibranchs shrimps which are more modest in size, as is the case for the *Miamira* (**53**) which has a specimen of *Periclimenes* close to the sea-slug's beautiful "bouquet". I noticed it threading its way through the nudibranch's gills and it was always difficult to distinguish its nippers and legs from the reddish lines on the gills.

Photograph **58** captures quite an amusing posture. Anata, who lived in India, said to me: "Tell me, is your shrimp having its yoga session?" Here it is, installed on the fringe of the mantle whose edge is wrapped around itself; in the foreground one can partially see the branchial bouquet.

The subject in photograph **52** reminds me of an unusual event which should be told, if only to prove once again that one should always be cautious. In a previous draft of this book, I had written about this shrimp-nudibranch relationship: "For as long as their host is alive, they will never leave it." But one day I happened to notice a couple of the shrimps on a sea cucumber or bêche de mer. This echinoderm resembles a very long hosepipe that is often seen in very shallow water or on tidal flats at low tide. It was even more surprising to find these brightly-colored shrimps on a background that contrasted so strongly with the gray/black shade of the sea cucumber. After bad weather, the large sea-slugs are washed to the shore completely exhausted after many hours of energetic swimming. They usually end up dying there and then their passenger-shrimps find themselves in trouble. I took the shrimps and sea cucumber to a tank in

the laboratory to recover and went to look for a large *Hexabranchus* that had been brought to me the day before. I was sure that on making contact with it the shrimps would immediately move from the sea cucumber to the slug. Despite frequent contacts between the hosts, nothing happened. I thought that this was so abnormal that I took out the bêche-de-mer, seized the two shrimps (with great difficulty because they held on very tightly) and placed them on the slug. They remained there, walked on it and even hid on it. Then about two hours later I replaced the sea cucumber in the tank. A moment later it came into contact with the slug and the two shrimps immediately abandoned the nudibranch and installed themselves quickly on "their" bêche-de-mer. The photograph shows the male and the female gripped tightly to it. The experiment was repeated several times and the result was always the same.

I had believed at first that it was quite an accidental adaptation of a shrimp to a sea cucumber, but that did not appear to be the case and there was still that element of doubt. Would this species of *Periclimenes* live commensally with an echinoderm in nature? I gave the divers for the Aquarium instructions to search, find and return. Two years after drafting my manuscript, Pierre Djemaoun and Michel Lavacry brought up a sea cucumber and a couple of these shrimps from a depth of 25 meters in a perfectly calm zone. Quite recently (1977), Pierre Laboute was showing us some magnificent photographs taken deep under-water. One of them showed us a *Pleurobranchus mamillatus* (Mollusks, **64**) which had a couple of these same shrimps near the edge of its mantle. There is obviously a remarkable diversity of organisms with which they live in symbiosis. But we have to admit that the concept that camouflage and mimicry are essential factors does not always apply.

Sometimes the shrimps in this group manage quite well with emergency adaptations when they are placed in abnormal circumstances. I have chosen this example: a young boy brought a specimen of the common *Periclimenes brevicarpalis* to the Aquarium. It has featured in many works and is very beautiful, with its ivory-white bands and pretty yellow spots on its caudal fan. It is also very unusual because of the translucence of its fine shell. Unfortunately the child did not think to bring the sea anemone on which it permanently lived. So that visitors were

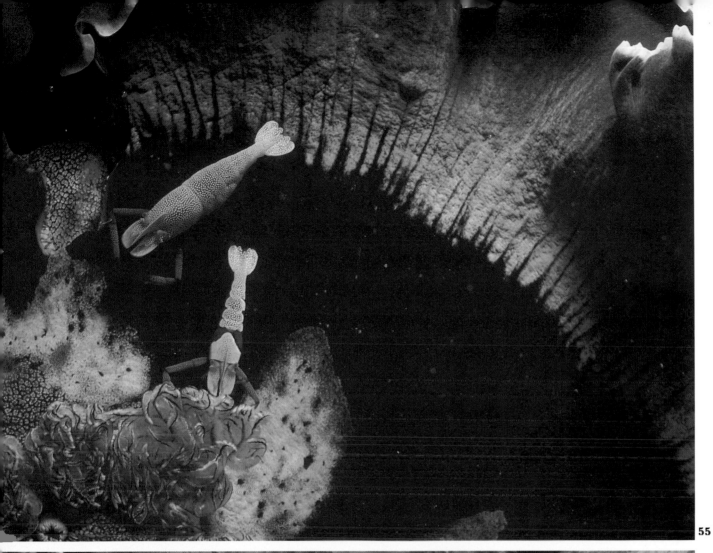

55 A *Periclimenes sp.* on a *Hexabranchus imperialis.* When this nudibranch is swimming, the shrimps can barely be distinguished because of the extreme rapidity with which they go from a clear area to a darker one.

56 A *Periclimenes imperator* on a *Hexabranchus flammulatus* harmonizing with the long yellow spots of the nudibranch. To the left, the small male is partly hidden under the gills.

57 *Periclimenes imperator* couple on the same nudibranch as 56. Magnificent example of camouflage and mimicry.

55

56

able to admire it right away, we placed it in a small tank. There it was deprived of anemones but was well supplied with other coelenterates. In less than ten minutes the small shrimp had installed itself in a soft coral (**64**) where it lived for nearly a year.

Having refered to the translucence of the *Periclimenes brevicarpalis*, I must also mention the *Periclimenes holthuisi* because its transparency results in the white pigment spots giving the impression that one is looking at broken pieces. The photograph which features a couple of these species is particularly striking (**60**). Another, where only the male is shown (**59**), highlights the tail fan. The sudden spreading out of the blades of this tail most often occurs when something has frightened the animal. I couldn't help but compare the appearance of the beautiful violet spots with that of certain butterflies (for instance the false-eyes of the *Caligo*).

The last example of transparency in certain shrimp shells is the *Leandrites cyrhorhynchus* (**62**). If the photograph had been taken with the animal moving across sand it would have been almost impossible to discern, so we placed it on an artificial blue background.

The different species of *Periclimenes* that we kept for a long time in our large tanks showed quite a curious side-sway, balancing movement of their body. It would be a little too simplistic to merely explain that this rhythm harmonizes with that of surrounding objects (like the algae that are stirred by the movements of water). As an experiment I completely closed off the water and air jets for a moment to obtain complete calm, but the balancing rhythm continued.

Another small shrimp, the *Thor amboinensis* (**61**), is characterized by quite a curious posture in which it permanently holds its abdomen in a vertical position. This odd pose is hardly necessary to be hidden in large sea-anemones *Stoichachtis* on which — or beside which — they permanently live. If this continuous abdominal erection was only done by one of the partners, one could conclude that it was a way of displaying to its partner, but this is not the case since both the male and female behave the same all year round (just like the *Periclimenes* with their curious side-sway balancing).

The shrimps called *Hippolysmata grabhami* (**68**) are beautifully adorned with long antennae

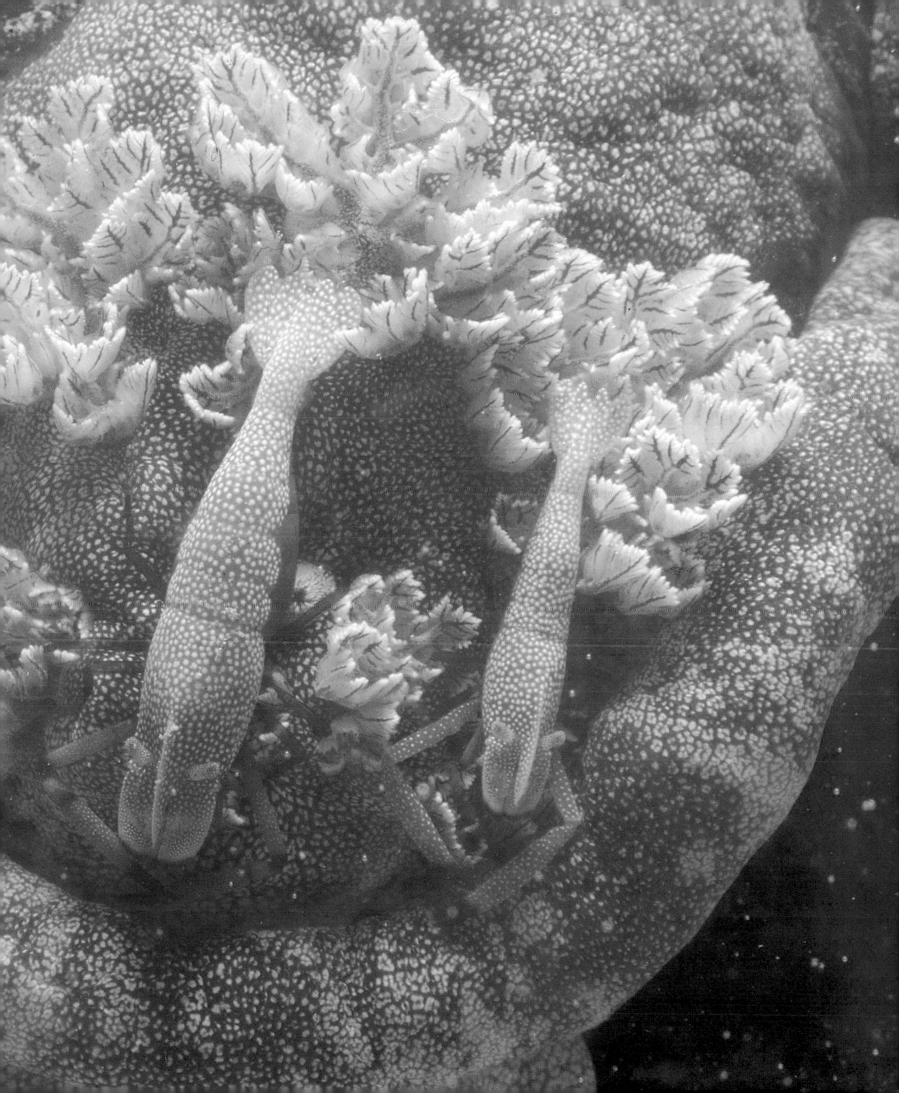

and display their superb colors fearlessly. These very pretty creatures are rare in our waters but not so in other tropic regions since there have been many publications with excellent pictures. Some private aquarists have been privileged to keep and observe them for some time in their tanks. There is no doubt that they would have been struck by the extreme grace of their movements and the delicate way in which they carry out their scrupulous toilette, especially when grooming their delicate, magnificent antennae which never seem to end. It is difficult to describe their tip-toe walk but when I look at these thin, extremely nervous, creatures I always have the impression that their slender legs are sensitively testing the bottom by simply brushing it lightly.

Photograph **63** shows us one of these *Hippolysmata* which has molted during the night and its old shell has been caught on the branches of a yellow sponge.

While on the subject of molting, there is one observation that will interest those specializing in the physiology of crustacea. I am referring to shrimps, such as *Stenopus, Hippolysmata*, and *Hymenocera*, that all carry out their molting process the night they arrive at the Aquarium. At first we could not see any link between the effects of transport — which would often be quite trying for shrimps — and the molting skin that occurred after such a short time in our tanks. We had only seen this as coincidental, thinking that these shrimps were molting quite simply because they were ready to do so. But gradually the frequency of these correlations intrigued us. And there was one other aspect that we also found particularly surprising; when the shedding of the shell took place before the end of the day. This was totally against nature because crustacea usually molt during the night.

Where the story becomes very ironic, at my expense, is that I should have seen the analogy between this phenomenon of early shedding of shells and my observations on butterflies made more than thirty years earlier. It all clicked one day when I read in a text by Pierre Grassé[81]: "Strong mechanical shakings during transport induce the caterpillars of butterflies (*Chrysiridia madagascariensis*) to metamorphose within a

58 A *Periclimenes sp.* (*Aesopius?*) on the fringe of the nudibranch's mantle in a "yoga" posture: this is quite common when the large sea-slug is at rest.

---

81   Grassé, P.P. *Pages choisies. Le fait social et l'effet de groupe* Ouvrage jubilaire. Masson, Paris, 1967.

58

59 *Periclimenes holthuisi.*
The tail fan (telson) is very open.
Generally this is a reflex of fear.

60 *Periclimenes holthuisi.*
Tail fan closed. These shrimps are
so transparent that they look like
broken pieces.

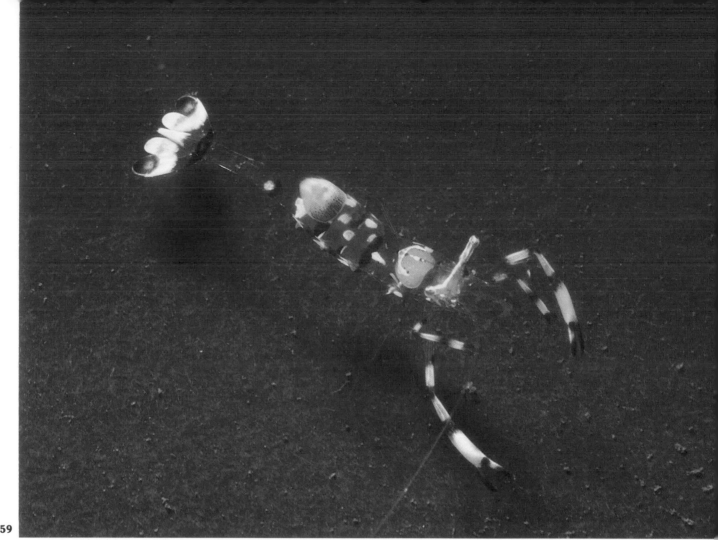

59

196

60

61 *Thor amboinensis* (couple). These very small shrimps walk along while continuously holding their abdomen in a vertical position. To the left, a large *Stoichactis* sea-anemone.

62 A *Leandrites cyrhohynchus* on an artificial background: it is nearly impossible to distinguish this species on the sand background where it lives.

61

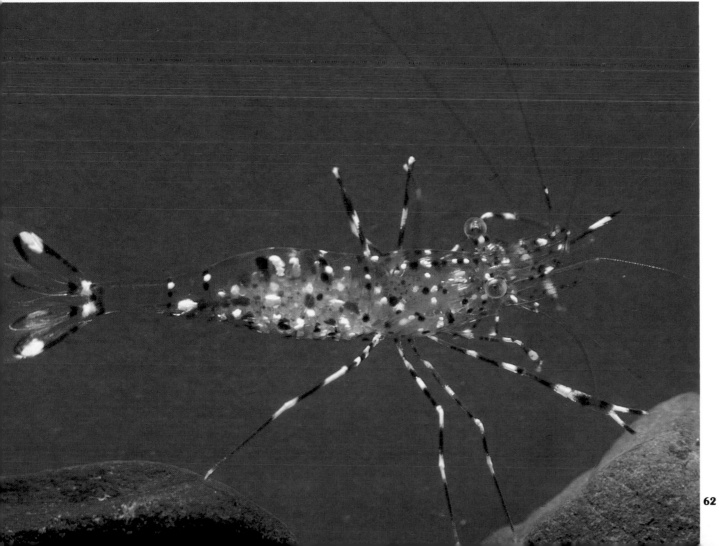

62

short period, and well before the normal time of their larval life (Catala 1939). It is probable that such mechanical disturbances change the endocrine secretions and that metamorphosis results from this."

Was I finding myself confronted with a physiological mechanism similar to those which had formerly allowed me to produce insect metamorphoses at will[82]? Why shouldn't the gland, whose hormonal secretions trigger off the phenomen of molting in crustacea, be affected by mechanical shudders just like the *corpora allata* of butterfly caterpillars?

These observations will perhaps stir young researchers to carry out many more experiments and, whether right or wrong, I think that investigators should concentrate on vibration factors rather than shock factors. I say this because I think of the incredible vibrations caused by the two powerful outboard motors on the boat used to transport containers with these organisms to the Aquarium.

Hymenocera elegans

In the book *Carnaval sous la mer*, and also in the film of the same title, I referred to the difficulties we had in trying to keep alive the first couple of these superb shrimps[83], despite the varied diets we offered them.

In 1967 a new couple, that had been caught at a depth of three meters, was installed in a small tank in the public gallery. This tank held a variety of miniatures: yellow, carmine or orange sponges, mauve soft-corals, red gorgonians adjoining lace coral, which are the violet bryozoans of the genus *Retepora* (Fish, **34**). In this garden of animal organisms, rich in shapes and colors, there was also a small but very common starfish called *Echinaster luzonicus*.

The next morning our two shrimps were clutching tightly to this starfish. What was the reason for this behavior and why was the small starfish so swollen?

Our observations were often made impossible due to the screen formed by the very large blades of the third pair of legs (**67**). These were so tightly clamped to the starfish that it was quite a battle to detach them without mutilating the shrimps. We took the starfish out of the tank and to our great astonishment we discovered that two of the arms had been nibbled at.

It has always been known that echinoderms, particularly starfish, are voracious feeders. But for crustacea to attack starfish was quite a new discovery for us. We also wanted to know just how the shrimps had began feeding. So an intact, fresh starfish of the same species was placed in the tank. Our two beautiful shrimps were walking side by side, in their very stiff manner, but after a few minutes they purposefully advanced towards the starfish. What stimulus had caused this to happen? Was it their communicating vibrations, or their sense of taste, or had they simply seen it at the same time? Whatever the reason, here is the sequence of their behavior: one shrimp grips one arm of the starfish and the other shrimp another arm and then they both frantically pull. They resemble ants tugging away at a twig, but instead of concentrating their efforts together they pull at the starfish in opposite directions.

The second pair of legs of the shrimp, which are extremely thin and slightly concave, have such tiny and tapered nippers that once they are closed they resemble an awl. Photograph **66** shows an example of this awl-like nipper on a small male shrimp. After several cautious prods on the arms of the starfish, these very fine daggers plunge into the skin. This "acupuncture" is what causes the astonishing swelling of the starfish skin in less than half an hour. One must also note that the grip of the other legs clearly contributes to this swelling reaction. I cannot explain how these perforations bring about such general swelling, but the distended tissues make it much easier for the shrimp to remove pieces of flesh for food. The loss of these bits has little immediate effect and a starfish of between seven to eight centimeters in diameter can survive the attacks of a single *Hymenocora* for one or two weeks.

In fact, it is not completely destroyed at all. When the last arm has become so small that the shrimp no longer has enough room on which to comfortably stand, it simply moves onto another starfish and the feast starts all over again. The remaining small arm stump of the mutilated starfish will gradually develop into a new starfish to be eaten again! This is why the survival of our *Hymenocera* no longer poses any problems for

63 A *Hippolysmata grabahmi* which has molted during the night. The *discarded* old shell remains caught on the branches of a sponge. To the bottom, on the left, a colony of bryozoans *(Retepora)*.

64 *Periclimenes brevicarpalis*. Not having a sea-anemone at its disposal, the shrimp has immediately adapted to a soft-coral.

65 *Hymenocera elegans*. The couple are installed between the empty valves of a *Chlamys* lamellibranch.

---

82 Catala, R. *Accélération, par des chocs, de la métamorphose des chenilles de Chrysiridia madagascariensis.* Comptes rendus de l'Academie des Sciences Paris, 1939, p. 1349.

83 Refer to *Carnaval sous la mer*, plate XXII, fig. 1.

198

63

64

65

us. From the very first pricks that the shrimp inflicts, the starfish does not show any defensive movements and is unhampered in its own mobility. One could say that it very quietly goes about its own business, yet lets itself be nibbled at. Everyone knows that in the insect world wasps lay an egg on, or in, the body of a caterpillar and then sting the main nerve center to anaesthetize it completely. The caterpillar remains perfectly alive and serves as food for the young wasp larva, but the caterpillar cannot move.

I should add that the *Hymenocera* have a partiality not only for *Echinaster luzonicus* (Echinoderms, **2**), but also for a small starfish which is equally widespread, the *Nardoa novaecaledoniae* (Echinoderms, **42**). One time our supply of both had temporarily run out so by chance we offered a specimen of large and beautiful blue starfish — the *Linckia laevigata* (Echinoderms, **6**) — to a single *Hymenocera*. This had been found by a young person on a reef (he must have overlooked the second shrimp because these shrimps always travel in couples). The shrimp, not having any alternate food source, was not put off by the large size of this starfish, but it did take more than two months to reach the end of it!

On this topic of feasting, I must conclude with this quite incredible story. In 1970 newspapers in the United States[84], Australia and Europe reported an observation carried out by a German zoologist: a couple of *Hymenocera* had completely devoured a specimen of *Acanthaster planci* in 24 hours! (Echinoderms, **1**). This is the giant starfish which is infamous for doing considerable damage to many coral reefs in the Pacific.

I will conclude with an excellent observation made by one of the boys who spend all their free time at the Aquarium. After reading a press article about this "feast" by *Hymenocera* on *Acanthaster*, the boy simply said: "An adult *Acanthaster* weighs more than two kilos, a couple of *Hymenocera* would only weigh a few grams. Where do they put these two kilos of flesh... and in 24 hours?!"

I haven't seen the film in question. But if it did show an adult *Acanthaster*, I maintain that its

---

84   And in particular in the Science page of *The Times*, May 25, 1970.

66 A *Hymenocera elegans* on the already very swollen starfish, *Echinaster luzonicus*. To the right, the awl-like nipper of the small male is quite visible.

67 *Hymenocera elegans.* Walking posture. Below the beautiful antennae, which look like large blades, the eyes on their stalks.

66

67

consumption in 24 hours (even in several weeks) by a couple of *Hymenocera elegans* is physically impossible. However it may have been a young *Acanthaster* at the stage where the starfish doesn't have thorns, but it is very rare to find a specimen as young as this, and if so they are found in depths of at least 30 meters or more.

This incident happened to us about ten years ago. The tiny *Acanthaster* was then only a simple disc of eight millimeters in diameter. We didn't even know that it was one of this species until about three months later when the arms began to take shape. There is something very important to mention here: the young *Acanthaster* grew in a tank in which there were corals of many species and, for several months, did not attack any of them, contenting itself with the algae growing on the panes of the tank. Unfortunately the observation did not go any further because the specimen crept out of the tank and we found it dried up on the floor of the service room.

Before concluding this section on our beautiful *Hymenocera*, I must tell you about a couple that were surprised one morning in quite an unusual situation. Not having any more starfish to nibble at, they found nothing better to do than install themselves between the valves of a *Chlamys* lamellibranch (**65**). The flesh of this bivalve had been completely devoured during the night, not by our shrimps, who had no taste for it, but by some cowries, *Cyprea eburnea* (Mollusks, **88**) which are fond of delicacies. The open valves were an excellent shelter for the shrimps and even more colorful because the top was decorated with beautiful sponges which so often grow on these shells. What a charming spectacle!

I received several letters from colleagues who were very excited at the prospect of a biological control for the scourge of corals, the abominable *Acanthaster*. "Your aquarium always possesses some *Hymenocera elegans*, as your film *Carnaval sous la mer* has shown us. You have reported on the ability of *Acanthaster* to rapidly destroy living corals so do you think that it would be possible to succeed in breeding *Hymenocera* to control them?"

My colleagues were quite disappointed by my reply: "The *Hymenocera*, of which we actually have several couples, have never reproduced, despite the excellent biological conditions that we have in our tanks. Also this species could be considered rare, if not very rare, in New

Caledonia. Finally, they have always shown a total repulsion for the large *Acanthaster*."

Many times we observed the behavior of our shrimps face to face with the "Crown of Thorns" (the English name for this dangerous starfish). We even made two couples of our *Hymenocera* fast for about ten days. Then we put them into a tank in which there was already a large *Acanthaster*. As the large starfish advanced, the shrimps moved aside. Another couple was accidently placed on top of the starfish and the shrimps literally went crazy, finding themselves in this stinging bush, fleeing immediately with great bounds. We repeated this experiment, but the next time we turned the starfish over so that its underside showed. The same desperate flight took place. Each time it was the same mad panic to escape. After their gallant attempts, and because we wanted to control the diet of our shrimps, we instantly offered them one of the small starfish mentioned before. They happily set about their first meal after twelve days of dieting.

Rock Lobsters

There are four or five widespread species of rock lobsters in the sub-tropical waters of New Caledonia. True lobsters with claws don't exist there and the numerous visitors to the Aquarium — particularly those coming from Europe — have often exclaimed: "Oh! these lobsters are more beautiful than the ones we have!" Léon Bertin, in his beautiful book *La Vie des Animaux*, had a ready answer for them: "Anyone confusing a rock lobster with a true lobster is a very bad observer."

The most common species of rock lobster in the Aquarium is the *Panulirus ornatus*.[85] But the *Panulirus versicolor* is only very rarely found. In certain regions near the urban centers, where there is a large demand for them, the stock is

---

85 In many southern hemisphere countries the common name of crayfish or crawfish is sometimes used, but the lucrative commercial markets for these prized crustaceans encourages the regular use of rock lobster or spiny lobster. Our two species, *ornatus* and *versicolor*, were originally in the genus *Palinurus*, so named after the pilot of Enée (and the Cape Palinurus also carries his name), but more recent taxonomists regrouped those species into a new genus *Panulirus* which is an anagram of *Palinurus*. They even contrived yet another anagram, Linuparus, for a third genus in the family Palinuridae.

68 *Hippolysmata grabahmi.* In brushing against the polyps of these corals, the shrimps have made them immediately retract in their calices.

69 *Dardanus megistos.* This superb hermit-crab is very soon going to make its elected abode topple over it (in this case, a *Charonia tritonis* shell).

70 *Dardanus pedunculatus.* Another hermit-crab. Its borrowed shell disappears under the sea-anemones (of the genus *Adamsia*).

71 The same species, staggering slightly under its load of sea-anemones.

72 In turn, the sea-anemones have also received their share of the daily feast (in this case, small mullet).

68

69

70

71

72

becoming even more rare, especially over the last few years. They would have totally disappeared if pot fishing had been successful, but this type of trap has never caught anything — even when abundantly provided with a variety of succulent baits.

These rock lobsters live in dense coralline formations and in the craggy rocks where they find excellent shelter. However accomplished divers soon spot the long antennae which gives them a good idea of numbers. Then they return to these locations at night, armed with electric torches, and easily catch the rock lobsters which, like most crustacea, have nocturnal habits.

While diving in virgin regions I have often seen absolute "forests" of rock lobster antennae. And I often wonder how they could find enough food to survive and prosper in such large numbers.

In order to grow in size, rock lobsters, like all crustacea, must shed their hard outer shell and then rapidly inflate a soft new shell which has been developing below the old one. These molts do not take place, as many believe, at equally divided intervals in time neither are they synchronised with phases of the moon. We carried out numerous observations on the frequency of molting and they are similar to the following sample of molting dates of a *Panulirus versicolor*. It entered the Aquarium on the 14th of October, 1958, and was observed for nearly three years.

25th October 1958	6th October 1959
3rd December 1958	3rd January 1960
11th January 1959	30th May 1960
28th February 1959	21st October 1960
17th April 1959	12th February 1961
3rd July 1959	15th July 1961

On this last date the specimen died. When this rock lobster first came to the Aquarium it measured eight centimeters (without antennae), and on the 15th of July, 1961, it measured 40 centimeters. These measurements don't have much significance for aquaculturists because these rock lobsters were never cultivated for breeding experiments in the Aquarium. Such experiments would have needed special isolated tanks.

I have never been able to determine if the more frequent molting in the warmer season was due to higher water temperatures or to the greater abundance of absorbed food. Perhaps the experts

203

73 The charming small "porcelain crab" (*Leucosia sp.*). So shy at the beginning, slowly becoming familiar.

74 An *Uca sp.* or fiddler-crab. The size of one of its nippers is always disproportionately large (refer to the observation in the chapter Mollusks under cephalopods).

75 *Parribacus sp.* (sea cicada). Strictly active at night. In the daylight hours it remains in the darkness of small caverns, mostly hanging from the ceiling.

76 *Zozimus aeneus* (captured at a depth of 25 meters). Reported as being one of the rare crabs whose flesh is poisonous (*Saxitoxin*).

77 *Zebrida adamsii*. A small crab which has extraordinarily rapid movements. Some writers have observed it as a host of sea urchins.

78 *Panulirus versicolor*. To the left, the old shell (*exuvie*), with the new one next to it. Notice the perfect regeneration of the antennae, formerly broken when being captured.

79 Cirripeds (*Lepas ansifera*) one of the rare, fixed crustacea. These cirripeds were considered to bc mollusks for a long time.

who have specialized in aquaculture of shrimps, rock lobsters and sea-cicadas can answer this question.

Our rock lobsters — along with the crabs — are the best cleaners in the Aquarium because each night they eat up all the remains of food and other residue in the tank.

The time of molting always takes place in the second half of the night and you can often see two identical rock lobsters side by side, but one will be old and empty and the other new and full (**78**).

When I say identical, this is not absolutely accurate because the new one is resplendent in its bright colors, while the old shell is covered with algae and many other fouling organisms, like barnacles, which have tarnished it.

The molting process is always impressive and one cannot help but ponder on the tremendous effort that the animal has to go through to perform the task. Through a dorsal split at the junction of the abdomen and thorax, the rock lobster frees all its appendages: antennae, antennules, jaws, first and second maxillae, first, second and third maxillipeds, then the walking-legs, and the swimmerets on the abdomen. Finally, situated right at the end of the abdomen, the five-piece tail fan. This casting off even includes the skin of the eyes.

There is another amazing miracle, and that is the regeneration of some organs. In the interval between molts, accidents can happen and a leg or two, or perhaps even an antenna, could have broken off. But whatever joints have been damaged or broken off will be completely restored at the next molt. This is what had happened to the specimen in photograph **78**. The two antennae on the old shell had snapped off at the moment of capture. And we see the new rock lobster with its two long completely regenerated antennae. It has been reported that if an eye has been torn out, instead of being faithfully regenerated it is sometimes replaced by an antenna (a phenomenon of heteromorphosis). I suspect that such a substitution by another organ only takes place occasionally, but we didn't have the heart to carry out any new experiments to verify this statement.

Molting is not always carried out without

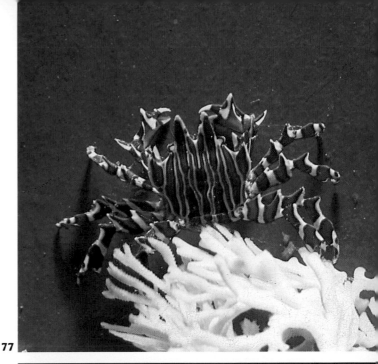

77

78

79

problems. Sometimes, in the large tanks of the Aquarium, there are many other organisms capable of annoying the rock lobster as it approaches the molting period, and they can delay the start of the process.

Also, a constriction in the shell, caused by a deformed joint or from another accidental cause, can hinder the proper release of an organ from its shell and trap the organ inside. The first few hours after molting, when the shell of the rock lobster is still quite soft and before the new chitinous coat thickens and hardens, are the most critical periods because this is when the animal is terribly vulnerable. From the first light of day, fish, crabs, starfish and other nibblers will quickly take advantage of this tender morsel unless secure shelter is found. What a feast it would make!

The table referred on page 160:

Branch	Class	Order	Type
Articulata or Arthropoda	Crustacea	Stomatopods	Mantis-shrimps no 1 page 161
		Cirripedes	Barnacles no 79 page 205
		Decapods	Shrimps no 54 page 188 Rock lobsters no 78 page 205 Hermit crabs no 69 page 202 Crabs no 45 page 182

Echinoderms

The large Branch of Echinodermata[86] is exclusively marine and is represented by five major groups which are readily distinguished from each other. In fact there is no resemblance between the Asteroidea or starfish, the Holothuroidea or sea cucumbers, the Echinoidea or sea-urchins, the Crinoidea or sea lilies and the Ophiuroidea or brittle stars. However, despite the profusion of forms and the diversity of structures, all these creatures have many common anatomical features which I will now briefly list.

— *Five-sided symmetry (Pentaradial)*[87]

The classic example of this group is the common starfish, shaped like a five-sided star. But even though it is sometimes less obvious among other echinoderms, this same basic architecture exists in all the groups listed above. The sea-urchin *Astropyga* (**4**) is a good example of this but the *Asthenosoma varium* (**50**) is an even more beautiful one. This symmetry of five sides or in multiples of five is not absolutely hard and fast. Among certain starfish we find 11, 12, 13 and 14 perfectly formed arms, like the infamous *Acanthaster planci* which is a great devourer of corals. However, there are other starfish which only have four arms, as we can see in the specimen *Protoreaster* (**3**). Many starfish also display arms that have curiously divided into two (**2**). This is due to regeneration following damage to an arm, or after autotomy — a spontaneous amputation by the animal itself.

— *An external skeleton*

This is composed of more or less linked calcareous plates. These skeleton-like elements composed of calcite or of aragonite are produced from a layer of internal tissues known as mesoderm. The chemical composition of this skeleton is different from that of the shell of gastropods which is produced from a substance called conchiolin secreted by the mantle.

— *A system of tube-feet*

On the underside of the starfish, for example, we can see a groove running along each arm, stretching from the central disk right to the extremity. In this groove an abundance of small fleshy tubes are continuously moving. These are the tube-feet or podia (**5**) which may or may not

1 An *Acanthaster planci*, the relentless destroyer of coral reefs. Young specimen.

2 *Echinaster luzonicus* (six arms, of which one is bifurcated). This small starfish is particuiarly appreciated by the famous *Hymenocera* shrimps (See chapter on Crustacea).

3 *Protoreaster nodosus*. This individual has four arms instead of five, a very rare anomaly among this species and probably congenital because no trace of any accident exists.

Page 207: A *Comanthus sp.* crinoid.

1

2

3

---

86   From *echinos* meaning spiny and *derma* meaning skin.
87   From *penta* meaning five.

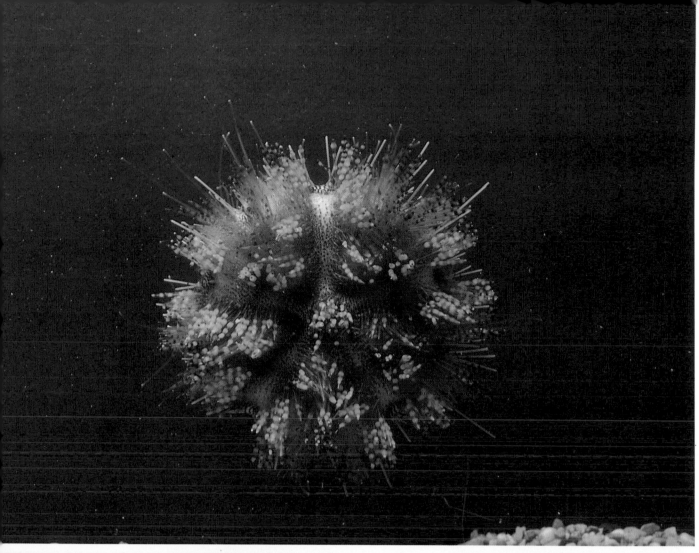

4 *Astropyga sp.* This small sea-urchin is a good example of a five-armed specimen.

5 *Halityle regularis.* A close-up of the oral face (ventral) to show the tube feet or *podia*.

4

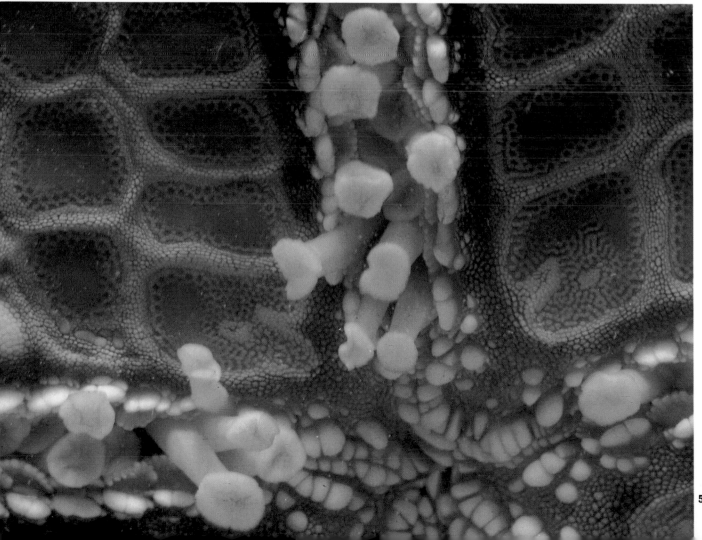

5

6

7

8

be provided with suction-cups, depending on the species. These tube-feet carry out multiple functions such as locomotion, sensory perception and often respiration. The adhesive power of these thousands of small tubes is so strong that the two valves of an oyster or of a *Chlamys* can be forced open and kept apart the whole time that the starfish feeds on the succulent flesh.

Among other groups of echinoderms, such as the sea-urchins and the sea cucumbers, the tube-feet are also useful for food gathering.

The underside of starfish, sea-urchins, brittle stars etc., is called oral because it is the surface carrying the mouth. When the animal lies naturally on the bottom, its mouth is underneath it. The upper surface has the opening for the anus and is called the aboral side.

— *An internal vascular system*

This is an exclusive characteristic of echinoderms giving them general communication through their tough skin to the exterior sea-water. The hydraulic pressure of this system can be controlled and it exerts a fairly strong turgescence on the tube-feet, making them expand or retract at will. On the upper surface is a small calcareous plate, pierced with holes, called the madreporite plate through which controlled amounts of sea-water flow into or out of the vascular system.

Unfortunately I must limit myself to this brief explanation of the major groups, although the world of echinoderms contains a vast array of other organs of an extraordinary complexity which again are exclusive to them.

For readers whose curiosity drives them to seek more detailed documentation, I recommend consulting one of the numerous manuals dealing more specifically with the anatomy of echinoderms. They will discover, to their astonishment, just how far nature has been able to demonstrate its inventiveness in adapting certain organs to various conditions of life.

Among other things, they will learn, of the existence of small organs called the pedicellaria which, even on the same individual, appear in many shapes. Jean Painlevé's famous and excellent film on sea-urchins shows an incredible arsenal of implements and weapons among the spines which are perfectly adapted to their respective functions. There are small, simple pincers and others with several jaws, hooks, tridents, etc., and all this fantastic machinery is controlled by muscles and ligaments allowing the

6 *Linckia laevigata.* A starfish which is quite common in the extreme South and East of New Caledonia. It is rare or very rare on the West coast. It achieved remarkable longevity in the Aquarium.

7 A *Protoreaster nodosus*, standing up on its arms to facilitate the emission of the sexual products. Among starfish, the sexes are separate.

8 A *Protoreaster nodosus* in the process of laying its eggs. (Apart from cases of sexual dimorphism, one notices a great variation of colors among the *P. nodosus*).

9 *Euretaster insignis*. Behavior that is even more strange — and very rare moreover — which has no relation to any activity associated with reproduction. See the X-ray page 243.

10 *Euretaster insignis* preparing a type of casing from mucus to which air bubbles attach on contact.

11 *Euretaster insignis*. Once finished, the casing will be lifted to the surface.

12 *Euretaster insignis* (aboral face), showing the osculum open to its maximum in the center.

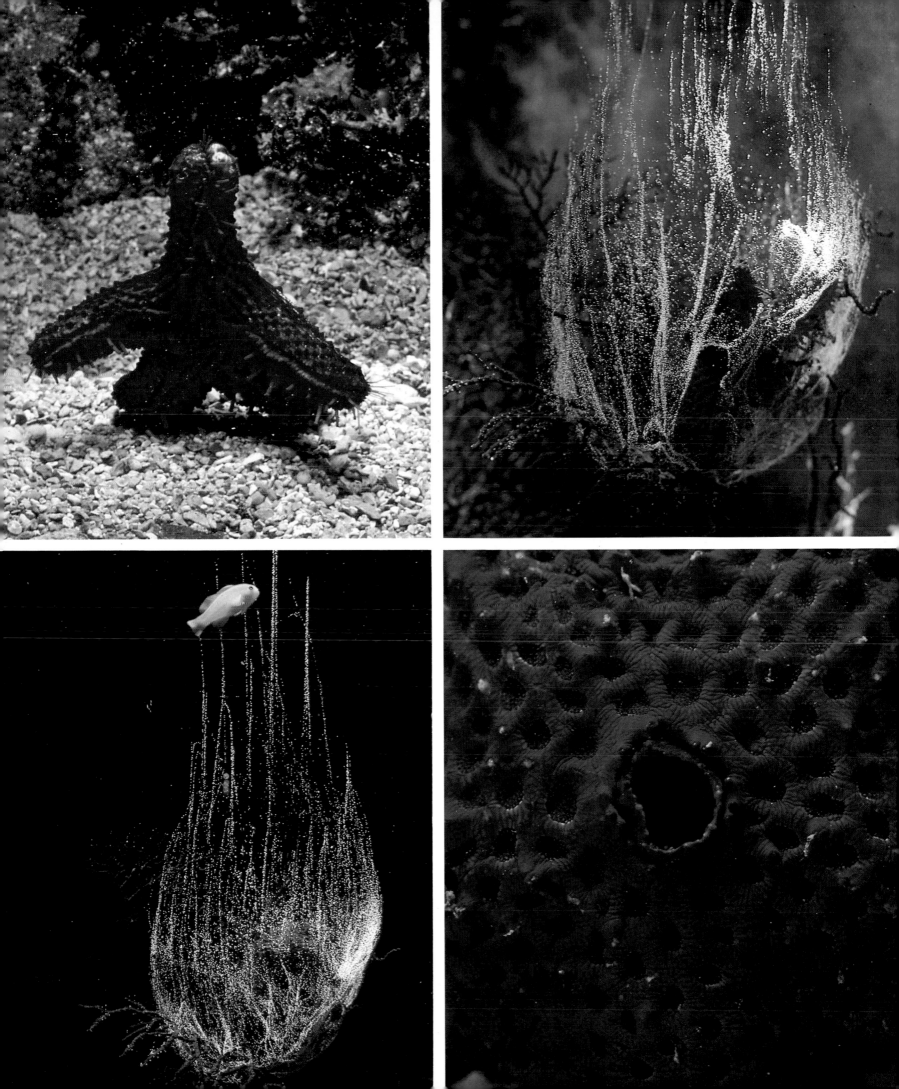

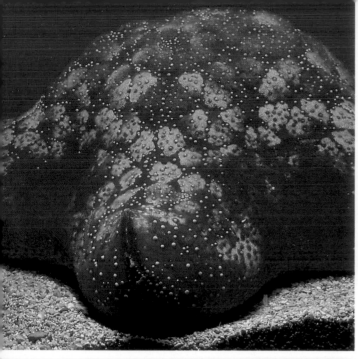

13 *Culcita novaeguineae.* The thickness of the *Culcita* is considerable, hence their common name "cushion". Average weight is 3 kilograms.

14 *Culcita novaeguineae.* W turned it over to see how it would behave in trying to get upright.

15 *Culcita novaeguineae.* The podia stretched to their maximum and looking for support.

16 *Culcita novaeguineae.* A few podia manage to come into contact with the sand.

17 *Culcita novaeguineae.* One of the arms, in the full effort of trying to bend over, will soon reach the ground.

18 *Culcita novaeguineae.* A close-up of the tip of one arm with the podia fully extended.

19 *Thromidia catalai.* The largest known starfish, 0·65 meters in diameter and 6 kilograms in weight. An adult hand gives an idea of size.

20 *Thromidia catalai.* It has been turned over so that its movements to turn upright again can be recorded. The starfish around it are *Protoreaster*.

21 *Thromidia catalai.* Taken 20 minutes after the preceding photograph: half-way to righting itself.

22 *Thromidia catalai.* A close up of the ventral face.

23 *Thromidia catalai.* The operation is nearly complete.

24 A *Choriaster granulatus* that we purposely placed in this position to show the dorsal face (aboral).

25 *Choriaster granulatus.* The ventral (oral) face beginning a general curvature, allowing it to get better leverage from support points.

26 *Choriaster granulatus.* Beginning to lift an arm.

27 *Choriaster granulatus.* A second arm is brought into contact with the first, but this does not seem to serve any useful purpose.

28 *Choriaster granulatus.* Maximum elongation of the first erect arm.

29 *Choriaster granulatus.* After having half turned over, the starfish finds itself in a position to completely right itself.

creature to open and close its varied arsenal at will. Some of these pedicellaria are equipped with poisonous glands and the toxins can be frightfully painful, even leading to death. In addition to their defence role, the pedicellaria of sea-urchins are also cleaning instruments. Without them, the excremental refuse and foreign bodies deposited by the whole marine world would accumulate among their spines. One never tires of the incredible display of coordination as this battalion of pedicellaria works the slightest impurity through the rows of spines to a position where it is deposited away from the sea-urchin. They work away so animatedly, one can imagine them saying to each other: "... hurry up, pass this on to the next one, quickly ..."

The spines are mainly used for protection, but in a good number of sea-urchins they also help with locomotion.

In all the textbooks you will find sketches of the masticatory organ of another masterpiece of architecture, Aristotle's Lantern.

My friend, the late Léon Bertin, gives a clear description of this famous Aristotle's Lantern in his book *La Vie des Animaux*[88].

"Imagine a pentagonal pyramid whose point would come out through the mouth and whose base would, as a consequence, be inside the body. Instead of being simple, this pyramid is made up of five triangular pyramids joined along their sides and retaining a tubular space in the center for the pharynx to pass through. Each one of these pyramids or jaw components is hollow and crossed by a substantial calcareous tooth which is shiny and hard and reinforced because of its T-section. The five teeth protrude beyond the top and can spread out, or close tight, according to whether the abductor or adductor muscles are functioning between the jaws and the semicircular calcareous rings, or auricules, which jut out of the outer edge of the oral membrane."

In most echinoderms the sexes are separate without there being any physical mating. The male sexual products create a chemical stimulus provoking egg laying by the female. Some authors point out that in many species male and female move closer together when they reach sexual maturity and this gregarious behavior increases the chances of fertilization.

Personally, I have only once noted a significant concentration of the starfish *Protoreaster nodosus* (**3**) in less than four meters

of water, and one fact struck me: these very beautiful starfish were quite flat on the sand, whereas in the large tanks of the Aquarium, where we have observed some over many years, they would stand up on their arms to facilitate the expulsion of their sexual products[89]. It's not easy to catch a starfish at the precise moment it decides to cock a leg (**7** and **8**).

The number of eggs produced by echinoderms is prodigious. Most reliable authors have provided very interesting estimations. Henrietta Hyman[90] quotes the estimation made by Gemmil of 2,500,000 eggs laid by the starfish *Asterias rubens* over a two hour period and adds that such a female lays more than once in a single laying season. The same author also quotes Mortensen who estimated that there were 200,000,000 eggs in the ovaries of a *Luidia ciliaris.*

Our great friend, Elizabeth Pope, who was Acting Director of the Australian Museum for a long time, and for whom the world of echinoderms holds no more secrets, wrote to me: "Echinoderms have a fossil past which is astonishingly long, and that might seem quite surprising when one thinks that the sea-water which surrounds them, and which circulates freely through the cavities of their bodies thanks to their water vascular system, makes them extremely vulnerable to all external physical and chemical factors and especially, nowadays, to the pollution agents created by man.

"However, echinoderms pursue their destiny with complete success. This success can be partly explained by the fact that at their larval stage, a great majority of the young, being part of the planktonic world, occupy an environment which is different to that of the adults living on the bottom. Therefore competition for food is not so great between the young and adults."

One can be justifiably enraptured by the incredible diversity and beauty of the larvae of crustacea at their different stages of growth and the larval stages of echinoderms do not pale in comparison.

88   Bertin, L. *La Vie des Animaux*, Larousse, Paris, 1949.
89   Not to be confused with the erect posture of the starfish *Luidia* (37) and *Euretaster* (9) among which this extremely rare behavior doesn't coincide with any emission of sperm or eggs.
90   *The Invertebrates*, McGraw-Hill Book Company, 1940.

OBSERVATIONS ON A FEW STARFISH

In *Carnaval sous la mer*, six drawings of characteristic attitudes of the starfish *Luidia* were given and it was also illustrated in color (plate XXII fig. 3), standing upright ... "dancing on tip-toe". This beautiful illustration was used again, but in a larger format, in *La Vie des Animaux*.[91]

Here is another *Luidia* (**31**), this time doing push-ups on two arms. The imagination can really run riot imagining what it resembles. Some people are amused by the fact that the position of one arm gave this starfish the look of the prehistoric reptile *Tyrannosaurus*, while others claim it reminds them of the silhouette of a large Borzoi dog. The important thing to note is that the *Luidia* maintained this strange posture for a whole day. Fish, and other co-inhabitants in the tank, would move around it and sometimes come within a few centimeters of it, but these comings and goings left it undisturbed. By evening it had resumed its normal position, flat on the sand and scarcely visible. But it must be remembered that, with the *Luidia* as with the *Euretaster*, an erect attitude does not necessarily herald a period of emission of sexual products, as is always the case with the *Protoreaster nodosus* (**7** and **8**).

Astropecten polyacanthus

As suggested by its specific name, this starfish has many spines, but what is peculiar to this species is that as well as two rows of "comb-like" teeth, one can find some spines in pairs, standing up at the inter-radial angles (**36**).

The *Astropecten*, like the *Luidia*, are considered by experts such as Horton and Millers, Fisher and Pope to be true living fossils because certain characteristics of their internal structure connect them to a very primitive family, the Stomasteroidae. It should be recorded that we have very often had *Astropecten* in the Aquarium and they have never shown the slightest tendency to erect themselves like the *Luidia*: in fact they tended to remain flat on the sand. The spines of the *Astropecten* are not venomous.

Gomophia egeriae

Many specialists in echinoderms have quoted numerous cases of both internal and external parasitism among starfish. We have often noted the presence of worms on the oral face of the *Euretaster*. Some mollusks also live as parasites on starfish, and we find gastropods on them too. I have preferred to choose the example of the starfish *Gomophia egeriae* (**32** and **35**) because the photographs clearly show the curious deformation on its arms caused by the two shellfish attached to it — one an adult and the other a juvenile — which remained lodged in the ambulacral groove for a long time.

Culcita novaeguineae

These very aptly named starfish — *Culcita* means cushion — are massive and very thick organisms. They can weigh up to three and a half kilograms. Because of their thickness and the hardness of their tissues I thought that if I turned these starfish on their back they would have a great deal of trouble getting upright again. But it was no trouble at all and I was quite astonished by the remarkable suppleness of their arms when they right themselves. To be sure, it sometimes takes them more than a quarter of an hour to complete the maneuver because it has not worked on the first attempt! Photograph **13** shows us the aboral or upper face of an adult *Culcita*. My Australian friends, Dr. Elizabeth Pope and Dr. Frank Rowe, both great echinoderms specialists, wrote to me of their surprise when looking at slides of this *Culcita*, because this specimen has a more definite star shape than the normal *Culcita novaeguineae*. They also told me that it was the first time that they had seen a species of this kind with a bright red color; normally they are brown, yellow, green or deep purple. And could I send them this specimen, prepared? The answer was sad. "A long time ago", I replied to them, "it was devoured one night by a large helmet shell that was an old inhabitant of the Aquarium!" For a while it was perhaps a new species. Whatever it was, I saw many others of this form and color which would, nevertheless, have been unusual among the *Culcita* of the Australian Barrier Reef.

Photograph **14** shows us the animal carefully turned over on its back to see how it would set itself upright again. Photograph **15** quite clearly shows the tube-feet stretched out to the limit, looking for something firm to attach to. Some of these, in photograph **16**, stick to the sand. In

30 *Culcita sp*. This starfish appreciates the coral polyps (several branches have been stripped of their polyps and gone white).

91 Grassé and collaborators. *La Vie des Animaux*, Larousse, Paris.

31 *Luidia sp.* This curious posture was maintained by the starfish all day (see another *Luidia* posture in plate 37).

32 *Gomphia egeriae.* Oral face. On the right arm, two gastropods have installed themselves on the edges of the ambulatory channel. Deformation by contraction. Photograph 35 shows the same animal viewed from above.

31

32

photograph **17** we see an extension of one of its arms and its efforts to bend over. This is the arm that will soon find a powerful enough contact on the ground to permit the starfish to turn itself upright again. The close-up shot in **18** highlights the skin and the tube-feet in detail. Like the dreaded *Acanthaster*, about which I have already talked and described the terrible damage they have caused to the coral reefs in many regions of the Pacific, the *Culcita* also occasionally devour coral polyps as shown in photograph **30**.

One can only hope that a biological imbalance, such as the one which must have originally caused the formidable population explosion of the *Acanthaster*, will not provoke the same demographic growth of *Culcita* one day.

Choriaster granulatus

At the end of 1976, one of our divers brought up a very curious starfish from about 20 meters at a location we called Duck Hole, close to a small island of the same name. Its external texture and its pink color made us immediately think that is was perhaps a juvenile form of the famous giant starfish that I will be talking about further on. So we were very excited. But before sending the duly prepared starfish to our friend Elizabeth Pope, at the Australian Museum, we sent her some typical photographs (**24** to **29**) for identification. Her answer did not take long ... and it was very decisive: "To your question: 'Could this pink starfish be a juvenile giant *Mithrodiidae*?' — the answer is no! It is a typical adult specimen of a separate species, the *Chriaster granulatus*. This species has already been seen in the Red Sea, the East Indies, Philippines, China, Japan and the South Pacific. It is also quite common in Fiji and exists in New Guinea. It was also once seen on a reef close to Green Island, Queensland." And Miss Pope added: "I think that is a *first* record of it in New Caledonia."

I have given you this long account to emphasize how many species can remain very rare in a region: for over 20 years our experienced divers have not seen any other specimens of that species.

Halityle regularis

The study of the names of animals — the science of taxonomy — has never been a strong point for me (probably because I prefer studying the living animal) but I must admit that without taxonomists we would sometimes be quite embarrassed. Here is one of many examples. One day, in 1965, divers were bringing up a superb starfish, the *Halityle regularis* (**40** and **41**), from depths between 20 and 30 meters, when one of them found a smaller starfish (**38** and **39**) whose underside looked like that of a large *Halityle*. However, the upper surface was completely different. Thinking that it was another species of *Halityle* (and perhaps unknown!), I sent some photographs to the Australian Museum for Elizabeth Pope to examine. She replied that without being able to examine the specimen itself (it disappeared from the Aquarium without leaving a trace!) she could not be an hundred percent certain, but it seemed fairly likely that it was a juvenile form of the *Halityle regularis*. It was then that I learnt that juvenile specimens of this family differ quite drastically from adults. This is also the case with the *Culcita*, in which the differences between the adults and the juveniles are so great that for a long time juveniles were placed in another genus! Finally, the most recent taxonomic research has assigned an intermediate place for the genus *Halityle* between the *Culcita* and the *Oreaster*.

Unfortunately, in 20 years we have not been able to find another specimen of this juvenile form of *Halityle*. I must also add that, despite various lighting combinations, both natural and artificial, I was never able to accurately photograph the beautiful purple coloring of the plates in the disk region. All my patience, imagination and time were taken up trying distant and close-up shots such as the one in photograph **5**. For the same reasons, I also found it impossible to reproduce the soft shade of purple of the beautiful spots on sea slugs. This is why I had to give up trying to produce one for this book.

Fromia monilis

This species is not particularly rare in our region. I believe that it is the most attractive of the starfish and it always captures the admiration of visitors because of the yellow or ivory white plates which stand out on a carmine background (**34**). I could not resist including one of the more unusual postures of this little *Fromia* in photograph **33**, which has conjured up a resemblance to cosmonaut Edward White floating outside Gemini IV.

33 *Fromia monilis*. An amusing posture evoking... Gemini!

34 *Fromia monilis*. Aboral face.

35 *Gomophia egeriae*, aboral face. The same individual as in 32. The left arm shows signs of strangling by parasites.

36 *Astropecten polyacanthus*. Note the spines which stand up in pairs at interradial angles.

37 A *Luidia sp.* "dancing on its toes". Among the *Luidia*, just like the *Euretaster*, there is no relationship between erect postures and the emission of sexual products.

36 and

Euretaster insignis

This beautiful, brilliant red starfish is fairly common and we have most often found it at depths of 22 to 25 meters in quite limited areas between the islands Ilôt Maitre and Ile aux Canards, about two kilometers from the Aquarium.

This particular habitat is mainly sandy bottom and the hard and soft-corals are not very dense in comparison with sponges. Very mixed areas of small clumps of seaweed, dominated by the *Rhodophycea*, contain many small crabs, shrimps and mantis shrimps as well as a quantity of bivalves of the genus *Chlamys*. It is on these clumps of algae that our beautiful, red starfish live.

For its size, the *Euretaster* is a thick starfish and I admire the talent of René Abgrall for being able to take such a fine X-ray as the one produced on page **243** of a preserved specimen that I had sent him. Like the *Luidia* (**31** and **37**), the *Euretaster insignis* adopt curious walking stances[92] just like the one shown in photograph **9**.

With the exception of times when the liberation of sexual products leads the animal to quite defined postures, we do not know what stimulus can provoke such erect positions which, we must point out, are only very rarely observed. These amazing stances can last a whole day. The starfish normally crawls flat on the sand or on a clump of algae. When sitting still it is easy to observe its regular inflating and deflating. The osculum (**12**), a large opening in the center of the upper surface, pulsates at a rate of about four times a minute. But this frequency can rise to 14 if the animal is irritated (these figures were recorded by our devoted and enthusiastic assistants, Martine Berger and Brigitte Martin). The term osculum is also used to identify the exhalent openings of sponges (Sponges, **2**). Henrietta Hyman, in her remarkable work on echinoderms[93], recalls what she calls a "special respiratory mechanism" observed among the specimens of the Pterasteridae family and in particular mentions the *Hymenaster pellucidus* from the North Atlantic. This respiration is, in fact, achieved by sea-water being pumped and therefore aerating the eggs in the incubating chamber. The larvae hatch and then develop into "baby starfish" inside the parent without having experienced free-swimming larval activities,

unlike the majority of starfish.

In addition to these minor observations, there is a much more curious one which is the production of a special mucus with which the starfish surrounds itself in a fine web. Once this has been completed, the animal rests at the bottom of this "bag", which in time will act as a balloon. Fine air bubbles gradually accumulate on the outside as well as the inside of the gluey mucus and eventually the balloon rises towards the surface where it makes an excellent float for the starfish. We have, of course, taken many photographs of the construction of the web and our first choice was when it was at the half-way stage (**10**) and our second, a few minutes after the release point (**11**).

This secretion of mucus is perhaps only a defense mechanism — like the loose cocoon which certain species of parrot-fish produce each evening. It is equally possible for such mucus secretions to have a repellent power towards dangerous organisms. These are only hypotheses on our part. Observations might have been published on the possible role of "repellent", but we don't know of any. One thing is for certain in all cases concerning the *Retaster*: the floating balloon has got nothing to do with any reproductive activity.

Other organisms also fabricate floating supports: for instance the gastropod *Janthina violacea* creates special bubbles for its egg-masses (Mollusks, **120**).

Protoreaster nodosus and Nardoa novaecaledoniae

I have already mentioned the voracious appetite of starfish. Examples have often been given of the considerable devastation they can cause to mussel beds and oyster farms. The strength of starfish arms, with their thousands of adhesive tube-feet, has the power to overcome the considerable resistance of lightly closed shells. After forcing the valves of the shell open they proceed to devour their prey by pushing the stomach inside out between the two open valves.

At the Aquarium, we often observe this behavior because of the many starfish that are permanently in all the tanks. *Protoreaster*

---

92   Refer to *Carnaval sous la mer*, pl. XXII, fig. 2 and fig. 22 (1 to 6).

93   Hyman, H. As before.

38 *Halityle regularis*, juvenile dorsal face which is so different from the adult specimen (41).

39 *Halityle regularis*, juvenile ventral face, has very few characteristics closely resembling the adult (40).

40 and **41** *Halityle regularis*, ventral and dorsal faces of the adult.

38

39

40

41

nodosus is our best example of a starfish which feeds off the most diverse prey but, nevertheless, its preferred diet is sea-urchin.

What a huge chapter one would need to relate all the episodes and adventures in the long pursuit and ultimate capture of sea-urchins by starfish. The starfish take their time to corner the sea-urchin, but from the moment that the tip of only one arm touches the base of the sea-urchin its fate is sealed. Only the long, needle-sharp points of the spines of certain species (*Diadema*), or the toxicity of the globular pedicillaria of certain others (*Areasoma, Toxopneustes*) allow the sea-urchin to survive. Photograph **42** shows us a *Nardoa novaecaledoniae* finishing off the flesh of a large *Heterocentrotus mamillatus* (pencil sea-urchin). You can clearly see the starfish still astride the calcareous shell of the sea-urchin with all the spines strewn around. Close by, another live and intact specimen of the same species seems destined for similar destruction.

Other prey are also very much appreciated by starfish whenever the opportunity arises. Photograph **43** shows a fish that was probably woken during the night by a wandering crustacean, then stumbled into the tentacles of an anemone to be stunned and find itself pinned against a pane of the tank by the arms of *Protoreaster nodosus* whose everted stomach is already partially enveloping this unexpected prey. In photograph **44** another starfish of the same species has pinned down a gorgonian that was close to the window pane; even though this plate is not as clear as it should have been, due to the thickness of the slab of glass, one can see the fine membrane of the stomach enmeshing two branches of this gorgonian to absorb its polyps.

Thromidia catalai

I will end my observations on starfish by reporting the discovery of the largest and the heaviest starfish in the world. On many accounts it is an amusing story. Our very good friend, Elizabeth Pope, one of the most distinguished personalities of the Australian scientific world, spends a few weeks each year at the Aquarium. So our team then concentrates more particularly on collecting specimens that could interest her and, by the time she arrives, our ponds and tanks are well stocked with starfish, sea-urchins, brittle-stars and other echinoderms. She is then able to make useful ecological and systematic comparisons with the species of the Great Barrier Reef in Australia. And then, because her study of classification does not mask her concern for living creatures, she can choose at leisure, night and day, to carry out many biological observations in the Aquarium tanks where all these invertebrates live at ease.

Having stayed up until dawn in the laboratory on September 14, 1969, she woke up a little later than usual. As she was finishing her breakfast my wife came to tell her: "Elizabeth, everyone is waiting below for you. The divers have just brought something that is quite curious (19) and that we have never seen before". She cautiousy added: "But it might be something common for you".

The "thing" had already flattened itself against the wall of the pond and her response to me was: "Listen you practical joker, when you make a starfish in gold leaf you could at least imitate an existing species." "Elizabeth!" I replied, "put on your glasses and come and have a closer look because this thing is alive."

I have rarely seen such amazement and such intense emotion from a specialist who was suddenly confronted with an unknown species of such gigantic size.

"No," she said, after a first, careful examination, "this starfish does not resemble anything that I know. Without doubt, it is a new species and a new genus. Perhaps it might also be a new family."

However, she was reminded of two species of starfish belonging to the family Mithrodiidae which had certain characteristics of our giant find. Her follow-up research proved her correct. But for us, who are not taxonomists, the most surprising thing about this starfish was its diameter: 65 centimeters, and its weight: 6 kilograms! It had been captured by Bernard Conseil and Georges Bargibant in about 30 meters of water.

Next it was necessary to decide what to do with such a precious organism. At the end of Elizabeth's indentification, scientific interest would require that the animal be anaesthetized and then preserved in alcohol. On the other hand, one could not deprive the public of such an astonishing spectacle. A compromise allowed the two needs to be reconciled and it was agreed to place this starfish in a large tank where visitors were able to admire it for about 10 days. We shot numerous reels of film and took many photographs, some of which were chosen to illustrate this book.

Photograph **19**, shows the upper surface of the starfish and allows the reader to appreciate its size when compared with an adult hand. Photograph **20** illustrates the underside and photographs **21** and **23** show the amusing postures of this starfish as it writhes to set itself upright again. Finally, photograph **22** is a detailed study of the underside. Each night the enormous animal was isolated in an enclosure with a plastic grating to shelter it from predators such as the large conch shell, *Charonia*, or the helmet shell, *Cassis*.

Elizabeth left for Sydney begging us to take care of it. A week later, because a large rock lobster had started to nibble at one of the arms of the starfish, it was anaesthetized with menthol crystals and preserved. Professor Gooding, an American scientist on his way through Noumea, took on the responsibility of transporting it. At Sydney's Mascot Airport, Elizabeth and her fellow-workers were waiting to greet this mysterious arrival.

X-rays and dissections were carried out immediately, along with bibliographical research, and our friend also informed many of her colleagues all over the world. After months of research she discovered that a small specimen, formerly found in the Hawaiian Islands, showed some anatomical characteristics quite similar to those of our giant starfish. However, there was still a long way to go before it could be assigned an exact place in the general classification.

The lay person could never imagine how much time went into the detailed preparations and histological examinations of this animal, as well as the correspondence and discussions that took place between international scientists to decide on the description and publication of this new species and genus.

Without wanting to spoil the publication which will be made by Elizabeth and her collaborators, it is interesting to quote from a small segment of her research results: "... in this new genus we are including the giant South African starfish (*Mithrodia gigas*) as well as a new species from the Seychelles. It is interesting that the giant red starfish from Noumea has already been referred to in literature dating to 1906 by Fisher who speaks of it as a peculiar *Mithrodia*

42 A *Nardoa novaecaledoniae* finishing off its meal of a *Heterocentrotus* sea-urchin, with only the skeleton and the spines remaining. Another "pencil sea-urchin" is still undamaged, but not for long!

43 *Protoreaster nodosus*. The stomach of the starfish (which is solidly fixed to the window pane) holds a partially-devoured fish.

44 *Protoreaster nodosus* about to absorb the polyps of a gorgonian. Notice the fine ramified striae of the stomach wall.

223

45 *Toxopneustes pileolus.* One of the most venomous sea-urchins. The beginning of the emission of sexual products (refer to 47).

46 *Echinothrix calamaris.* A close-up of the anal cone. The ringed brown and white spines show that it is not yet adult.

45

46

specimen but does not put a name to it. Later, but without precisely giving its locality of origin, it was compared to a Hawaiian specimen (*Mithrodia fisheri*), but in reality, it does not really resemble it. The peculiar specimen seems to have been lost, because we have never been able to locate it in any other American collection."

The purpose of this lengthy story is to show the difficulty sometimes encountered by even the most experienced specialists in assigning an unquestionable place in the classification for a recently-discovered specimen. On the other hand, it is interesting to point out that the opportunities to discover unknown species are not as rare as one might think.

Another very good friend, Mrs D. Reed, who acquired powers of remarkable observation from her father, Professor Maurice Mathis of the Pasteur Institute in Paris, said to me while looking at numerous photographs of the giant starfish: "During our stay in Guam my husband and I saw two specimens of this species while diving, but thinking that they were known we preferred to let them live." Despite our numerous dives over the next six years we were never able to find other specimens. However, in July 1975, Pierre

Laboute — a gifted naturalist and underwater photographer — showed us a wonderful photograph of a second specimen of this starfish from the same locality, also lying on the sand but in slightly shallower water at 20 meters. "Hampered by all my photographic equipment, and with only just enough air in my aqualung to take one photograph, I was not able to bring this animal to the surface," he told us. "But if I run into it again I will bring it to the Aquarium."

Meanwhile, Pierre Laboute and Alister Birtles were exploring the reef near the sandy zone in question and one evening brought up two specimens! This was much to the great astonishment of Elizabeth Pope who had just arrived. One specimen was immediately preserved for new studies to be carried out on it; the other was put into the largest tank in the Aquarium. Although its weight did not exceed five kilograms and its diameter was 53 centimeters, it nevertheless was one of the great attractions for visitors to the Aquarium ... and for ourselves as well. Our distinguished colleagues Elizabeth Pope and Frank Rowe were kind enough to name this famous starfish: *Thromidia catalai*.

SOME TYPICAL SEA-URCHINS

A little girl had just read *Tripneustes gratilla* on the label of a tank containing three small sea-urchins (**54**) and she commented: "I suppose *gratilla*, refers to its thousands of little spikes." But I explained to her that this Latin name means a small round edible cake — fortunately without any venomous spikes — which was cooked by the Ancient Romans. Before we knew the scientific name with which naturalists had baptised them, we used to call them "the little melon sea-urchins". Moreover, in certain regions of the Pacific this sea-urchin is highly prized as food by the natives.

These pretty creatures of the coast are very widely distributed throughout the western region of the Pacific and right up to the Hawaiian Islands. For the past 20 years there have always been some at the Aquarium. Their behavior is quite curious, as shown in the middle ground of photograph **54** where one of them has almost completed its disguise using a *Caulerpa* seaweed. But their taste isn't limited to algae: they camouflage themselves with all kinds of debris,

from dead coral to fragments of shells and even a complete bivalve shell. Sometimes they will only use grains of sand but, no matter what refuse they decorate themselves with, it is rarely sufficient to give complete protection.

The sea-urchins' efforts are a far cry from the perfection of camouflage by seaweed crabs when they don their superb living or artificial adornment. I can well imagine a *Camposcia* chatting with a *Picrocerus* (Crustacea, **16** and **22**), both dressed to the nines and perfectly invisible under their total disguise: "Have you seen that dress? The old 'hedgehog' looks quite dowdy, doesn't she?"

Isn't it true that the "chance ornaments" worn by sea-urchins often make them more visible — to our eyes at least — than if they didn't adorn themselves with anything at all? I still remember one that rigged itself up with large spines of a pencil sea-urchin (*Heterocentrotus mamillatus*). Sporting this disguise it became more obvious than ever: a case of involuntary exhibitionism!

Moreover, isn't it wrong to try and find a

meaning for *everything*? The so-called camouflage of these *Tripneustes* perhaps has nothing to do with the concept of trying to conceal itself or hide from sight; after all, we seem to be sensible beings and often decorate ourselves simply for our own pleasure!

While writing this passage on disguises, and imagining different echinoderm specialists reading it, I can see them smiling at my false interpretation and astonishing ignorance. In actual fact, there is a completely different explanation about sea-urchin camouflage. From numerous observations made by experienced biologists it is claimed that sea-urchins demonstrate an intolerance to bright light and therefore they place objects between themselves and the light to act as a sunscreen. Even though this argument seems quite reasonable, it has not convinced me simply because of our many observations over the years.

Photograph **54** shows three *Tripneustes*. Only one of them has twisted some seaweed around itself. The other two, equally intensely illuminated, felt no need to protect themselves even though there are plenty of objects around to provide cover and most of these objects are easier to grip than the seaweed. We have often noted this difference in behavior. How many times did we also notice a sea-urchin belonging to one species or another — because it isn't only the *Tripneustes* species that dresses up like this — that had no screen during the course of the day but, once night fell or during the course of the night, applied whatever covering element it could find. I don't want anyone suggesting that it was in anticipation of the next day's sun!

Another small factor continues to intrigue us by its frequency: every overflow pipe in the tanks is protected by a small plastic cylinder grating which covers the water exit pipe. This is an essential precaution to avoid having small, rare fish — or useful ones like the cleaner *Fissilabrus* — sucked away by the force of the current. These gratings are removable because they clog up quite quickly with algae and other refuse, and daily cleaning is necessary. Now, in certain tanks where these sea-urchins live, not a week goes by without one of them forcing off the grating and walking along with it on its back the next morning. Here again, light has had nothing to do with it because this operation takes place during the night. I could quite easily quote other examples,

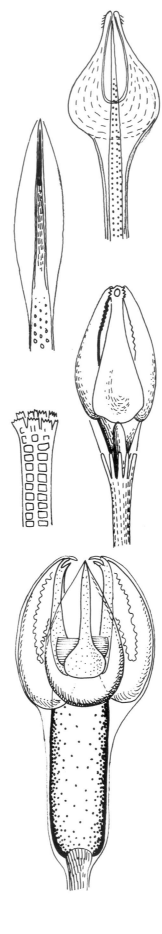

Pedicellaria of sea-urchins (from H. Hyman)

both from the Aquarium and at sea, but those that I have given show how risky some interpretations can be. It is because of these controversies, caused by hasty deductions, that I have left many notes taken over the years in my files. Flagrant contradictions would take away all their value.

Another observation concerns a *Tripneustes* sea-urchin, photograph **53**, which carries around a fragment of purple living lace coral (*Retepora*) and two pieces of green gravel. This is actually high-grade nickel ore (four to five percent) which the sea-urchin had been transporting like this for weeks. This sea-urchin is perfectly comfortable and so bears witness to the complete indifference to the so-called toxity of heavy ores, of which mention is made in the deplorable commentary to the film by the Cousteau team: "*500 million d'années sous la mer.*" Many newspapers referred to this same film at the time under a title which was equally unfortunate: "*The Noumea Lagoon, Cemetery Of Deal Corals Where Only Venomous Snakes Survive*".

I will have more to say about the many inaccuracies in this film (and I am choosing my words very carefully) which have given a completely false impression of the lagoon.

Toxopneustes pileolus

I have mentioned the amazing pedicellaria earlier and their astonishing shapes. Many authors have talked about the toxicity of the poison in the venom glands of the globular pedicellaria. It seems that the sea-urchin *Toxopneustes pileolus* is the most dangerous. Thus, H. Hyman quotes the observation made by Fujiwara in 1935 that the pricks of only seven or eight pedicellaria on a finger were sufficient to provoke very severe pain, followed by dizziness, facial paralysis and respiratory difficulty. Other authors have mentioned fatal cases. A number of books have shown close-ups of the pedicellaria of this sea-urchin in which they appear like little flowers. Here I have preferred to illustrate *Toxopneustes* during the emission of sperm. The first picture (**45**) shows the beginning and the second (**47**) was taken an hour later. But a third photograph, taken an hour later, is not produced because the whitish cloud had become so dense that one could not make out the perpetrator of such a profusion of semen. It became so abundant that the 4,000-liter tank of running water remained intensely milky for more than three hours.

47 *Toxopneustes pileolus*, sperm diluting about half an hour after photograph 45.

48 *Araeosoma sp.* Aboral face. A dangerously venomous sea-urchin. The blue-violet on some spines could not be captured.

49 *Echinothrix calamaris* in its entirety. The same comment can be made on the ringed spines as in 46. Depth of origin, 25 meters.

50 *Asthenosoma varium*. Aboral face is a remarkable illustration of pentagonal symmetry, the five fields being clearly demarcated.

51 The same individual; a close-up of the periproctal region.

52 *Echinothrix calamaris*. Transition between juvenile and adult stages. A few spines are completely brown. They will all be like this within a year.

52a A juvenile *Diadema setosum* with ringed spines.

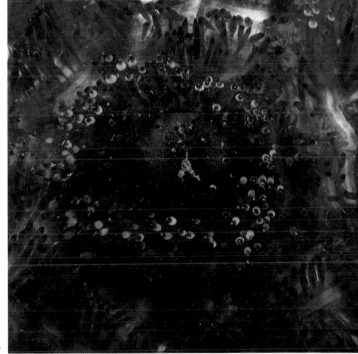

48

51

52a

49

52

53

54

55

56

Araeosoma sp.

This sea-urchin has left me with vivid memories. One day, leaning on the edge of one of the large tanks of the Aquarium, I was taking out some plankton when a small jar slipped from my fingers. Wanting to catch it, my hand collided, full on, with an *Araeosoma* near the concrete partition wall. You could never imagine the pain I went through and, despite applying Hydrocortisone cream, the pain persisted for several hours. I even had fever and an increased heart-beat.

Despite all of this discomfort I must admit that I still have a soft spot for this elegant and fine-spined sea-urchin. I was never able to take photographs of all the superb color variations produced in the different light conditions. The photograph of the upper surface (**48**) only gives a hint of this beauty ... it is still paler than in real life.

While on the subject of *Araeosoma*, we note that some of the pedicelleria have three jaws which function just like sugar tongs which are opened by the pressure exerted by a thumb on a central plunger. I wouldn't be surprised if their inventor was also a specialist in echinoderms!

Asthenosoma varium

This is also a very beautiful sea-urchin and some species are as large as a plate. I know it is venomous but the pain that I experienced twice through mishandling them was not as strong as that from other sea-urchins. However, such a remark does not mean very much because sea-urchins can be more venomous in certain seasons just as some people can be more sensitive than others and their sensitivity to the poison changes with every experience. Photograph **50** shows us one of the most beautiful examples of five-sided symmetry on the upper face so clearly are the five fields defined. A close-up of the same face (**51**) allows the reader to fully appreciate the complexity of its texture; at the center the anus, as one can just see, is about to ... open up.

Echinothrix calamaris

Only twice in 20 years did we have the great satisfaction of letting our visitors admire this magnificent specimen of a sea-urchin. Three pictures which are shown here (**46**, **49** and **52**) represent the juvenile forms when the spines are ringed in brown, white and red. At the adult stage these long spines become very dark uniform

53 *Tripneustes gratilla*. This small sea-urchin — as well as many other different marine organisms — moves around on a bed of nickel ore (green). It has even attached some pieces on its test (refer to anecdotal text and Epilogue).

54 *Tripneustes gratilla*. Only one of the three specimens has wrapped a *Caulerpa* alga around itself. The others remain "bare" despite the same luminous intensity.

55 It only took this perforating sea-urchin three years to hollow out this cavity in the concrete side of a tank.

56 *Echinometra mathaei*. This species is fairly common. With a magnifying-glass one can distinguish secondary spines, as well as the long white spines.

57 A sea-urchin from the family *Cidaridae* showing the co-existence of two very different types of spines.

58 *Heterocentrotus mamillatus* or "pencil sea-urchin". Contrary to nearly all species of sea-urchins, this has thick spines with triangular sections.

59 A close-up of a sea-urchin of the *Cidaridae* family showing the difference between "bare" spines and encrusted ones.

brown which changes their juvenile beauty. It is interesting to point out that the darkening does not occur on all the spines at the same time. In fact, over a period of two years, during which we were able to follow this gradual change of pigmentation, a certain number of spines already had the uniform coloring of the adult, while others were still ringed like the juvenile (52). Surrounded by primary ringed spines and the very fine secondary spines — but quite separate from them — one can see a small white-spotted sphere speckled with black. This is the anal globe or "anal cone" as English authors term it[94]. Even those with only a passing interest in marine life would be forced to admit that the small sphere in photograph **46** is not lacking in style, and I doubt if one would find an anus as hansome as this in any other organism, marine or non-marine!

Biologists who have been able to patiently observe these remarkable sea-urchins have no doubt noticed the curious rotatory movement of the little sphere, which is more active among the *Diadema setosum* than the *Echinotrix calamaris*[95]. Everyone I have asked for an explanation of the movement had no answer.

A nice person to whom I had gladly given up an hour of my time for a detailed tour of the Aquarium said to me while looking at the small central sphere: "I can see that eye turning like a radar and observing." I had to explain that sea-urchins are not cyclops and what that organ was for. It was then that I pointed out the real eyes — or more precisely, what acts as those — superb points of brilliant blue which change to violet under certain lighting.

To return to our *Diadema setosum* sea-urchin (**52a**) we notice the same ringing of spines in the juvenile as in those of the *Echinotrix calamaris*. At the adult stage they become uniformly black.

Heterocentrotus mamillatus

This is a common sea-urchin but one of great beauty and is clearly distinguished from all the others by the form of its thick, primary spines which are practically triangular in section, while its white secondary spines are very short and have a flat extremity. Certain specimens have a shell with white dorsal protuberances like the one shown here (**58**). Others have a test which is uniformly black. Many specialists whom I questioned on whether it is a matter of two

different species or of sexual dimorphism were unable to give me an answer.

Echinometra mathaei

Extremely widespread in all areas of the Indo Pacific, it is most often embedded in hollows of a reef. It uses its jaws and the scratching of its spines to slowly excavate the rock and certain reef areas are literally riddled with these indentations. H. Hyman tells us that "when the holes are not too deeply hollowed, the sea-urchins can leave them temporarily to look for food when the level of the tide is favorable, but these echinoderms seem to remain permanently in deep cavities and find difficulty leaving because of the narrowness of the entrance which they had used when they were younger and smaller. In such cases their feeding is dependent on the arrival of nutritive materials which the waves and the tides bring into their holes".

This long quote was necessary because our observations do not strictly agree with this. Certainly it seems presumptuous not to agree with an author who has received such universal homage. That some sea-urchins are really imprisoned must have been observed because such an eminent author tells us so. But we do not remember having noticed such an irreversible cloistering as this. Most of the holes of the sea-urchins, even those that have been deeply hollowed out, still retained wide edges to allow their occupant to stretch its legs once night has fallen. The one illustrated in photograph **56** is seen in front of a beautiful encrusting sponge called *Cliona schmidti*. Even when they appear to be absolutely stuck in their cavity, they have always extracted themselves quite easily by lying down their spines close against their shells. What must also be noted is that at the time of extremely low tide, when the numerous resting places of sea-urchins are high and dry, their occupants are no longer to be found. Finally, the influence of twilight and evening are probably a more important factor on the comings and goings of a sea-urchin than the changes of tide.

The same author tells us of the conclusions by Otter, who established that the rock cavities

60 Nature's inventiveness. A large *Chlamys* lamellibranch has attached itself above a large *Cassis* helmet shell: a *Siphonochallina* sponge is growing on the valve of the bivalve and a *Comatella sp.* crinoid is attached to the sponge.

---

94 Hyman, H. As before. "The periproct is naked with a conspicuous anal cone".
95 These two species belong to the same family of *Diadematidae*.

protect sea-urchins against strong waves and that these cavities are consequently found to be limited to areas subjected to excessive action by these waves. In addition he states that these sea-urchins enlarge an existing rock cavity by the rotating movements of their spines.

The first observation is oversimplified because in many areas influenced by moderate winds — in other words, that are rarely hit by waves of high intensity — one can still find sea-urchin cavities and their occupants.

As for the second remark, it is contradicted firstly by the observations also quoted by Hyman and confirmed by Irving on the Californian coast; considerable damage is inflicted on steel pillars by *Spongylocentrotus purpuratus* which, amazingly, were lodged in hollows which they had excavated themselves. Secondly, it is contradicted by observations made inside our own Aquarium. Some of our sea-urchins (*Echinometra* and *Parasalenia*) hollowed out holes in the smooth concrete of the tanks just above the surface of the water — in a place that was constantly splashed by the overflow pipe. These hollows (like the one shown in photograph **55**) were not chosen by the sea-urchins because of an existing depression; the cement was quite smooth. In her superb book on the Australian Great Barrier Reef, Isobel Bennett[96] writes about these excavating sea-urchins such as the *Echinometra mathaei*: "One doesn't know how long it takes them to hollow out their cavity, which could be the result of a scraping action by the jaws and spines of many generations of sea-urchins." The cavity shown here (with the occupant who was responsible for it) is the result of three years' work. Many cavities have been started on other tanks, but in places where it would have severely damaged them so we couldn't allow resident artisans to make them any bigger.

Cidaridae

These are very curious sea-urchins which give the impression of great age because of the calcerous encrustaceans covering a large proportion of their spines. I will restrict myself to only showing here two specimens of the cidarid family. The one in photograph **59** (*Goniocidaris?*) clearly shows very fine secondary spines in small

61 *Comanthus sp.* which seems to be quite rare. Found at a depth of 25 meters.

62 An undentified bicolored crinoid. Same depth and locality as 61.

63 *Comanthus sp.* which is extremely fragile and not very frequent in the areas already studied in the region of Noumea.

61

62

63

96   Bennett, Isobel. *The Great Barrier Reef.* Lansdowne Press Pty. Ltd., Melbourne, 1971.

clumps at the base of its large primary spines. And the second (**57**) shows the natural red color which are probably new spines. That is my interpretation at least, and perhaps a specialist might give me a completely different explanation for the disparity of color in these spines.

SEA LILIES

Standing in front of one of our most spectacular tanks, where the sea lilies are kept, visitors are often heard to comment: "Oh, what beautiful little ferns!" and are astonished to find out that they are actually animals. However, looking at them more carefully they notice the innumerable little "fingers" or pinnules (**67**) working all along the arms. The movements of these little prehensile organs are even livelier when the plankton happens to be denser than normal. Sometimes visitors have a chance to see a sea lily swimming — one of the most graceful spectacles in the marine world. How lucky they are to witness this dazzling balletic scene. Fortunately I have been able to shoot several film sequences, even though movement happens without any warning so it is impossible to predict. Sometimes we have been able to provoke swimming by carefully detaching them from their support. Movement itself is caused by the constant vertical pulsating of their arms. Sea lilies with many arms, like the specimen in photograph **69** (*Pentiometra andersoni*), move very rapidly, but the species with few arms, such as the *Antedon* illustrated in photograph **68**, are comparatively slow.

Certain sea lilies grip the corals, gorgonians, sponges or rocks by means of "crampons" called "basal tendrils" (**69**). They can remain fixed to these for days or even weeks, their delicately curled arms bent towards the center. And then suddenly, for reasons which escape us, the flight takes place. But it never lasts more than a few minutes at the very most. We have often noticed that if a sea lily fixes itself on a hard coral of the *Porites* group it will stay longer than on other supports, probably because the tendrils find a better grip on such a firm support. Other sea lilies, which do not have these basal tendrils, move in a sort of jerky crawl with the aid of their arms.

Sea lilies in the shallow coastal zones are only rarely seen during daylight hours, because the majority of species avoid light and shelter in crevices or under corals with large horizontal plates. But by evening, or during the course of the night, you would be surprised to see how many more of them move out in the open. One of many such examples is the *Comatella maculata* (**60**). On the other hand, all the sea lilies living deeper in the lagoon, between the 25 and 35 meter mark, do not hide during the day. And this gives all our visitors a chance to admire them in all their beauty because the tanks in which they live are exposed to sunlight.

Most of these species from the deep water of the lagoon are, as one can see, very prettily colored. Some have two areas of different colors on the same individual, (photographs **62** and **63**). As these sea lilies do not have basal tendrils, the prehension power of their many arms is used to anchor the animal firmly to the surfaces of sponges, seaweeds and gorgonians etc. Moreover, they hold themselves there with such strength that it is quite difficult to remove them without leaving a great number of pinnules behind ... and sometimes even a whole arm breaks off. However they have the ability to regenerate amputated limbs just like starfish.

These organisms are so delicate that we are faced with all sorts of problems in trying to bring them to the Aquarium intact. Our aim was to keep them alive for a long time and in perfect condition and to achieve that we had to perfect a device that fed their high oxygen needs with a voluminous flow of water, and yet caused their fragile arms no damage with turbulence.

Most of the sea lilies illustrated here were identified by Dr. Frank Rowe of the Australian Museum in Sydney. The *Pontiometra andersoni*, holding tight to a coral in photograph **69**, is one of the swimming species that moves with remarkable speed.

In the close-up of the *Comantheris briareus* in photograph **73**, we can see a little commensal crab, *Galathea elegans*, which lives on many sea lilies. The *Comanthus benneti* is one of the most beautiful specimens, showing golden reflections under certain lights. Picture **67** is a study of the arms to show the pinnules in detail. And in photograph **77** of the upper surface of *Comanthina schlegeli*, the black area surrounding the center is none other than a couple of

64 An undentified crinoid. To the right, the pink and white organism is a *Spongodes merleti* soft-coral. At its base there is a "Venus lace", a colony of bryozoans (*Retepora*), which is alive because it is violet colored.

65 A *Comanthus benneti*, one of the most beautiful species of crinoids. Reproduction in print cannot show the golden brilliance of its arms.

66 The same species, with the oral face of the crown showing the arms carrying numerous lateral branches called pinnules.

67 A close-up of the arms and their pinnules. On the bottom one can see how they appear on either side of the channel.

64

65

68

69

70

68 *Antedon sp*. One of the "swimming" crinoids, but unlike those of the *Pontiometra* group (plate 69), it swims slowly.

69 *Pontiometra andersoni* clearly showing its tendrils for fixation. It swims extremely rapidly.

70 An undentified crinoid attached to a *Clathria* sponge.

commensal shrimps, *Synalpheus*, which are so well camouflaged that only an experienced eye can spot them. Finally, photograph **79** once again shows us a close-up of their basal tendrils. It must be pointed out that this species is very fluorescent under ultra-violet rays.

For a non-specialist the photographs and drawings of sea lilies in taxonomic publications are quite disappointing because the preserved specimens themselves were usually in a piteous state. I have tried many different methods of preservation myself, but without great success; the problem is that these echinoderms lose color rapidly and the arms break up into small fragments. Certainly it is possible to overcome the latter problem by first anaesthetizing the specimen, but it is a long process and we just never had the time to experiment. Only once, when we needed to photograph the wonderful fluorescence of the sea lily illustrated in number **78**, did we do this. We anaesthetized it in royal style by allowing a few grams of menthol crystals to dissolve in its tank. Otherwise it would have been impossible to stop all movements of the animal for the eleven minutes of exposure that we needed. Several other species also fluorescence when subjected to ultra-violet light (of 3650 angstrom wavelength). This is the case with the beautiful *Comatella stelligera* (**79** and **80**), seen here in the light of day.

Many sea lilies give shelter to, or provide homes for, different types of organisms which live happily together with them. Among these are nudibranchs, flat worms, small crustacean isopods and even tiny gastropod mollusks, not to mention the small shrimps, *Synalpheus*, and the charming crab, *Galathea* (Crustacea, **47**).

I have reserved a most unusual spectacle, illustrated in photograph **60**, as a finale. A caption saying "just as we planned it" would be justified here because such a pile of superimposed organisms would never have had a chance of being produced in the sea. In fact, it was necessary for many different organisms to be present in the same tank for the erection of this balancing pyramid. I first noticed this incredible piece of mounting early one morning. I hurried to take the photographs for fear of having the ensemble break apart, because it was soon time for the creature forming the base to bury itself under the sand. This was a large helmet shell called *Cassis* to which a *Chlamys* lamellibranch

71 *Comantheris briareus* (depth of origin, 25 meters), attached to a sponge which is entirely hidden by the abundance of arms.

72 The oral face of the same organism. The lowering of arms, while others raise, enables it to swim at quite a pace.

73 The central region of the same subject. One of the small commensal crabs (*Galathea elegans*) is easily recognizable below. Its spouse is barely visible above right.

71 and 72

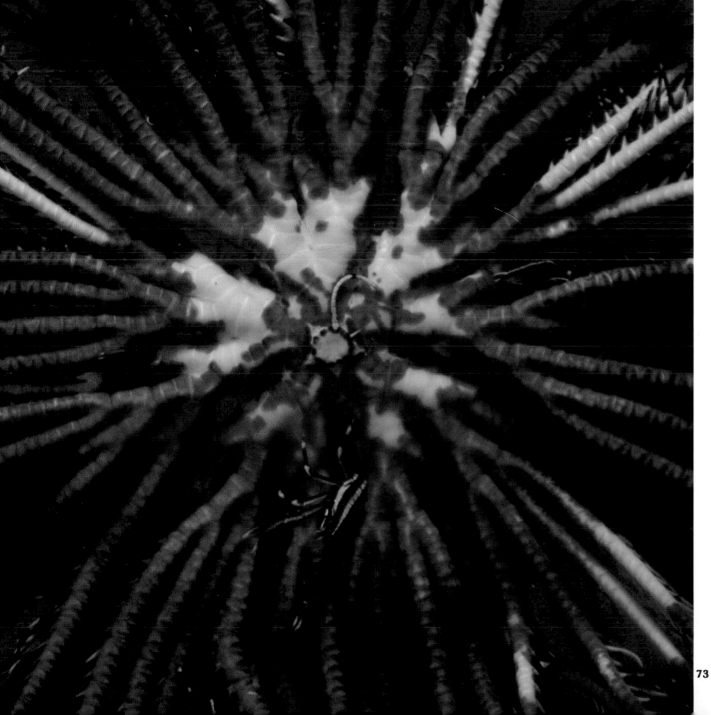

73

237

74 A crinoid of the *Tropiometridae* family. It seems to be extremely rare.

75 *Comanthina schlegeli.* Again we can clearly see the radial arms divided into five groups.

76 A crinoid which has just landed on the polyps of a coral which has not been retracted for long. To the right, a reddish sponge (probably a *Clathria*).

77 A *Comanthina schlegeli* (opposite face). A couple of *Synalpheus* shrimps form a black ring around the center (camouflage).

78 A crinoid in fluorescence under ultra-voilet light. The reddish fluorescence is calcareous algae.

79 *Comanthina stelligera*, to show the importance of the attachment tendrils.

80 The same specimen's aboral face. This species, which is very fluorescent under ultra-violet light, is shown here in daylight.

75

76

77

had attached its sticky threads during the night. This bivalve, as has already been illustrated in the chapter on mollusks, had some *Siphonochalina* sponges over it. And then, sitting like a crown on top of all of this was the *Comatella maculata.* I was only able to take one photograph because the first flash made the *Chlamys* flee and so the sea lily immediately let go as well. This photograph would have been even more remarkable if it had also been able to record the little symbiotic crab living in the *Comatella.* But we shouldn't ask for too much!

THE BRITTLE STARS

These echinoderms generally resemble starfish but their body is made up of a central disk from which five arms radiate. However, these cylindrical arms are very thin. They writhe like slender snakes, and it is from these movements that they have gained the alternate common name of "serpent star".[97] The arms are more brittle than those of the starfish but there is the same regeneration if one happens to be broken off.

Certain species, and in particular the little ones that are brought up from depths of 20 to 40 meters, live in small colonies on sponges and on gorgonions and the light of day doesn't disturb them. On the other hand, the shallow-water species prefer the darkness and remain in the cracks of rocks or under stones all day. This is the case, for example, with the beautiful *Ophiarachna incrassata* (86). My radiologist friend, René Abgrall, took some admirable X-ray photographs of them which I am delighted to reproduce here (page 243), to pay tribute to a great specialist and also to thank him for his generous and spontaneous collaboration.

In spite of its aversion to light, the brittle star does eventually take the risk of putting out a few arms from its hiding spot to forage for fallen bread-crumbs intended for the fish swimming around in its tank. The keeness of this brittle star's senses has always surprised me, as has its ability to know exactly where on the bottom this small tasty morsel has fallen. One of the arms immediately wraps around the crumb and brings it to its mouth which tears it to pieces. Having no anus, brittle stars expel waste from their digestion through the mouth.

---

97 Their scientific group name is Ophiuroidea, from *ophis* meaning serpent.

81 A *Gorgonocephalus* (*Euryale*?) or giant brittle star. In the diurnal hours, the arms and ramifications of the animal roll and shrivel up, making it very difficult to see.

82 *Astrobrachion sp.* brittle star wrapped around the branches of a gorgonian.

81

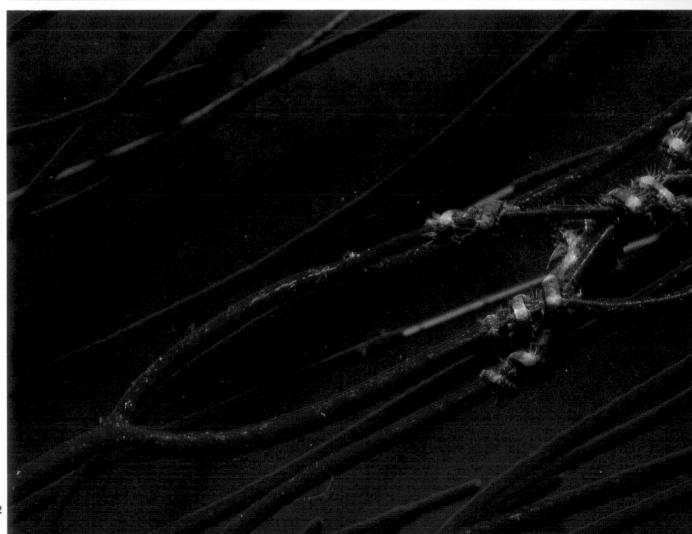

82

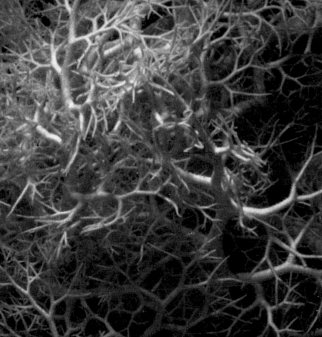

83 A brittle star supposed to belong to the family of *Trichasteridae*, attached to a gorgonian. Beautiful example of mimicry.

84 A very small brittle star which has decided to make its home in the cloaca of a solitary living coral (*Fungia*).

85 A close-up of the central ramifications of a *Gorgoncephale*.

83

84

85

There is, of course, much more one could say about this group of echinoderms and many illustrations to show the diverse species. I have chosen to illustrate a tiny one here (**84**)[98], which lives on the inside of the cloaca of a *Fungia* coral. Another of the *Astrobrachion* genus, in photograph **82**, is scarcely any bigger and has wrapped itself around several branches of a gorgonian brought up from a depth of 40 meters. Photograph **83** also shows a very rare brittle star which the specialists believe probably belongs to the family *Trichasteridae*. The flash has made it possible for us to see it more clearly in the photograph than in real life since it blends in so well with the deep-water gorgonian to which it is firmly attached. As for the pretty *Acanthophiothrix purpurea* (**87**), found at a depth of 35 meters, its forest of very fine spines gives it a very dangerous appearance, but in reality they are harmless. Finally I come to the basket star or "Gorgon's head", *Gorgonocephalus* (**81**) which lives at depths varying between 20 and 40 meters and measures about half a meter across the arms. In daylight its arms are curled up and no one looking at this immobile ball would think that, once evening has come, it would emerge in full "bloom" as shown in the photograph. All the fine branches on its arms twist and writhe to search the bottom and sides of the tank for anything edible.

SEA CUCUMBERS

Although these echinoderms are of great scientific interest, one can hardly say that they are aesthetically appealing — even though certain species have most unusual designs and delightfully bright colors, like those presumed to belong to the *Aspidochirota* (**88**). This creature was found only once, at a depth of 25 meters, on a giant sea-squirt (*Polycarpa aurata*[99]). The loss of this specimen was a great shame because it was probably a new species according to specialists.

When these animals crawl slowly across the sand, by extending and contracting their bodies, they resemble enormous caterpillars. Such is the case for the *Stichopus variegatus* (**92**) and *Holothuria aculeata* (**91**). But it is said that even the least elegant of marine organisms possess some form of beauty. Certain sea cucumbers can

98   Not yet identified.
99   Refer to *Carnaval sous la mer*, pl. III, fig. 1.

241

86 An *Ophiorachna incrassata*, able to reach a size of 20 centimeters. It is found over a very wide area. It remains hidden during the day (refer to the X-ray of it opposite).

87 *Acanthophiothrix purpurea*. Despite the impressive forest of very pointed thorns, this magnificent brittle star is not venomous. Depth of origin, 35 meters.

86

87

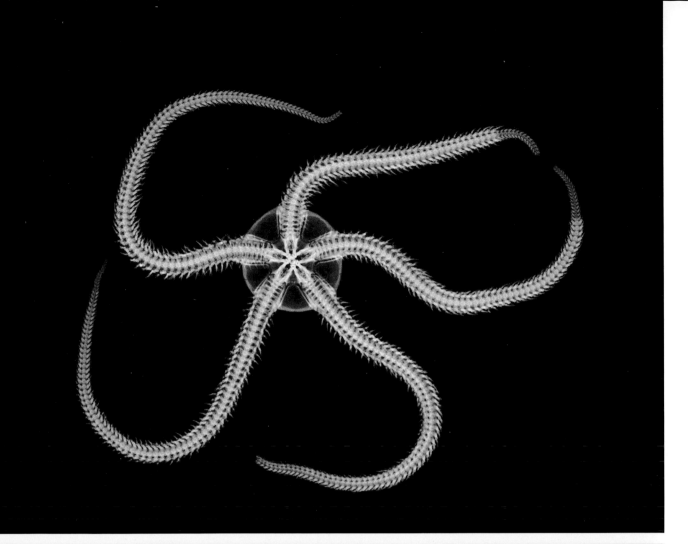

Above: an X-ray of an *Ophiorachna incrassata*. Below, an X-ray of an *Euretaster insignis*. Negatives: R. Abgrall.

243

88 An unidentified sea cucumber. It was found at a depth of 25–30 meters on a giant sea-squirt (*Polycarpa aurata*), presumed to belong to the order of *Aspidochirota*.

89 *Aspidochirota sp.* (*Actinopyga?*). This group of sea cucumbers includes dangerously toxic species which the native fishermen on many of the Pacific Islands use to capture fish on the reefs. (Refer to chapter on Fish).

90 *Phyllophorus magnus*. The animal buries itself under the sand with only the retractile tentacle showing.

88

89

90

91 *Holothuria aculeata*. This relatively common sea cucumber is very inactive.

92 *Stichopus variegatus*.

91

92

245

produce very beautiful "bouquets" when their oral tentacles are fully expanded, like the *Phyllophorus magnus* illustrated in photograph **90** and those of the *Holothuria sp.* (**93**). Usually the animal is completely buried under the sand and only reveals its presence with a "sheaf" which, at the slightest external disturbance, instantaneously retracts deep inside the body. There are also very peculiar postures. In one of the large tanks of the Aquarium where we had kept some large specimens of *Holothuria* for a number of years, we surprised some during the night and found them standing bolt upright. This perfectly immobile posture would remain for several hours. I do not know whether any observation of this kind has been made before, but I think that there is some correlation between this erect stance and sexual activity because I have only noticed this behavior during September and October, the southern spring.

Numerous books on reef fauna have illustrated the classic behavior of a sea cucumber defending itself by expelling quantities of long, white and sticky filaments through its anus. These expulsions are called "Cuvier tubes" and they neutralise enemy attack. On numerous occasions we have all personally experienced the effectiveness of these sticky tubes when we have disturbed sea cucumbers through our carelessness or curiosity. I can't tell you what trouble we had, and what patience we needed, to extricate ourselves from this ultra-sticky "vermicelli" which adheres to the skin and wetsuit!

Another well known but very strange behavioral feature of sea cucumbers is their ability to eject a part of their gut; this disembowelling does not bring about the animal's death because the organs regenerate again in a few days. Among other strange phenomena, one must also mention the strong and intimate association sea cucumbers have with a small, long and translucent fish called *Fierasfer*. This fish lives in the sea cucumber's intestines and when it re-enters the anus it usually does so in reverse.

Embedded in the skin of the sea cucumbers are tiny calcareous structures which have an infinity of pretty shapes. These are called spicules. Finally, a photograph of the toxic sea cucumber of the *Aspidochirota* (**89**), about which I make further reference in the chapter Fish (refer to The breeding of trevally).

Synaptes also belong to this group of echinoderms; they are extremely long, and astonishingly extensible. It would have been superfluous to illustrate all the *Synaptes* again in this book because they have appeared so frequently in popular works. And to learn more about the association between *Synaptes* and *Periclimenes* shrimps, the reader should simply turn to photograph **52** in the chapter on Crustacea.

93 *Holothuria sp.* The attractive expansions of the retractile tentacles.

93

246

Fish

Right at the outset of this chapter I must warn the reader that most of the observations presented here are deliberately directed towards fervent aquarists. For those thousands of professionals and hobbyists I must repeat that observations on "the world of fins"[100] will lure them for life — as they have me. Detailed description[101] is necessarily lengthy and as Miguel Zamacois said in his *Redites-nous quelque chose*: "You can't just hook up a fish story on a fishing line."

More observations on the leopard-sharks[102]

In 1969 I contributed a large number of photographs taken of life in the Aquarium to the magnificent book, *La Vie des Animaux*, published by Librairie Larousse under the direction of my old friend, Professor Pierre Grassé.

I was delighted at the remarkable quality of the color reproductions of the chosen subjects. But I was greatly disappointed to discover in the third volume, including the chapter on fish, that one of my captions had been altered ... the one which accompanied the photograph of a newly-born leopard shark, *Stegostoma fasciatum* (**2**). The text that I had carefully composed for the baby leopard shark was: "Close to it, the large egg case from which it came." The caption in *La Vie des Animaux* had become: "Close to it, the large egg case from which it perhaps came."

If this alterer of captions had glanced through *Carnaval sous la mer*, he would have read these lines: "... as it is probably the first time that the hatching of such a shark has taken place in an aquarium ... it was necessary to illustrate the new-born creature next to the large egg case from which it has just come. Thanks to the translucence of the keratinous skin of the egg case, we had observed for months the regular growth of the small embryo as it moved and changed position".

Each year, for the two decades that this Aquarium has been functioning, many visitors have been able to follow for themselves the regular growth of a few embryos which we kept in a specially lit shadow theater. I was able to shoot many movie sequences on extremely sensitive 16 mm film (**1**) and, besides the "foetus", you can distinguish the umblical cord which connects it to

the vitelline mass (photograph **3** also shows this). If that isn't enough to convince "Mr Perhaps" I must add that it would be very difficult to see how one could have a new-born *Stegostoma* in an aquarium tank without having the egg first.

I had written to our friend Grassé in August 1970: "... we have concluded that as soon as they have come out of the egg, they swim for the open sea (like several newly-born fish of other species) and into quite deep water, probably on the outer edge of the barrier reef or in the trenches of the lagoon".

This hypothesis was proved a short time later. For many years, when collecting shallow water fauna and flora, we and all our helpers had spent thousands of hours rummaging about amongst the algae looking for the *Stegostoma* egg cases that we knew had been laid and solidly fixed there. However, new-born sharks were never observed nor did we ever capture any in the numerous drag nets in these same habitats. And baby leopard sharks never took the fishhooks of the natives who spend the whole day in these shallows fishing for *Thalassoma*, *Apogan*, *Glyphisodon* and other small fry. This is at least to my knowledge, and after much research, the case.

We only know of one exception which, in my opinion, confirms the rule: one evening some fishermen from Noumea laid a long net to the edge of a large plateau and therefore quite close to the outer drop off. The next morning they found a dead newly-born *Stegostoma*, all tangled up and in quite a sorry state after having made so many efforts to attempt to reach the open sea before dawn.

A short time later two excellent divers reported that they had noticed a few young *Stegostoma* in a trough in the lagoon about 50 meters deep and on a muddy sand bottom. These were quite tame so the divers were able to get sufficiently close to realize that their size was similar to those of our new-born specimens in the Aquarium.

100   An expression which has been taken without shame from a colleague, M. Roby, who gave this good title to one of his numerous books on aquatic fauna — books which should be read. (See Bibliography).
101   Like trevally, barracuda, and other fish which are attracted by shiny lures.
102   *Carnaval sous la mer*, p. 108 and pl. XXVI, fig. 1.

1 *Stegostoma fasciatum*: 16 mm frames showing the almost continuous movements of the embryo through the thick egg case.

2 *Stegostoma fasciatum*: leopard-shark. On the top right, the large egg from which it came a few hours earlier.

3 *Stegostoma fasciatum*: embryo, yolk-sac and "umbilical cord".

4 *Stegostoma fasciatum*: a live two-meters specimen showing adult colors. The black spots remind one of a leopard.

Page 247: A *Centropyge flavissimus* of the family Pomacanthidae.

2

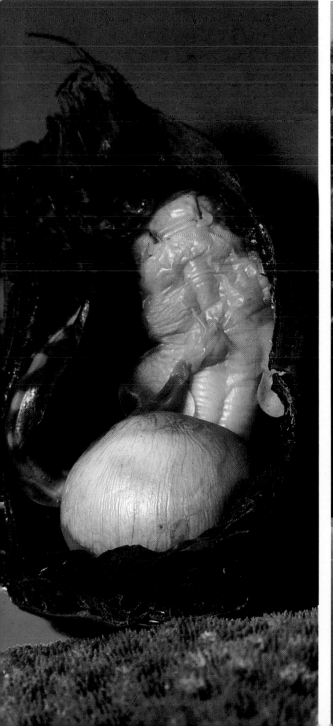

3 and 4

5 *Aetobatus narinari*. Eagle ray in motion. It remains concealed under the sand for hours with only its eyes emerging.

6 *Sphyrna sp*. Juvenile hammer-head shark. The eyes are positioned at the end of the cephalic extensions.

5

6

In March 1976 a young 80 centimeter leopard shark, which already had its adult color, was installed in the largest of our tanks. It was brought to us by a fisherman who caught it on a line in about 30 meters and in the same region where our divers spotted the babies. Certainly it would be too much to conclude that this zone was the only nursery area, but such a capture should, on principle, be pointed out.

This young *Stegostoma*, with its adult coat, rarely moves in the middle of the day but shows a vigorous appetite by evening. It is just as well that feeding takes place so late because the other large fish in this tank (snappers, groupers, etc.) have already found their retreats and will not come and disturb its meals. Such a schedule is understandable because *Stegostoma* are short-sighted, but this is compensated for by their highly sensitive taste buds.

I have heard it said that keeping a *Stegostoma* in a tank should be avoided because the water becomes toxic to other fish. We have never observed the slightest inconvenience among any fish, whether large or small, which swam in the tanks where our leopard sharks were kept. This was even the case when some sharks measured more than two meters. After that size specimens don't feed properly and decline in health so we put them back to sea. However, we have kept three beautiful adults in the Aquarium for longer than two years now and my wife, once again, has succeeded in taming them. She has incredible patience and strictly observes their eating hours, hand serving them "*a la carte*".

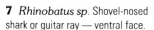

7 *Rhinobatus sp.* Shovel-nosed shark or guitar ray — ventral face.

8 *Aetobatus narinari.* Ventral face.

Hammer-head shark

I have taken a photograph of the head of a juvenile hammer-head shark, *Sphyrna* (**6**) to show its mouth which is in the shape of an arc. It seems quite small in comparison to the enormous head, but the jaws beneath are very dangerous. One will also notice the position of the eyes at the extremity of two lateral extensions of the head which give these sharks such a strange appearance, like a perpendicular hammer-head on a handle.

Stingrays

One of our most popular living stingrays on exhibition at the Aquarium are the very common small *Dasyatis*. They delight the visitor because of their near-constant movement and great appetite. Covering a piece of fish or a clam with their wing-like fins, they arch over the food taking on the appearance of a miniature aeroplane hangar. Once the meal is over, and after a few very graceful "flights", these stingrays stretch out on the bottom and raise clouds of sand with very rapid beats of their fins: on settling this covers them completely except for their eyes which show through the surface like small black balls. How many visitors have passed a few centimeters from these stingrays without even realising they were there? They are very hardy and some of them have been in our tanks for more than ten years.

Unfortunately we can't say much about the beautiful *Aetobatus narinari* (eagle rays, **5**) whose lash-like tail is more than twice the length of the animal, nor can we say much about the unusual guitar rays (*Rhinobatus*, **7**). They do not adapt well to captivity, even in our very large tanks. Both species probably need even larger tanks — a facility which does not exist at the Aquarium in Noumea. We have never had the ambition to be a showcase for large animals. Most books only illustrate the top surface of stingrays and guitar rays. I have preferred to show them from underneath (**7** and **8**) because that angle always seems quite funny.

Barracuda (Sphyraena barracuda)

The magnificent barracuda, also called a sea-pike because of many similarities with the fresh-water pike, looks like a superbly hydrodynamic silver spindle. It is one of the most impressive fish that there is. In certain regions it can reach two meters or more.

This terrible torpedo is feared by divers and the formidable teeth in its powerful jaws can sever an arm. Several times during my long stay in Madagascar I met one-armed men in the east coast fishing villages and would ask them: "*Asan'sa*" (shark)? and they would reply: "*Aloua!*"

(barracuda)."[103] One old man even told me: "A very long time ago a large *aloual* attacked a diver so furiously, and plunged into his stomach so deeply, that both man and fish died." (sic)

I have always doubted the truth of that story. A large barracuda certainly has enough strength to penetrate an abdominal cavity, but it would still need to strike the same place several times and its jaws would have to be closed to form a pointed muzzle. Since, a charging barracuda normally opens its mouth wide, the story was probably a question of personal hatred![104]

Many times in the largest tank in the Aquarium we tried to keep barracuda of between 40 and 70 centimeters which had been caught with a lure or in a fishing-net. Perhaps some were eaten by large groupers, but we have concluded that a barracuda over a size of about 20 centimeters is already too big to adapt to captivity.

Other carnivorous fish needing space, such as the trevally that we successfully raised from tiny specimens, were easily captured with a sweep-net close to shore. But it is very difficult and extremely rare to capture tiny barracuda because they live in thick seagrass meadows, in small groups of about five or six individuals. We have only captured two very small specimens. The first measured only three and a half centimeters and we placed it all alone in a laboratory tank, feeding it with small white-bait (*Lebistes*). This small creature already showed the same surety and the same ferocious determination as adults when attacking. Day after day we noted its regular growth. At the end of one and a half months we had to shift him to a larger tank. It grew even quicker when we began feeding it small mullet. We also immediately noticed that unlike greedy species such as scorpion-fish (*Synanceus*), angler fish (*Antennarius*) and other predators of living fish, this barracuda would not snap up its food unless it was hungry. At the end of the afternoon (the third "restaurant" service of the day) we would always put in about ten mullet. It would catch three or four of them in rapid succession, leaving some in case it had hunger pangs later. One morning to our sorrow we discovered it dead — and in an unfortunate manner. While hunting it was used to executing magnificent vertical climbs to avoid banging against the side walls of its tank, and this time its momentum must have been so vigorous that it had caught its snout in the

wire-netting mesh covering its tank, and was suspended there. Sadly, all that was left for us to do was to measure it precisely. In 85 days it had grown from 3.5 centimeters to 20 centimeters.

The following year M. Cogulet[105] brought a second specimen to the Aquarium, but this already measured nine centimeters. Even though it was placed by itself in a half cubic meter tank, it continuously thrust itself against the panes of the tank, and with such painful perseverance that it was even wearing out its snout. We had decided to release it back into the sea but, by luck, a net fisherman had caught some very small mullet. Our baby barracuda, that until then had taken no interest in food, began chasing vigorously. We therefore kept it and benefitted greatly because, as it turned out, it was to teach us quite a few things.

What has always struck divers is the perfect immobility of the barracuda, resembling the freshwater-pike lying rigidly in wait. While watching our guest at a standstill we observed that, from time to time, it wriggled its whole body. This "limbering-up exercise", which only lasts a few seconds at a time, shows astonishing flexibility which one would not have thought possible from this long, normally rigid spindle.

Having transferred Cogulet to a bigger tank of several cubic meters (which was not a very easy task because these creatures are a bundle of nerves), he rapidly grew in his new home. In a year he had reached 50 centimeters and the large, characteristic black spots had already appeared towards the sixth month.

During daylight hours our barracuda had no desire to hunt (except if he did not receive

---

103 Written phonetically. The spelling is *aloalo*. During a stay with fishermen in the Fiji islands I was surprised to note that barracudas have the same name as in Madagascar. Hundreds of words are identical or very close. A mystery (for me) of human migration.

104 On the other hand, I believe this terrible story that I was told to be perfectly plausible. A fisherman was lagging behind (in Marakeï, Gilbert Islands). His little canoe was low in the water and the sail was making it go very fast. Then a very large swordfish (*Xyphias gladius*) took the lure that was jumping about at the end of a line about 100 meters long. The battle between fish and man lasted a long time. Other fisherman watching this scene saw the swordfish charge the canoe and its immense snout pass completely through the fisherman's body.

105 Even though we are not in the habit of giving our fish nicknames, this second juvenile barracuda was called "Cogulet" by all of us to distinguish it from its predecessor.

breakfast, due to an unforseen interruption). The diet alternately consisted of *Tilapia*, mullet, and, when there was the chance to catch some, young trevally. The prey are always swallowed tail first, as shown in photograph **69**.[106]

The small fish go down easily, but when Cogulet is swallowing *Tilapia*, whose hard dorsal fin spikes are so long and sharp, one is amazed that he doesn't lacerate his throat. Watching these painful efforts one often feels for him and wonders: "Why doesn't he start with the head so the spines fold down as the fish progresses along the throat."

Our young friend, Serge Leroy (a man of great logic), had suggested: "When one of these large, carnivorous fish is in full chase, it is the tail of the pursued which faces it, and that explains why the prey that is fleeing is inevitably caught in what we consider to be the wrong way." The argument certainly makes good sense. Ever since there have been barracuda that chase other fish in the sea, they have, over time, become so accustomed to catching their prey from the rear that they no longer know how to do otherwise (oh! anthropomorphism!). But the following observations run counter to Leroy's explanation.

Sometimes Cogulet caught a mullet or a *Tilapia* at an angle — or perpendicular to his jaws. The teeth would grasp solidly, but not bite into the flesh. Loosening his grip slightly, and with small lateral jerks, he turned the fish into a more convenient position to be swallowed. There was nothing to stop him from swivelling it around to face head first. Sometimes the live prey would escape — but it would not get too far away, such is the lightning speed of barracuda. When the prey was too big it was cut in two and the rear half swallowed at once. The front half was usually caught immediately before reaching the bottom. Swallowing the tail half was sometimes a little difficult and Cogulet, not having had the time to catch the front half, would then plough the sand with his muzzle. This is somewhat degrading behavior for the noble barracuda, and something which would, of course, never happen at sea.

Our barracuda certainly knew how to recognize his trainer from other people. The person in charge cleaned the tank and served its three daily meals. I am not saying that he could actually recognize the face of the trainer, but his behavior was not the same when strangers came to peer in.

The roof of this outside tank is made up of slabs of thick, heavy glass designed to withstand typhoons, with a small opening for feeding in prey, vacuuming the sand and cleaning glass panes. The latter task is carried out with a metal brush fixed onto a long handle which removes the fouling organisms and prolific calcareous algae. The small opening is sealed by a heavy brick which makes a frightful scraping noise on the slab of glass when moved. For the first few days Cogulet was very frightened by this. Then he very quickly understood that the noise heralded feeding time.

But scraping and cleaning the glass panes was a completely different story. Despite all the precautions taken, Cogulet was panic-stricken by the arrival of this little brush and, I believe, even more terrified by its long handle. He would hit his snout wildly against the walls of the tank. I tried many cleaning techniques to keep him calm, and after a few days I succeeded. Having overcome his fears, he became curious and followed the movements of the brush from less than 20 centimeters. He also quickly recognized that the cleaning took place every ten days (once we even let a fortnight go by) and he showed no fear. However, if another person carried out the same operation, Cogulet would once again become very worried and would retreat to a dark corner. Was this because the brick was moved differently, or because he could see that the face of his housekeeper was unfamiliar?

When he only measured about 20 centimeters, and was still in a laboratory tank, I would amuse myself by placing my hand high above the glass which covered the tank and, as I lowered my hand very slowly, Cogulet would bow down just like a submarine beginning its dive. Raising my hand slowly, I would watch my "submarine" return to the horizontal.

How can one predict what his behavior will be when we release him to the open sea? Freedom is magnificent, but he is suddenly going to explore an unknown world. We believe that the best thing to do is to put him back in the same seagrass meadows where he was born. We know

---

106 For more than a year, and with an average of three captures a day, I only noticed three swallowings "head first". In these three exceptional circumstances I saw how easily the prey slipped down.

that at the beginning he will not dare launch himself like a torpedo at sardines, mullet and other living fish, for fear of hitting a glass panel, but it probably will not take long before he understands that there are no more obstacles. After spending a few days lurking in the high *Sargassum*, *Cystophylla* and *Hormophysa* algae, he will venture towards areas that are more and more open to finally discover the splendors of the immense lagoon. However, he will also discover its dangers. Well, dear Cogulet, look right, look left ... and good luck!.

Color and pattern changes as fish grow

Certain species belonging to very different families go through quite curious transformations between the juvenile and adult stages. Many remarkable cases have been discovered by scientists through careful study. But during the last two decades considerable progress has also been made by enthusiastic aquarists and in the public aquaria. These results of color changes have been amply illustrated in many popular books, journals and magazines of all types. Among the more classical ones are the *Pomacanthus semicirculatus* (**9** to **12**) and the *Pomacanthus imperator* (**13**, **14** and **15**). It is quite amazing that these two species, which are so dissimilar at the adult stage, show so such a close resemblance when younger. The most striking marking of the *P. imperator* is the complete white circle which is only a semi-circle in other species. This is indicated by the scientific name that was so well chosen for it. The progress of these variations of designs is slow, taking several months. At certain intermediate stages there is a mixture of juvenile and adult coats, as shown by photographs **10** and **14**.

Other changes are even more surprising, like those of the *Coris angulata*. I have already given an interesting illustration of this in plate XXVII in *Carnaval sous la mer*. It is shown again here in photographs **30**, **31** and **32**.

The *Novaculichthys bifer*, belonging to this same family of Coridae, shows us not only that the designs simplify with age until they almost disappear, but displays a more curious anatomical transformation. Long tufts of the first two dorsal spikes, which belong exclusively to this fish in its juvenile stage (hence the specific name *bifer*), undergo a progressive reduction until they are absent in the adult (**16** to **21**).

The transformations in another species of Coridae are equally surprising. Many visitors to the Aquarium cannot believe that a juvenile *Coris gaimard* (**23**), swimming around in one tank, is the same species as an adult in a nearby tank (**24**). Some say: "Are you really certain?" or: "How do you know?" We explain to them that the adults they see all entered the tanks when the coats were still red and white and that we had many opportunities to see the transformation happening in less than a year. We can also offer illustrations in books showing the two patterns that are so different from each other. Moreover, we can also tell them that authors who thought that they were dealing with two different species previously called the young form *Coris grenovii*, and the adult form *Coris gaimard*.

The same quite excusable incredulity is inspired by the *Acanthurus olivaceus* (**35**). We have had young and adult specimens in the same tank and I succeeded in taking a single photograph showing the young one, which is uniformly yellow, and the adult gray-black one with its magnificent slash of orange.

Behavior and age

Other surprising variations are demonstrated by the *Plectorynchus chaetodonoides*[107], when the adult coat only appears at the end of three years — at least this was so in the Aquarium. Illustrations **25** to **28** need no comment. The behavior of this species also varies a great deal with age. As a juvenile (**25**), it continously undulates and whirls about in broad daylight. But once it reaches the stages of transition (**26** and **27**), it settles down, becoming quite timid; in the daylight hours it only makes very brief forays from its preferred hiding spot. Having become a creature of the dark its outside activity is only freely carried out at dawn and dusk.

In the case of parrot-fish (family Labridae), one would need a large album to illustrate all the variations of color and designs that accompany growth of the two sexes.

---

107 Lacépède described this species in 1800 and therefore named it. I have always wondered what particular character in this fish could have led this famous naturalist to find a resemblance to a *Chaetodon*.

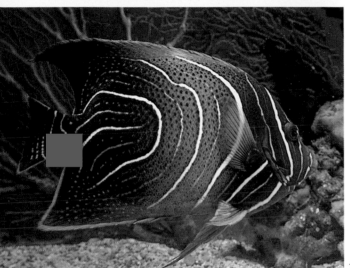

9 *Pomacanthus semicirculatus*. A juvenile coloring to compare with that a *P. imperator* (13) at the same age where the circle is complete.

10 *Pomacanthus semicirculatus*. Coexistence of juvenile and adult coloration.

11 *Pomacanthus semicirculatus*. Last remains of the semi-circles.

12 *Pomacanthus semicirculatus*: adult coloration. All traces of lines have disappeared.

13 *Pomacanthus imperator*: juvenile coloration: The small white circle is complete.

14 *Pomacanthus imperator*. The first elements of the horizontal and oblique bands make their appearance.

15 *Pomacanthus imperator*. Definite adult coloration. Example of variations between juveniles and adults that are even more astonishing than those in the *P. semicirculatus*. (Photo. B Conseil).

9

10

11

12

13

14

15

16 *Novaculichthys bifer,* juvenile. In fact, before this stage, a coloration exists which is even more complicated but the photograph has been lost.

17 and 18 *Novaculichthys bifer.* Coloration of juvenile. This variation is before the loss of two dorsal spines.

19 *Novaculichthys bifer.* Adult coloration. At this stage the two dorsal spines disappear.

20 *Novaculichthys bifer.* After a night under the sand, the animal cautiously emerges at dawn.

21 *Novaculichthys bifer.* Reassured, it completely frees itself in one undulating movement.

18 and 19

20 and 21

Color variations other than those due to growth

Many coral reef fish which are mottled and pale slowly turn to a darker color as night falls, and this change of hue generally affects the entire body of the fish. On the other hand, at the end of the day some species show definite areas of intense darkening which appear on the same areas of the body each evening.

Some very typical examples of this can be seen among the Chaetodontidae family. The most striking of these are the *Chaetodon melanotus* (**44** and **45**) and the *Chaetodon trifasciatus* (**46** and **47**).

When photographing, even a very weak light — which is necessary to focus on such a subject — is enough to make the spots and the black patterns of the nocturnal coat disappear. These photographs can obviously only be taken with a flash. But a single flash is enough to make the daytime coat reappear, and one has to wait at least an hour for the characteristics of the night coat to return in all their intensity.

Another quite curious variation is seen in the *Lo vulpinus* from the Siganidae family (*vulpinus* = fox, but the English call it "rabbit fish" and their terminology is better). The daytime coat of *Lo vulpinus* can be seen in photograph **36** and the nocturnal coat in **37**. Black spots also appear (and in the same places) when the animal is angry or very frightened, whereas with the *Chaetodon* such emotional states never bring out similar changes in pigmentation. On the other hand, fear in certain pomacanthids produces curious pale spots which give the impression that the animal has been scrubbed. As it gradually gains confidence its normal looks return.

Carnivorous fish need very long tanks (at least ten meters) to launch themselves at living prey such as mullet or sardines. This is the case with the groupers *Plectropomus maculatus melanoleucus*, called "independent grouper" by Noumea fishermen (**48**). These fish swim so fast that we have often seen two specimens smack against each other very hard when chasing the same prey. Once, in a triple collision, the force of these creatures made the impact so violent that a fourth one took advantage of the situation.[108]

---

108 We never observed such collisions among the trevally which, in similar circumstances, also move at great speed.

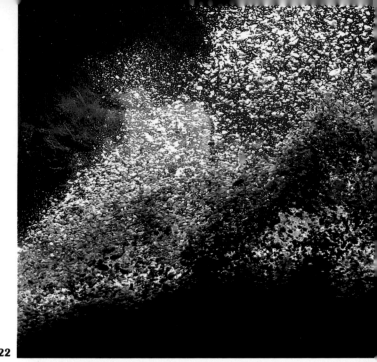

22

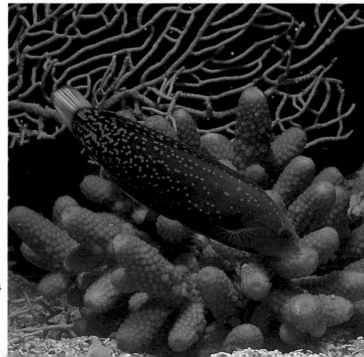

23

24

One day the professional fishermen of Noumea, who have captured thousands of "independent grouper" over the past two decades, brought a curious adult specimen to the Aquarium. This was quite rare since the usual yellow bands were non-existent. It was therefore more suited to being called *melanoleucus* than the nominal variety (**49**)[109]. And it wasn't an albino because the black bands were as clearly marked as those in normal individuals.

Color development

We were very keen to conserve this unique specimen for as long as possible and were quite fortunate that it survived to show us its gradual color development. It entered the Aquarium on January 27, 1967 and on May 15, some yellow spots appeared on its lower jaw and on the tips of the fins. These showed a perfect bilateral symmetry. The spots enlarged regularly until March 1968, and by the month of May of that same year one could no longer distinguish this specimen from its peers.

Seeing the interest we showed in these specimens with abnormal coloring, the fishermen brought us two more that behaved differently again (**51** and **52**). They exhibited no change in their diverse coloring during two years living at the Aquarium.

Small sand-burrowing fish

One of the large tanks in the Aquarium contains fish which the initial visitors immediately nicknamed "bulldozer fish" because of the large quantity of sand they can shift, whether it be for food or to hollow out underground galleries.

These are called *Gergobius taeniura*, and even though they have recently been renamed *Valenciennea longipinnis* by taxonomists, I will still use their old name here. This is not so much clinging to a habit of several decades, but in

---

109   Photographs of this aberration, and that of others which follow, are not very clear because fish of such size can only be placed in large-capacity tanks with very thick glass panes. This makes it very difficult to focus properly.

25

26

27

28

deference to the numerous people who also call them *Gergobius* after observing them in our tanks for more than 20 years.

The dawn-to-dusk activity of these fish is an astonishing sight and provides amusement for visitors who rarely spend enough time to study all their action. But their complex behavior has much to entrance the biologist.

In addition they are very pretty creatures, as shown by the close-up photographs of the head (**53**), the patterns on the body and even more, the tail fin (**53a**). Their eyes are like two deep black pearls, each surrounded by a magnificent gold circle.

These *Gergobius* can grow to about 20 centimeters long and the adult females are slightly more corpulent than the males. In the simulated surroundings of our tanks their growth is quite rapid and young individuals double in size in less than a year. Their basic nutrition is micro-plankton which they absorb while filtering the sand. However, certain food which is new to them — and which a natural habitat would not provide — is very much appreciated. This includes the meat of crabs and bivalves which is cut up very finely and fed several times a day to the other fish living in the same tank. But no matter how attractive, these morsels are only like cocktail snacks because their mouths are not made to chew. Let's say that they only squeeze the juice from them.

Gergobius taeniura always live in couples, but if one accidentally loses its partner it will then carry out all its "household duties" alone. We have also noted that after isolating a couple in separate tanks for a few weeks, each would carry out these tasks with the same perseverance and the same daily routine. However, they must move forward the timetable for their pre-dawn labors; tackled solo their tasks take a little longer and you will soon understand why.

Throughout the day their behavior and activity is fairly routine. But towards the end of the afternoon they start the tasks which will ultimately make them disappear under the sand. The timing of this activity is controlled by the intensity of the fading daylight, but to a lesser extent than for other fish like the *Coris*, for example, which also bury themselves each night.

Although *Gergobius* are common in shallow, muddy-sandy areas at a depth of about two meters, capturing them is extremely difficult. At the slightest warning they disappear into one of their underground galleries. These galleries usually wind into and through calcerous slabs of stone. But sometimes a couple happen to choose to make their main shelter under the overturned shell of a large *Tridacna* clam (Mollusks, **127**). This is a godsend for us because we are able to cover their refuge with a special nylon cloth, forcing the edges into the sand all around the shell ... like tucking in bedclothes. We must be quick because the emergency galleries are sometimes extensive. A small crowbar lifts the shell a little at a time, allowing us to progressively slide the net under it. If the maneuver is carried out methodically and quickly, both the house and inhabitants are caught.

Sweeping fins

The fish are soon installed in a large tank where their own home has already been placed (**55**). After a few small exploratory tours, they waste no time in getting down to work. This includes distributing sand around and on top of their shell, removing annoying but useful materials to another place, clearing things here and burrowing under things there. The two mouths never cease scooping up shovelful after shovelful of matter which they spit out again in the appropriate places. For further work they use their beautiful, spear-shaped fins to sweep, level out and toss the gravel about. We are always amazed by their diligence, as well as the methods they use.

The impetus seems to say: "Let's hurry, let's hurry," because it is imperative that everything be ready for the underground hiding before nightfall.

It is also interesting to note that they are perfectly indifferent to the presence of all the other long-term residents in the tank. Yet, many of these organisms — fish, crustacea, mollusks, or echinoderms — never haunt the type of muddy-sandy regions where, in nature, the *Gergobius* live.

Apart from feeding, the major activities of our new residents fall into three categories during the day. Firstly, the excavation, rebuilding and consolidation of the main underground tunnel — a task which they sometimes extend to secondary emergency galleries. Secondly, the transportation of sand from many areas of the tank close to their residence and, finally, the late afternoon enterprise of camouflaging their night-time residence and their own final burial.

Each of these activities deserves to be expanded upon. The permanent elements in the house occupied by our *Gergobius* consist of a "living-room" which they reach through a main underground tunnel, and two, rarely three, smaller galleries.

Extra security

These secondary tunnels, which are closed at all times, are perfectly hidden. They will only be used in cases of sudden danger or if some very large organism, such as a massive starfish, a lumbering sea cucumber or a large crab, obstructs the main opening for a long time. This normally remains wide open all day and there are never two tunnels open at the same time. However, in our two tanks, and also at sea, we have seen that a minor supernumerary gallery is sometimes dug out at some distance from the main house. It provides another resting place which is just a simple and temporary makeshift shelter. It seems that it is an extra security precaution in case of imminent danger or if a large obstacle prevents it from quickly reaching its main gallery.

Each morning, after having left their dwelling, our *Gergobius* busy themselves in clearing away all the sand which has caved in due to their morning exit. It is nearly always the male that assumes the heaviest duties. However, on certain days the female companion pushes up shovelfuls of matter which its partner then scoops up and transports far away. It seems that he is very careful just where he unloads since he often hesitates a few times before tipping out the mouthful.

During the course of these transportations all obstacles littering the bottom are also removed. These include pieces of dead coral, pebbles and fragments of molted crustacean and bivalve shells. The removal of this debris is necessary to make sure that the bottom is sufficiently smooth, and even to avoid having its delicate lips damaged when it plunges into the sand. To fully appreciate this, one only had to see the force displayed by *Gergobius* when excavating for food or transporting sand or debris.

There are many daily feeding sessions during which the fish work over the whole bottom of the tank, and so the surface layer of sand is sifted through many times a day. The two partners either glean separately or side by side, sometimes head to tail and sometimes so close to each other that they are touching and rhythmically diving in the sand. Photograph **54** clearly shows the suppleness of the body arched to dive. The synchronous chewing of the jaws, and the pulsing of the gills as the sand comes out, is very rapid. At full pace the normal rhythm is about 50 beats in about ten seconds, but it can vary depending on whether the fish is greedy or just simply a gourmet. Sometimes the micro-plankton is very dense and they linger longer, perhaps even rummaging in the same hole together and gorging themselves. Then suddenly they scatter up the high walls of the tank. The thick algal felting covering these concrete walls is rich in micro-organisms. Although too small for our eyes to distinguish, the fish know how to locate them very well. But they only peck at them, and these forays last a short time: they are not comfortable so far away from the sand and they hurry to return there.

With each feeding dive, *Gergobius* only take a small mouthful because if their mouth is too full they are unable to sift through the sand efficiently. Once I saw them do the job in triple-quick time. It was on a day when we completely lifted off their large clam shell home so they had to complete a considerable repair job at great speed. But I will talk more about this later.

It would be tedious for all but the dedicated aquarist if I related here the 80 or so recorded observations made during the months of March, April and May, from 4:30 in the afternoon until the two Gergobius buried themselves each day at about 5:30 pm.[110] It is during this final hour or so that their activity is most sustained — sometimes even feverish. I will try to highlight the more striking aspects, but this can only be very schematic because, not being robots, these animals change their behavior from one day to the next, especially when they face unexpected circumstances. At those times their very deliberate

---

110   It was the exception to wait until six o'clock.

30 *Coris angulata*. Juvenile coloration in September 1959 (5 centimeters long).

31 *Coris angulata*. Young adult in September 1961 (15 centimeters long).

32 *Coris angulata*. Adult coloration in September 1965 (50 centimeters long).

30

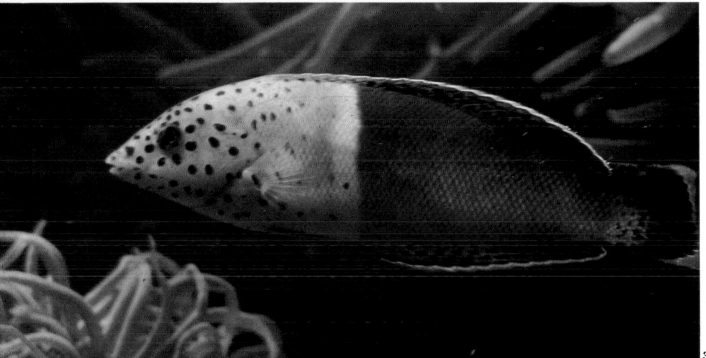

31

32

actions bear testimony to an unquestionable judgement which often seems incomprehensible to us.

In the course of an afternoon our *Gergobius* enter their abode many times through the open gallery. They carry up a few shovelfuls of sand from the bottom and throw these on top of the secondary openings, which are now closed all the time. As time goes by the frequency of these visits increases, and the effort and care they take to put the primary opening in order becomes more intense. If one of the two *Gergobius* — most often the female — finds some more unwanted matter to clear out of the gallery, it pushes it to the entrance and its partner transports it to a place which becomes the "refuse dump". The location of this refuse dump remains constant for several days but when it becomes too crowded another is started, generally opposite the first one. The major objects in the dump are usually covered by sand — but not always. In the course of two weeks we observed the following take place three times: a small colony of lace coral, *Retepora,* (**34**), was deposited on top of the layer of sand that was camouflaging the dump. This delightful, calcareous lace was alive, as proven by the beautiful violet color of its tissues (in death they turn black very rapidly). Many times this colony was shifted a few centimeters and, despite its extreme fragility, suffered no damage. It was never covered with sand.

Sometimes the female moves so much sand while working underground that a small cave-in takes place on the surface. The male immediately

34

refills this spot. However, these incidents only happen rarely.

After several trips in and out of the gallery, the female finally disappears inside until the next morning. Immediately its spouse works furiously to bring scores of mouthfuls of sand (sometimes more than a hundred double shovelfuls in less than ten minutes) and completely seals the entrance to the tunnel.

The first time we saw this happening we thought it was a stupid thing to do because it was sealing its own retreat from the outside! Once the opening has been blocked it continues its sand-carrying and, if the abode is a clam shell, literally buries its home. Some sand slides occur on the slopes, so it again loads up until all traces of the shell disappear (**60**).

Then it habitually devotes itself to a mysterious task (in 70 days it missed out doing so on only seven occasions): it hollows out a semi-circular trench about 15 centimeters away from the base of the large pile of sand. The shovelfuls taken from here are also deposited on top of the dome. I have searched in vain to find some logical reasoning for this broad trench which is less than three centimeters deep. Was it a moat for other organisms to topple into? Certainly not, because it wasn't deep nor steep enough. Someone suggested: "Perhaps the small ditch in the form of a circular arc might help these creatures to receive vibrations from above when they are buried underground." To that I replied: "It would matter very little to them to know what is happening on the surface because they are so snug in their underground dwelling that no one would know how to trouble them there."

The imagination can quite easily get lost in such a maze of analysis. Another observer added: "Perhaps it is to mark the boundary of their territory." The idea is good but it doesn't really hold water because many animals, including echinoderms, crustacea and mollusks, move easily over this obstacle as if it were not there at all.

Finally, I must point out that other couples of our *Gergobius,* when placed in similar conditions and surroundings, have never hollowed out a gutter — very puzzling! But these particular *Gergobius* make sure that their gutter is in perfect order. When a large *Culcita* starfish ploughed up

34 *Retepora sp.* A colony of lace Vermidians Bryozoans. In the middle distance, *Axinissa* and *Clathria* sponges.

35 *Acanthurus olivaceus.* The uniformly yellow color of a juvenile specimen. Below, the adult form.

36 *Lo vulpinus.* Adult with diurnal color.

37 *Lo vulpinus.* Adult with noctural coloration which occurs also during the day when it is frightened or angry.

38 *Zebrasoma veliferum*. Juvenile color. (The small accidental tear of the ventral fin will be repaired in a few days).

39 *Zebrasoma veliferum*. Adult coloration. Its dorsal and anal fins are extended like sails (*veliferum*).

40 *Cetoscarus bicolor*. Juvenile color. The outline of the ocellus of the dorsal fin is well defined. It will become blurred as the fish grows older.

41 *Cetoscarus bicolor*. Adult coloration. The melanization of scales is even more dense among very old specimens.

42 *Lepidaplois perditio*. Juvenile coloration. In this species, also, the outline of the spots is clearly defined.

43 *Lepidaplois perditio*. Adult form. The colors are blurred. The general color is often a beautiful dark red. The paleness of the fish here is due to the presence of the small *Fissilabrus* cleaner.

40 and 41

42 and 43

44 *Chaetodon melanotus.* Diurnal coloration. Some species of this genus offer us the most remarkable examples of variations.

45 *Chaetodon melanotus.* Nocturnal coloration. The blackish areas and white spots always occupy precisely the same areas.

46 *Chaetodon trifasciatus.* Noturnal coloration. Among this species, the areas of variation are not exactly the same as those in the *C. melanotus.*

47 *Chaetodon trifasciatus.* Diurnal coloration.

48 *Plectropomus maculatus melanoleucus.* Normal coloring. The length of this adult specimen is 70 centimeters.

46 and 47

48

49 *Plectropomus maculatus melanoleucus.* A rare variety which didn't have any yellow spots, even though an adult.

50 *Plectropomus maculatus melanoleucus.* Much darker coloration due to the emotional state of the fish.

51 and **52** *Plectropomus maculatus melanoleucus.* Extremely rare aberrant forms.

49

50

51

52

a section of it our male immediately put everything back in order again. Another time it was a *Calappa* crab (Crustacea, **49** and **50**) that had nothing better to do than to hide at the bottom of the hollow. With a determination that one would not have believed possible, the *Gergobius* managed to drive away the intruder and then immediately set about repairing the damage.

As the day comes to an end, we are soon to find out how and where the male is going to rejoin its companion. It certainly tests our patience to the limit, because it continues to load up here and there, sifting through a few mouthfuls. But then it rises up for a better view of the whole situation in the tank. Perhaps it wants to assess the positions of the other animals and judge perfectly the moment to disappear without being noticed by them.

Suddenly it dives, with lightning speed, making a hole in the ground precisely through to the opening of the tunnel. Despite the force of the impact, only a few grains of sand flutter about, and then there is no trace to give away the spot that it has just struck.

We said to ourselves: "When the time comes each evening to dive into its tunnel, the Gergobius swims up high enough to have the power to penetrate the sand. But in the morning does it dive out again? From such a cramped space?

At 5.30 the next morning we are able to make out only the contours of the rocks, corals and gorgonia ... and the small mound belonging to our *Gergobius*. In the semi-darkness we can distinguish a few fish, still fixed in their night-time shelters among the gorgonian labyrinths and craggy rocks, or even against the concrete walls of the tank. All is quiet except for the normal noctambulants — hermit-crabs, sea-cicadas and rock lobsters — which return to their favorite hideouts within half an hour, remaining there for the rest of the day.

Caving in

We focus our attention on the *Gergobius* mound and say: "Perhaps they are slowly trying to clear a passage and gradually we might see the first part of the head of one of our troglodytes appearing." But no! It is the complete opposite to what we are expecting. The sand caves in to form a little hollow; exactly what an hour-glass does when it has just been turned over. A minute later the caving in begins again and then stops. So it goes on. Eventually, a complete excavation has been dug as far as the underground chamber. At the last sandslide we notice the male's mouth. He doesn't go towards the light; he makes the light come to him.

Each little cave-in occurs at about 50 to 90 seconds intervals, which might relate to the distribution of sand in the living-room and maybe in the secondary galleries too. Do both partners cooperate in the distribution of the sand? This is probable and it would explain why the time intervals are a little longer when this work is carried out by a lone widower or bachelor fish.

Although this procedure is very simple and ingenious, it burdens the species with a never-ending job each day of their lives, bringing up all that sand to the surface again. We have calculated the quantity of sand shifted by a couple of these *Gergobius* many times. We estimate the total annual shovelfuls at 900 kg for the male and 600 kg for the female, one and a half tons a year for both of them. I am certain that we have under rather than over-estimated the real figure.

We devised the following method to make the calculations. A glass partition was placed between their general living quarters and a large pile of sand that we had deposited at the end of the tank. A narrow passage was left for them, and they quickly learned where they could go through to draw on this sand pile. But because they followed a straight line to return they would bump against the transparent panel and pour out the entire contents of their mouths. A plastic furrow-drain, closely placed against the glass partition, would collect all this regurgitated sand. It was easier and more accurate to measure the male's regurgitation because it is the less nervous. It will come and go, even though I sit less than a meter away from the tank. Its spouse is always very wary and waits for me to move to about seven or eight meters from the tank before coming out and setting about her work again. I can see this timid little creature observing me from the bottom of its shelter. The visual acuteness of these fish is quite remarkable: at a distance of ten meters they are

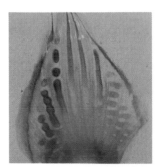

53a

53 *Gergobius taeniura*. Average total length of 15 centimeters.

53a *Gergobius taeniura*. Designs on the caudal fin.

54 *Gergobius taeniura*. Showing the remarkable suppleness of their body.

53

54

still able to follow my movements with the greatest attention.

Gergobius taeniura makes an exceptional subject for behavioral studies because it demonstrates perseverance and ability in overcoming many problems that other fish would be incapable of resolving. A biologist with a lot of time available would be able to carry out numerous experiments. I will tell you about one. It is 5.30 in the afternoon and there is still an hour to go before nightfall. The two *Gergobius* are definitely inside their clam shelter. We lower a hooked rod to the bottom of the large tank and grip the edge of the shell near the "arcades" (photograph **55**). It is very slowly lifted up to a height of about ten centimeters from the ground. I am able to observe the two fish huddled next to each other, not making the slightest movement. Imagine their surprise when, all of a sudden, their walls and ceiling came away from the floor.

The immobility of the partners only lasts a minute. Then they both swim out and around their domain very slowly, attentively considering the extent of the damage. Less than five minutes later there they are working frantically, plunging their mouths into the sand, transporting not two consecutive mouthfuls at a time but three. They have to hurry because it is no easy task to fill in the large space around the length of the shell! They operate with such a rhythm that in less than half an hour no trace remains of the effects of the upheaval. The job is not as perfect as if they had had an hour or an hour and a half to work at it, but none of the essential principles are missing: laying the foundation, forming tiers to avoid sandslides and re-covering the clam shell. It must be pointed out that on this occasion they re-entered their shelter by striking one behind the other. The next day, and those to follow, we lifted the edge of the shell another ten centimeters and the "arcades", which formerly opened onto the galleries, now formed almost vertical holes or chimneys. Our *Gergobius* are now faced with problems which their fellow-creatures do not have to tackle in natural surroundings. A clam shell lying in such a position in the open would not suit them at all. There are enough natural fissures in rocks and other forms of excavations which they can use. But the creatures in our tank have no other choice.

Search for a screen

They carry out their work with a dedication which seems to grow with the difficulty confronting them. But when they reach the chimney level they become quite perplexed. The male never ceases to bring sand to try and block the openings, but this sand keeps disappearing. The female, now at the bottom, evacuates it through a very low lateral opening right on the edge of the shell. The male quickly realizes the situation and ceases his useless endeavors. Is he going to abandon the job and leave the holes open like that for the night? Certainly not, because he starts to look for twigs of algae or gorgonians and other elements that will form some sort of screen. However, the bottom of the tank has been perfectly cleaned out and there is no debris anywhere.

One of us puts his head over the tank and the *Gergobius* immediately disappears. This is the moment to take advantage of its temporary absence and send down some small, empty *Chlamys* shells (a bivalve like a scallop) so that they scatter everywhere. The male again comes out, notices the shells and, ignoring the little ones, chooses one that matches the diameter of the hole. He grasps it with his jaws and puts it directly into place (**58**). The female, who has also come to work on the outside, adjusts the shell a little as if not happy with its initial position. However the male, in a sort of frenzy, rushes back and changes the position again. His companion is content apparently, although to our eyes the correction she had made was better. However, this does not matter to them as both then throw shovelful after shovelful on top of the bivalve and in a few minutes it disappears under the sand cover.

It doesn't take them long to locate the other *Chlamys* which they gradually bring together to have close at hand when necessary (photographs **56** and **58**) and we observe the same procedure for the other two chimneys. However, the last aperture isn't completely closed because they have to get back in themselves. This outlet is obviously not going to be covered by sand, as it would have been if the clam shell was flat on the ground.

In the course of these maneuvers a serious sandslide occurred because the slope was too steep. We were once again able to admire the ingenuity demonstrated by our *Gergobius.* Transporting (**57**) a few of the small *Chlamys* shells that were held in reserve, they stuck them in on the side of the mound (**59**). Some were a little lopsided, but thanks to these props the sand which was then brought along did not slide. The bivalve shell thus became a building tool.

Since we have had the *Gergobius,* and seen them at work, we have observed many examples of amazing acts and initiative. If we are sometimes baffled by their behavior it is quite often because of our inability to understand them.

There are other fish which are also good excavators. For example, the *Calleleotris strigata* (**65**) (which have recently become *Valenciennea strigata*) and another very close species (**62** and **66**), both classified recently under this new genus, *Valenciennea.* When alarmed, or because night has fallen, both of them take refuge under the edge of a rock or in a very simple tunnel which is quite rudimentary compared to the meticulous work of the *Gergobius.* Among the *strigata* species the beautiful blue stripe under the eye passes from the mouth to the gills. Under certain light rays the brightness of this blue is so intense that it brings to mind the brilliance of the wings of the Brazilian *Morpho menelaus* butterfly.

Invulnerable eyes

A phenomenon that has been intriguing me greatly is the amazing force with which some fish crash into the sand once nighttime has arrived. And this happens every day of their lives. Their eyes have no lids and therefore they must rub against the grains of sand each time. If these fish were species like the balloon-fish (*Arothron,* **138**, or *Ovoides*), one would be able to understand because their eyes can sometimes disappear in deep folds of skin. However, this is not the case with *Gergobius.* The cornea of their eyes never gets scratched, and yet it is just as fragile as that of other burrowing fish. We know how the slightest bacterial infection can produce an opaque cornea. And we see the same invulnerability with the *Novaculichthys bifer* (**20**) and among all the species of *Coris* which vigorously bury themselves each evening — or when danger threatens. To give you an idea of the force of this

penetration, in photograph **22** I have illustrated how the sand flies about everywhere at the moment of impact when the *Coris angulata* crashes into it. As the light levels fall at dusk the energetic burying urge comes into play, and after a violent dive the animal wriggles along under the ground, probably to lose any eventual follower. While moving underground its eyes are constantly rubbing against the sand granules. Just imagine the pain from this scraping on the cornea.

To close the subject of eyes, one word about those very strange flathead fish, *Platycephalus.* The close-up photographs of their eyes (**125** and **126**) show a ciliary fringe which seems all golden under certain light rays. One day, when a flathead had jumped overboard and was found dead in the service-room, I tried to separate its eye-lashes with the point of a pin. To my great surprise this pretty fringe does not cover the cornea, but is situated behind it. The numerous movie films I took of the living creature do not show any mobility in these "eyelids", but no conclusions can be drawn from this because it was necessary to use a constant light intensity for the film sequences. I say this because many authors believe that these "eyelids" are a mobile screen to soften the light. In other regions flathead species may not have this ciliary fringe.

Coris angulata

In the section explaining color pattern changes as fish grow, I mentioned the astonishing transformation of the *Coris angulata* (**30**, **31**, **32**). Visitors to the Aquarium always remember the "Lord", which deserves its noble title because it features on three New Caledonian stamps, each showing a typical color phase. In other words, three absolutely different looking fish with one name. The largest individual that we saw while diving and, unfortunately, the largest killed by underwater hunters, measured over a meter in length.

There were two of them in the Aquarium, one of which died after 18 years with us — probably from old age. It was a superb animal, specially remembered by regular and tourist

55 *Gergobius taeniura.* A clam shell (*Tridacna*) serving as shelter for a pair. The female observes.

56 and **58** *Gergobius taeniura. Chlamys* shells gathered by the *Gergobius* and transported to close their "doors".

57 and **59** *Gergobius taeniura.* Shells placed as props to prevent the sand from sliding.

60 *Gergobius taeniura.* Props and cupola are now covered. Pouring out the last mouthfuls of sand.

55 ar

57 ar

59 a

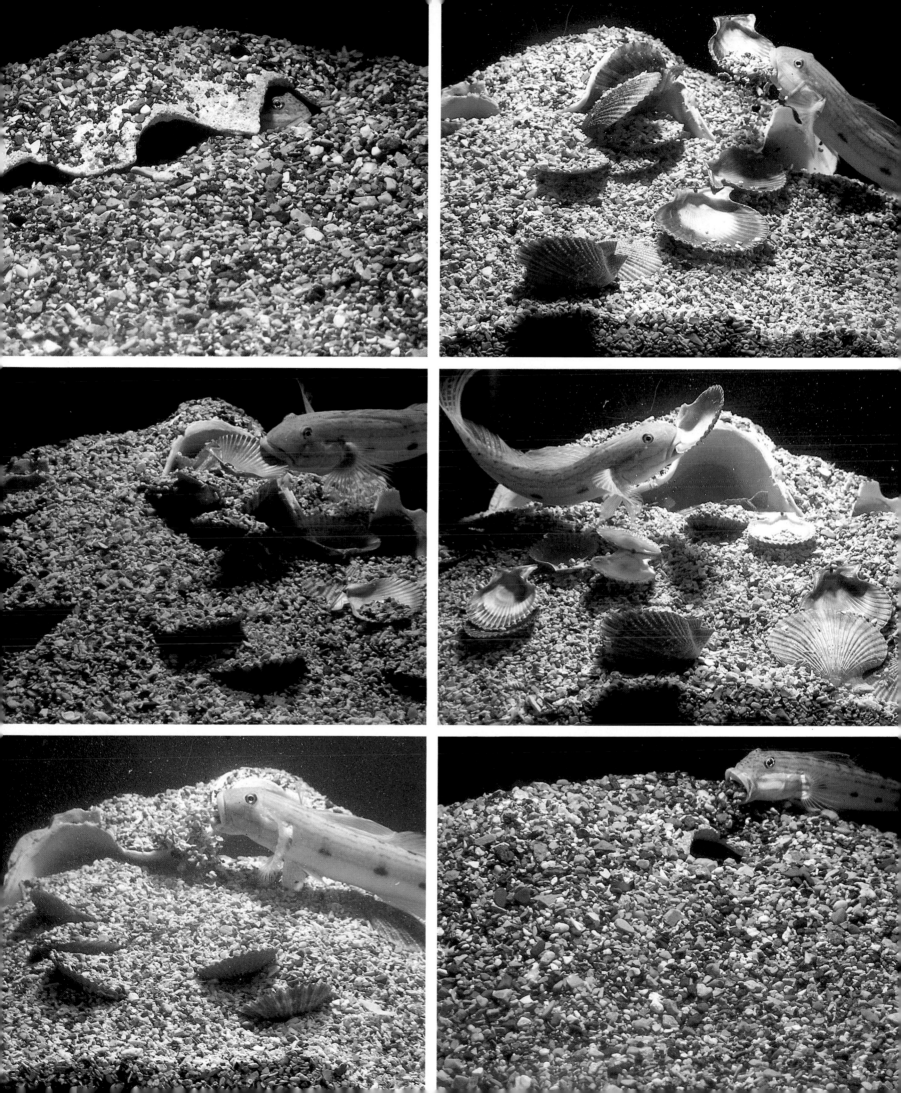

61 *Apogon orbicularis*. This species has become rare in our regions. Photo taken during the day.

62 and **66** *Valenciennea sp.* Even though they are sand excavators, they are not as fervently industrious as the *Gergobius*.

61

62

63 *Apogon orbicularis.* The same couple photographed during the night.

64 *Apogon catalaï.* Depth of capture: 25–35 meters. They withstand decompression quite well.

65 *Calleleotris (Valenciennea) strigata.* The intensity of the blue of the sub-ocular band is reminiscent of effect of the thin stripes of the Morpho (*Lepidoptera*).

67 *Vireosa hanai.* Photography cannot adequately illustrate the iridescence which adorns this 6 centimeters long fish with its very beautifully colored reflections.

68 *Vireosa hanai.* The same specimen yawning. The membrane is perfectly transparent.

69 *Sphyraena barracuda* (barracuda or sea pike) A young 20-centimeter long specimen which has just caught an *Abudefduf.* The prey is swallowed back to front.

63

67

64

68

65

66

69

visitors alike because of its very attractive behavior. It swam steadily and gracefully with a serious and reflective solemnity which prompted many observers to say: "Truly, it has human features." It displayed perfect indifference to the crazy games and antics of the other fish in this immense tank. One can also state that it did not mix with any of them.

The great attraction for visitors was the moment when we would throw some clams (*Atactodea*) in its tank. The first one would be snapped up before it hit the bottom. Then the *Coris* would "stand up" in an oblique or vertical position to accurately place the shell at the bottom of its throat. Its powerful, grinding pharyngeal teeth would crush it there. When the clam was large, and therefore harder, it would make several attempts to use its very impressive "nut-cracker" and the sound of this cracking could be clearly heard through the thick glass panes. The clams which landed on the bottom were skilfully picked up so cleanly that not even the slightest grain of sand was disturbed.

One day, little five-year-old Valerie Conseil was munching on some sugared almonds and asked: "If I give it one, do you think that it would catch it?" And in fact, it caught the candy underwater, put itself in the same upright position it would for a clam, and to Valerie's great joy, crushed it. However, much to her dismay it then spat out all the bits.

"Was it the sugar or the almond that it didn't like?" Very alert children always ask such impossible questions, but I got out of it by saying to her: "We tricked it and that's not what we should have done."

Some visitors would occasionally stay back late, simply to watch the "Lord" going to sleep. Certainly a lot of patience was needed because, even at the end of the day, a small cloud reflecting the last rays of the setting sun would mean an extra wait of between ten and 20 minutes after it normally dug in for the night.

The sensitivity of the *Coris* eye must exceed our best photo-electric cells. The *Coris* usually buries itself in the same place for weeks and it knows exactly where it will strike the bottom. It must know where the surface of the sand is soft enough to avoid the risk of hitting a buried rock or other hard body on which it could smash its head

70

71

72

70 *Caranx (Gnatanodon) speciosus.* A trevally rapidly adapting to life in captivity.

71 *Caranx (Gnatanodon) speciosus.* Note the extraordinary protuberance of the jaws which are about to yawn here.

72 *Caranx sexfasciatus* moving about in the largest tank at the Aquarium.

or at least seriously hurt itself, so great is the force that it uses to disappear.

It turns and turns again, just like the movements of a dog when it is looking for a good place to lie down. At least 20 times we thought it was going to plunge down, and each time it slowly circled for a new tour, always with the same regular, swaying rhythm. It was as if it wanted to observe where all the other fish were in the tank to be certain that it wouldn't be seen burying itself by too many. Then it would reach the right height and suddenly make a rapid dive, disappearing in a cloud of sand (**22**). Sometimes, the burial would not be quite so rapid and we would be able to see the body undulations in the full effort of penetration. Usually, however, it would plunge into the ground at the speed of a javelin thrown by a powerful athlete. That would always bring to mind the famous verse from Virgil: "... *et aducto contortum hastile referens immitit ...*"

Immediately after the dive the *Coris* undertakes an undulating crawling beneath the sand, sometimes travelling as far as a meter from the point of impact.

Together with our friend, the late Yves Merlet, I once tried to capture a *Coris* for the Aquarium by placing a small draw-net over the precise spot where the spray of sand had signalled its point of entry. Having buried the edge of this net we were very confident of capturing it. But while thoroughly searching the sand with our hands we noticed that the *Coris* was already calmly moving about outside the net.

We often came to the Aquarium at dawn to watch how our *Coris* would carry out its exit after spending the whole night under the sand. Just like the *Novaculichthys,* (**20**), it does not emerge in a single movement. First its muzzle, then its head, slowly showed and only when one third of its body was exposed and it had had a good look around would it free itself completely. Then it would shake itself violently so that not one grain of sand was sticking to its mucus-covered body.

One day Stucki said to me sadly: "The Great Lord *Coris* hasn't got up." These few words caused considerable anguish. We had lived so closely to such an admirable creature for 18 years so it is easy to understand what we felt. Three days later it finally emerged, very slowly, but

remained lying down on the sand alongside a rock crevice. It was to die in the early dawn. I will never forget the sorrow I felt holding the superb, lifeless animal flat in my hands. The hundreds of visitors that had remained faithful to it, and would often come to admire it, felt the same sorrow until the day when it was replaced by a new *Coris.*

Growing trevally in captivity

For a better understanding of this subject, I will repeat the essential circulatory characteristics of our Aquarium. The seawater, pumped from the edge of a small coral reef, continually supplies our 40 tanks to the tune of about one and a half million liters *every* 24 hours.

All the tanks are lit by natural daylight. The capacity of two of the largest tanks is 10,000 and 22,000 liters respectively. And the water temperature is the same as that at sea.

The sum of all the factors listed has made possible the survival of a quantity of invertebrates collected from different depths (three to 60 meters). The most remarkable lifespans[111] are those of the corals and fish, the oldest ones of which celebrated 20 years with us a few months ago (November 1976).

In spite of this, overall, we had bitter disappointments for the first ten years each time we captured trevally in the lagoon. And we only ever kept specimens that were apparently intact. Except for the *Caranx speciosus* (often placed in the genus *Gnathanodon*) which we kept for several years, none of the other species of trevally survived more than two or three days. We were especially disappointed when rare or very decorative animals such as the *Alectis indica* died.

It was always the same pathological process. Small areas lost scales and skin and this spread slowly to eventually expose the flesh. Another sign was an opaqueness of the eye which would

---

111   Catala, R. *Longévité d'organismes marins à l'Aquarium de Nouméa.* Bulletin du Muséum national d'Histoire Naturelle, vol. 42, no. 6, 1970–71, pp. 1311–1314.

fairly rapidly cause blindness. We are not able to supply any data about parasitic or bacterial infections. This deficiency isn't the only thing that we have regretted since opening the Aquarium in Noumea. The low numbers of tourists in New Caledonia does not provide sufficient funds (this is a private establishment) and because of this and extremely high salaries, we have had to spend most of our time working away like slaves to keep the Aquarium running at a basic level.

Contagious diseases

Such shortcomings, and the grave danger of contagious diseases spreading to other families of fish, forced us to give up trying to keep all the other species of trevally except the *C. speciosus* (**70**) in our tanks.

On the other hand, beginning in the laboratory, we had tried to raise *Caranx sexfasciatus* (**72**) and *Trachinotus blochi*, starting with specimens of about one to three centimeters which we captured with fine-meshed casting nets.

It was demanding work to raise them because it was necessary to procure and provide fry of *Lebistes* (whitebait) several times a day. After a few days one could also get these baby trevally accustomed to a very fine purée of the flesh of Clovisses (*Atactodea glabrata*). The *Trachinotus* also took advantage of this purée because this species never chase living flesh, whether when young or adult.

After about two months these young trevally quadruple in size, but even though they are still as voracious their growth stops. This is quite a well known phenomenon as their limited habitat brings about the situation. Transferred into a bigger breeding tank they immediately begin to grow again. This growth progresses even more rapidly once they are big enough to eat small mullet or finely shredded fish flesh.

After being raised for 13 months in this breeding-place, our trevally had reached an average of about 20 centimeters. The time had definitely come to install them in one of the larger public tanks.

Some of our long-term inhabitants came from the most diverse families. Among those were some serranids with constant, voracious

73 and **74** A *Caranx speciosus* remaining in contact with its chosen jellyfish.

73

74

75

75 and **76** *Caranx speciosus.* Very laborious penetration attempts. The fish has become too big.

77 The *Caranx speciosus* has nevertheless succeeded in installing itself inside, its caudal fin acting as a scull.

76

77

appetites such as *Plectropomus maculatus*, *Plectropomus maculatus* var. *melanoleucus cylindricus*, *Epinephelus kohleri* and also a large *Lutjanus argentimaculatus*.

It was necessary to supply all these fish with an abundance of their preferred food — mullet and small crab — until they were no longer hungry and would not devour our new introductions. One night we carefully captured 20 *Caranx sexfasciatus* and two *Tachinotus blochi* and, one by one, put them into the large tank.

They gradually gathered together to swim as a group, but the next morning ten were already missing. There were only seven left the following day; however, from this moment on there were no more losses to lament. We repeatedly observed that when young fish have survived in these large tanks by successfully escaping from these greedy, carnivorous fish, a happy co-existence is firmly established. Evidently there are a few exceptions like the bottom-living flathead *Platycephalus longiceps*. It lies on a flat rock or on sand and knows how to take advantage of its camouflage to swallow prey passing within reach. The victims are nearly always absent-minded *Chaetodon*. The trevally don't really run much risk from this flathead because they move in groups and in midwater levels.

One and a half years later, when our *Caranx sexfasciatus* were therefore three years old, they measured abut 40 centimeters. But for the last few months their growth had been very slow. These magnificent creatures were very healthy and their appetites so constant that the cost of their food weighed heavily on the Aquarium's budget, especially at times when the number of mullet captured with the cast net was very low.

Sometimes — usually from May to July — these trevally are subject to a loss of appetite which can last for several weeks. These fasts have also occurred among fish of other families, and during the same season. We know that it is not attributable to the temperature of the water, nor its "quality"[112] but we have never been able to discover the cause.

In my report on the longevity of marine organisms in the Aquarium[113] I mentioned a serious epidemic which raged in this same large tank in June 1970. We attributed this to the introduction of a small balloon-fish, *Ovoides*

implutus, that had been captured on a barrier reef in an area which later proved to have been polluted by *Oodinium*[114].

First victims

At the time we had already succeeded in raising eight *Caranx sexfasciatus* (**72**) which reached the age of three years and seven months. Their weight was 2,500 grams, and size 52 centimeters. Of all the fish in this large tank, these superb trevally were the first victims of the infection caused by *Oodinium*. Since this epidemic did not break out in any other tank the pathogenic agent responsible for it could not have come from the reef where we collect our water and then pump it through to all the Aquarium tanks.

The virulence of this infection extended to nearly 90 percent of the fish in this tank and we lost three specimens of *Plectropomus maculatus* with individual color variations that were extremely rare (**51** and **52**).

All the *Chaetodon* were also exterminated, along with two *Cheilodactylus gibbosus*, nearly all the scarids, all the pomadasyids and even two specimens of the flathead, *Platycephalus longiceps*, which is normally so robust. All these fish had been there for several years.[115]

Of course, before starting the second attempt to raise trevally we waited for several months to

---

112   This is a lack of understanding of a phenomenon which we come across regularly: when professional fishermen in Noumea complain that the fish aren't biting we find that the fish in our tanks show the same tendency to neglect their food. Should we be looking at solar or lunar charts? A discussion of this would take us far from our subject.

113   Catala, R. *Longévité d' organismes marins à l'Aquarium de Nouméa*. Bulletin du Muséum national d'Histoire Naturelle, vol. 42, no. 6, 1970–71, pp. 1311–1314.

114   Correlation or coincidence, certain species of colonial Madrepores coming from this region would present, next to healthy polyps, completely discoloured polyps whose sensorial reactions were extremely weak. (Refer to Coelenterates).

115   It must be remembered here that no treatment can be tried: the continual "flow" of sea-water which passes through our installations each day (1,500,000 liters), prevents the introduction of any antiseptic product. This is the other side of the coin with a circuit which is so wide open. On one side it brings all the plankton necessary for the survival of the invertebrates, but on the other, it lets in all the pathogenic elements which endanger the fish. It must be noted, however, that an outbreak of such severity was the only one in the past 20 years.

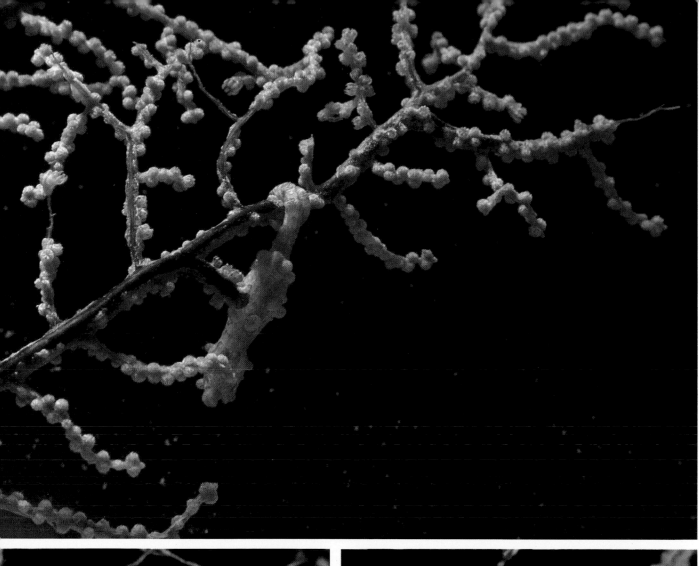

78 *Hippocampus bargibanti.* Adult: 1·5 centimeters. The smallest sea horse known. Here the female is suspended by the tail from a gorgonian.

79 *Hippocampus bargibanti.* Hooked to the main ramification. There is remarkable mimicry between the fish's protuberances and the retracted polyps on the gorgonian.

80 *Hippocampus bargibanti.* The male with its tail wrapped around a secondary ramification. Towards the end of the tail, the incubating pouch is still dilated after the birth of about 40 little ones (about one millimeter in size).

78

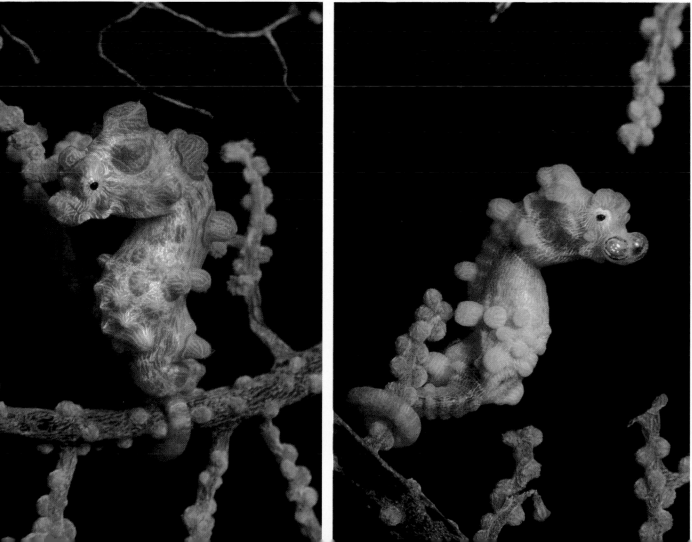

79 and 80   279

test the conditions and gradually introduced a few specimens of other fish at a time. These fish were deliberately chosen from the more vulnerable species like certain *Chaetodon* and, more especially, the very common *C. flavirostris* (99) which are particularly sensitive to *Oodinium*.

When this plague had finally disappeared our second try at raising trevally succeeded remarkably well, confirming that fish belonging to families of "pelagic wanderers" can adapt to confined surroundings, as long as one starts with very small individuals that do not know what life is like out in the open sea.

Further decimation

It is quite obvious that these raising techniques mean that the person in charge must be constantly available to remedy any technical or biological problem that might occur. How many thousands of times during these two decades has my wife got up during the night to go down to the Aquarium for fear that something was amiss? Relax for a moment and we have a sad repeat of the deaths of nearly all the fish in that famous large tank. Later a quantity of fish of different species, including the superb trevally from the second raising which had lived with us in perfect condition for so long, were decimated in only a few hours by the thoughtless introduction of a toxic sea cucumber of the genus *Aspidochirota* or *Actinopyga*? (Echinoderms, 89). Relaxing our constant care only a few weeks earlier had resulted in the annihilation of all those precious organisms that had demanded so much from us, and which represented a major interest for aquarists on the biological scale.

Since 1880, the toxicity of certain sea cucumbers has been noted and described by numerous authors (Saville-Kent, Matthei, Gardiner, Yonge, J.W. Wells, Halstead, Nigrelli, etc.) and we have therefore been very careful in our choice of species. We also knew that some other species of sea cucumbers were being deliberately used by the natives of the Pacific to stupefy fish that they encircled in their nets or surrounded by stakes of coconut palm trunks.

The death of these handsome trevally from the second raising experiment was particularly regrettable because there had been great interest created to see how long they would live beyond those eight years. The only consolation from this fatal accident of August 1977 was the knowledge gained, first about the development of intoxication, and secondly by being able to weigh and measure the trevally (verbal report by P. Djemaoun).

In less than 30 minutes after the introduction of this pernicious sea cucumber, and despite the huge volume of water running freely into this long 22,000 liter tank, the trevally exhibited great panic, trying to jump out of the water to escape from the rapidly spreading poison. At the same time these bright silver fish began changing to a darker color just like other fish (for example the *Lutjanus sebae* and various scarids) that had been their companions for such a long time. Despite the prompt withdrawal of this deadly sea cucumber, the trevally died — some late in the evening and others in the early hours of the next morning. Curiously, the oldest of the *Platax orbicularis* (93), which had been in the Aquarium for 21 years, and a young *Cheilinus undulatus*, which was only a few years old, survived.

The weight and size of some of these unfortunate trevally were as follows:

number 1: 2,320 grams and 50 centimeters in length

number 2: 3,450 grams and 55 centimeters in length

number 3: 5,710 grams and 60 centimeters in length

number 4: 5,820 grams and 66 centimeters in length

One might be surprised at such disparity in weight and size since all these trevally were raised at the same time (similar results were observed during an earlier raising experiment[116]). I think that this is explained by the simple fact that certain specimens quickly get the upper hand on their fellow fish as they are better at chasing and capturing prey.

---

116   Catala, R. *Longévité d'organismes marins à l'Aquarium de Nouméa.* Bulletin du Muséum national d'Histoire naturelle, Paris. vol. 42, no. 6, 1970–71, pp. 1311–1314.

81 *Dunckerocampus caulleryi.* Row of eggs under the male's stomach. Its caudal fan tail is entirely extended.

82 *Dunckerocampus caulleryi.* These beautiful Caullery pipefish form into couples and remain faithfully together.

83 An unidentified pipefish displaying instantaneous adaptation to an *Isidae* gorgonian.

84 *Corythoichtys fasciatus.* One of the finest portraits of a pipefish. A very widespread species in littoral areas.

81

82

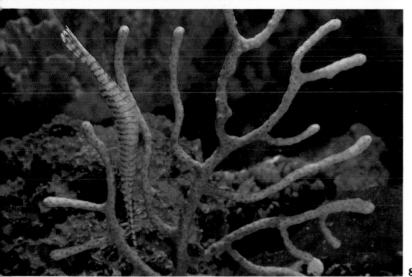

83

84

I have perhaps talked too long about the *Caranx sexfasciatus,* whose success in captivity astonished more experienced aquarists. But there was great satisfaction in finding out what would happen to them.

The symbiosis of a Caranx speciosus with a Rhizostoma jellyfish

Naturalists and sailors have known about this curious association between fish and jellyfish for a long time. Large *Rhizostoma* shelter young *Decapterus* or small trevally under their umbrella. The fish skilfully avoid the dangerous, venomous tentacles of these jellyfish and dash headlong in and out of the middle of this mobile shelter without the slightest danger. One often sees a transparent flotilla of tiny fish moving very actively inside *Rhizostoma* (Coelenterates, **80**). An aquarium within an aquarium!

These superb jellyfish, however, quickly harm their gelatinous umbrella against the sides of our tanks as I have described. The trevally stay in their shelter for as long as possible, but are obliged to evacuate when their protective host dies.

While out in the lagoon one day, my 13-year-old friend Yves Thurneyssen, who is always on the lookout for original things to collect, brought us "something which is amusing and unusual". It was a little violet jellyfish, *Phyllorhiza*, with "its very own trevally" (**73** to **77**). After placing them in a large tank we were able to observe a very absurd exhibition by the outsize trevally and the small jellyfish for several days.

We can imagine that somewhere in the large lagoon, about six or seven months ago, a tiny *Caranx speciosus* discovers a large dwelling place which happens to be this pretty violet jellyfish. A very harmonious bond is established between the two; a harmony which unfortunately is not going to last forever because the trevally will outgrow the jellyfish which has already reached its maximum size. In our Aquarium we were able to witness the continuing burlesque show as the outsized trevally was still trying to penetrate inside its jellyfish at all costs. The farce was that each time the fish forced its way under the umbrella with a tenacious frenzy, its head stuck out from

85 *Pervagor melanocephalus*. A magnificient trigger-fish spreading its caudal fan tail to the maximum. The post-cephalic spur is slightly raised.

86 *Pervagor melanocephalus*, displaying the fins. Spurs (first dorsal) are inserted in their channel.

85

86

87 *Pervagor melanocephalus*. It is rare for the dorsal spur to be erect at the same time that the caudal fan tail is spread out.

88 *Osbeckia scripta*. (Sub-adult). Photographic reproduction doesn't allow the beauty of the blue of the *scripta* to be shown.

one side and its tail stuck protruded on the opposite side. And instead of the jellyfish propelling itself by the rhythmic contractions of its umbrella, it was the trevally that was providing all the propulsion.

The jellyfish survived for only a few days, but the trevally lived on for almost two years until it accidentally jumped out of its tank one day.

The research results from this small study on raising trevally in captivity were published in the *Revue Française d'Aquariologie* (3rd term, 1974). I thank my great friends B. Condé and D. Terver (Aquarium Tropical of Nancy) for having taken so much care with the text and the reproduction of color photographs.

The smallest seahorse in the world
(Hippocampus bargibanti)

In 1970 our associate, Georges Bargibant, brought back a huge living gorgonian fan from a depth of 45 meters destined to feature in one of our largest tanks. Before being installed in the large tank, this beautiful animal colony was placed in a large sink so we could examine it more closely and comfortably. The thick "foliage" conceals many small organisms: crustacea, shellfish and other symbiotic mollusks which are often very difficult to distinguish because of their camouflage and mimicry. Such examinations are always passed onto my wife because her patience and attention to detail lets nothing go unnoticed.

I can still hear her calling to me: "I must get stronger glasses. There are two minute things on this gorgonian which I cannot unhook." A moment later she cried: "Come quickly, I think they are two little seahorses. One has voluntarily detached itself and is swimming around; what a pity that we don't have the parents to be able to identify the species of such babies!..." Then she looked more closely at the one that still had its tail clamped around one of the branches of the gorgonian. Picking up a strong magnifying glass, you can imagine her amazement at discovering that it was an adult male carrying eggs in his swollen brood pouch. What we had in front of us was a mature species of dwarf seahorse. Our thought was that perhaps this was an unknown species! Immediately we took numerous

photographs of these two little creatures measuring no more than 13 millimeters. The size of the baby seahorses that the male released a moment later would have been about one millimeter. Photograph **80** was taken after the release. One can still see that the two lips of the broad pouch are parted and swollen.

Our old friend Gilbert Whitley from the Australian Museum had published an excellent book on seahorses and their relatives[117] a few years earlier and he was the logical person to ask whether this dwarf species was known or not. If it was something new, we also asked him to dedicate it to the person who brought up the living gorgonian.

The smallest seahorses in the world were soon to be the subject of a special display in the Australian Museum, next to the one featuring the largest starfish, discovered by Bernard Conseil in the Noumea lagoon.

Visitors to the Aquarium in Noumea were able to see these dwarf seahorses clearly, thanks to the magnifying glasses that we attached to the glass pane of a small tank especially assigned to them. Installing a branch of the original large gorgonian allowed them to remain hooked to it, and everybody was justifiably surprised by the display of mimicry. The little bumps on their body replicated retracted polyps of the gorgonian and their colors harmonized perfectly with their support (**78**, **79** and **80**). Other specimens of this seahorse have since been found many times, always on the same species of gorgonian and at the same depth. However, we were unable to keep any of these dwarf seahorses alive for more than about a fortnight. They refused all the types of food offered, including the *Artemia* larvae. So we stopped trying to keep them alive to display at the Aquarium. A survival rate of two weeks does not justify sacrificing such a remarkable species.

Pipefish

Pipefish are first cousins to seahorses: they, however, swim horizontally while seahorses move about vertically. Their numerous species mostly have simple colors of

---

117 Whitley, Gilbert and Joyce Allan: *The Sea Horse and its Relatives*, Georgian House, Melbourne, 1958.

89 *Amphiprion clarki*. The Amphiprion living in symbiosis with sea-anemones, do not fear the thread cells of their tentacles, so dreaded by other fish.

90 *Amphiprion perideraion*. The couple moving around in contact with their sea-anemone *(Physobrachia)* whose cloaca is visible. Their offspring (above right) will soon be turned out to go and "start a home" in another available sea-anemone.

89

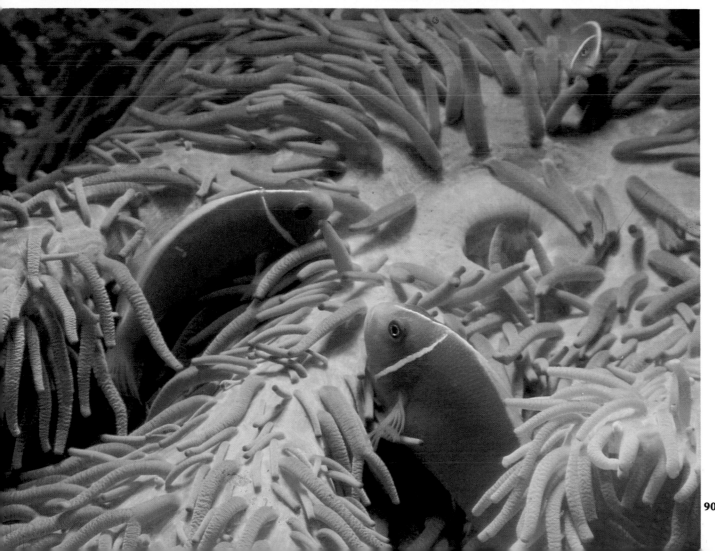

90

285

91

white, gray, black or green but sometimes the designs are very pretty as shown in the fine portrait of a small *Corythoichtys fasciatus* (alias *C. intestinalis?*) (**84**).

But in the waters of New Caledonia there is a special pipefish of great beauty. It is a species of *Dunckerocampus* which was dedicated to my teacher and friend, the late Professor Maurice Caullery. This *Dunckerocampus caulleryi* (**81** and **82**) is brown, ringed with black bands, and its erect caudal fin is a ravishing red and yellow blade. One could say it resembles the Belgian flag! This species is fairly rare and its capture is not always easy because of the remarkable agility and ease with which it threads its way deep into the smallest rock chinks. These *Dunckerocampus* always live in pairs. At the Aquarium we are able to keep them in tanks for quite a long time and we place them in prominent positions where visitors can see them clearly.

The only food that is suitable for them is live prey. In fact, many times a day we bring them tiny plankton raised at the laboratory. These are the famous *Artemia,* well known by all aquarists[118]. We receive the dry eggs from the United States, then we pour many spoonfuls of this "powder" into basins with aerated sea-water. The eggs hatch after about 36 to 46 hours, depending on the water temperature. The tiny crustaceans which hatch out are called nauplius larvae and they are so small that the naked eye can scarcely distinguish them.

Millions of these *Artemia* larvae are therefore cultivated by us each day in the Aquarium laboratory. *Artemia* occur naturally in the United States where they are collected from large marshland habitats that provide excellent conditions for full growth and development to the adult shrimp stage. However, in the laboratory the survival of nauplius larvae is no more than about 100 hours. Although many other coral reef fish are also fond of *Artemia* larvae, they willingly accept other food: but we have found that for *Dunckerocampus* the only satisfactory food is this plankton. Their way of gulping down the larvae, with small, jerky bursts of their long pot-like beaks, always amuses visitors.

92

93

94

118   Refer to *Carnaval sous la mer*, p. 103, fig. 40.

91 *Glyphisodon xanthonotus.* One of the jewels of the coral reefs. It is very difficult to capture because its reflexes are so rapid.

92 *Cirrhitichtys falco* showing the small "feather dusters" at the tips of its dorsal spines.

93 *Variola louti.* This beautiful moon-tail cod likes to sprawl in this manner. Behind it, four old *Platax orbicularis,* the most senior members of the Aquarium.

94 *Chaetodon speculum.* Equally as common. Clumps of the algae *Cheilosporum spectabile* are fixed to the rocks.

95 *Stethojulis casturi.* This eternally restless fish is seen here passing in front of a *Clathria* sponge. To the left, an *Axinissa* sponge.

96 A *Lepidaplois axillaris* looking in the mirror. The other fish are waiting their turn. The reactions are very different according to the families.

95

96

Sometimes my young and capable volunteer assistants have only been able to bring the male or the female of a couple they have spotted to the Aquarium. However, the mate that had escaped would never be too far away from its habitual site and the next day, or even several days later, my boys would succeed in capturing it. We would then place it in the same tank where the first one stood patiently waiting. The reunion of these two little creatures is one of the most rewarding sights in nature. They rub against each other, make slight jerky movements forwards and backwards, swimming together or in different directions, approaching each other again and touching in a parallel position, or even touching when criss-crossing. During this choreography, whether together or separate, they both display the magnificent colored disc on their caudal fin. The beauty of these small, unfolded flags is even more striking when the two creatures are head to tail. To see them habitually stiff, like sticks, one would never believe them capable of such suppleness and undulating postures. You can therefore understand one of the frequent comments made by visitors: "Oh! Look at those funny little snakes." Sometimes their behavior looks like a fight, but then you see clearly that it is only play. These dances and counter-dances are all fantasy and grace, a simple parade of love, even outside the normal mating season. You can see the double row of eggs under the abdomen of the two subjects in photographs **81** and **82**. Even though the *Dunckerocampus caulleryi* eggs are much smaller, their color is the similar to the eggs of salmon — the favorite of gourmets. Before we realized the conjugal fidelity of the *Dunckerocampus,* it so happened that we mixed up two couples while cleaning the tanks, and then coupled them wrongly. There was an immediate battle that would have ended in death if we had allowed it to continue. *Dunckerocampus* are very selective in their choice of partners!

We cannot leave this charming family of pipefish without recounting an amusing case of instinctive and fortuitous camouflage. A diver brought in a pipefish that had not been seen before (and whose identification I still don't know). I asked the young man to place it directly into the tank where there was already a mixture of corals, sponges and a deep-water gorgonian that I was in the process of photographing. This pipefish moved about in this completely new environment, but as soon as it arrived near the gorgonian t slipped in between its branches and sat, vertically, not moving at all. The reconnaissance of its surroundings and taking up of its posture had not lasted more than two minutes. So I had all the time necessary to focus and take the photograph reproduced here (**83**). The almost immediate adaptation of this pipefish with the only branched organism that best-suited it for urgent camouflage is interesting. Also interesting is the curvature that its body took, as if to harmonize with the branches of the gorgonian. Here again, one can see an analogy with the behavior of certain insects.

Pervagor melanocephalus

Two species belonging to the family Aluteridae are considered elite subjects by us. The first, the *Pervagor melanocephalus* (**85, 86** and **87**), is not rare in the coralline formations of the outer reef, but being wild and fast moving it is difficult to capture. One meets it most often in couples. The chance of keeping these pretty fish in an aquarium is excellent, as long as they don't feel too confined and are able to continuously pick away at the small crabs or minute shrimps found in the multiple nooks and crannies of calcareous rocks. Fortunately for us they very quickly appreciate the rich purée that I have already described. These *Pervagor* are usually very active creatures, but when they move around in complete peace of mind their caudal fin is compressed like a small brush. But at the slightest excitement it suddenly stretches into a superb reddish fan with bronze reflections. This is a very good example of what one calls flag display. The sudden appearance of the bright caudal flag, whether as a warning sign or as a defence mechanism, is quite often more effective than the first spine of the dorsal fin which stands up simultaneously (**87**), giving the animal a menacing look. Erection of this spur, and the unfolding of the fan, occur together during the brief playtime interludes or during courtship before mating. Photograph **85** shows that the spur has slightly come out of the groove in which it is completely encased when at rest (**86**).

The other alutid is the *Osbeckia scripta* (**88**). The individual illustrated here is a juvenile of about 20 centimeters, but it can reach a length of

97 A *Heniochus acuminatus* with a "branched" banner (accidental abnormality. Refer to text).

98 *Zanclus cornutus*: the very long banner is a sign of excellent health.

97

98

one meter: its overall color becomes darker as it grows. The characteristic hieroglyphic pattern which justifies its specific name, *scripta*, appears brown if the fish is seen horizontally, as is the case when a visitor observes it through the glass wall of the tank. However — and this is the case with many fish from the coral areas — these colors change if we look at it from above. The *scripta* then seem to metamorphose into a remarkably deep blue. I have not succeeded in taking good photographs, even with a polarizing filter, because the reflection of the sunlight on the surface of the water considerably weakens the brilliance of this blue. The same comment is valid for certain mollusks, especially the clams whose flesh appears quite dull when viewed horizontally compared to the fairyland of colors that they reveal when seen vertically.

In the large Aquarium tanks the appetite of the adult *Osbeckia* is enormous. We sometimes amused ourselves by cutting long strips of flesh from the fillets of mullet. The large *Osbeckia* would rise close to our hand, just at the water's surface, and would immediately snatch the first food strip and swallow it like a strand of spaghetti. A second and third would be offered to it — and so on, without end. What amazed us is that, despite the quantity of food absorbed without interruption, the *Osbeckia* maintained its waistline. The same thing can be said about my young barracuda which swallows abnormally large prey for its size, but without altering the slimness of its spindle-shaped body.

Amphiprion or Clown-fish

Over the last 15 years, most encyclopedias, books and popular journals have written about these fascinating symbiotic hosts of sea-anemones, and illustrated them profusely. I also dedicated a few pages and two good photographs to them in *Carnaval sous la mer*. It gave a good opportunity for me to quote the excellent description of egg-laying that Jean Garnaud[119] had observed in the tanks of the Monaco Aquarium when he was director.

119 Garnaud, J. *Nouvelles données sur l'éthologie d'un Pomacentridae Amphiprion percula Lacepede*. Bulletin Institut d'Oceanographie. No. 998, Monaco, 1951.

In our tanks in Noumea, we introduced a few specimens of *Amphiprion ephippium* in 1963[120] and they are still happily alive today (1976). Other species of the same genus are also quite comfortable there even though they were introduced more recently. This is the case with *A. xanthurus* (today called *Amphiprion clarki,* **89**) and *A. perideraion,* (**90**). In the latter photograph one of the babies is some distance from its parents. This is normal stratagem by the parents to progressively make the small ones move away from the anemone where their infancy was spent. Soon they will be made to understand — and sometimes quite bluntly — that the time has come to move out; there are always other anemones without hosts, and now is the right time to lay the foundations for a new home. This is why we always allow several sea-anemones to fix themselves in the tanks with *Amphiprion,* ready to welcome the younger generation.

It is interesting to note that in all the years of close confinement in our tanks they behave quite naturally, never leaving their anemone or its immediate surrounds in spite of all the interferences which may disturb them. The courage that they demonstrate in defending their territory always rouses our admiration. One observation deserves to be made on this subject. This was experienced many times by the diligent person who always cared for our residents and provided everything necessary for their comfort. Whenever she put her hand in the tank where the *Amphiprion* lived, for housekeeping reasons, they would immediately come to bite it. Their attack would be even more vigorous during the egg-laying period when they were watching over their clutch. But, after many years of handling highly toxic marine organisms, she would sometimes be obliged to wear thin rubber gloves to protect herself from painful skin reactions. The *Amphiprion* would approach to bite once or twice, but the contact with rubber would soon put them off. However, they very quickly worked out how much of the arm was protected ... and that it was more rewarding to bite just above the glove!

120   Catala, R. *Longévité d' organismes marins à l'Aquarium de Nouméa.* Bulletin du Muséum national d'Histoire Naturelle, Paris. vol. 42, no. 6, 1970–71, pp. 1311–1314.

99

100

101

99 *Chaetodon flavirostris*. A common species in the lagoon region close to Noumea. Extremely sensitive to *Oodinium*.

100 *Naso lituratus* belonging to a group of surgeon-fish (see *Acanthurus* plate 35 and *A. dussumieri* plates 152 and 153).

101 *Chaetodon ornatissimus*. Not a very common species and very difficult to keep for a long time at the Aquarium.

102 *Chaetodon reticulatus*. The same observations as for the *ornatissimus*, but it also needs the corals of the *Poritidae* family to be frequently replaced.

103 *Chaetodon (triangulum) baronessa*. A very delicate species requiring particular care, especially with feeding.

102

103

104 *Cephalacanthus orientalis*. A gurnard, its fins totally extended and its cephalic spur erect. The thinness of its "wings" is shown by the fact that they scarcely cast a shadow on the ground.

105 *Cephalacanthus orientalis*. A close-up profile clearly showing the digited lateral fins (dactylos) and their "scraping nails".

106 *Cephalacanthus orientalis*. The "sabre antenna" is erect; "rotation" take-off.

107 *Cephalacanthus orientalis*. "Swing-wings and full speed ahead?"

108 *Cephalacanthus orientalis*. "Forced landing" (16 mm cinematographic shots).

104

105 and 106

107 and 108

Chaetodontidae

Of all the very beautiful coral fish, two widespread species always attract much attention because of the magnificent white banner flowing from their dorsal fin. These are the *Zanclus cornutus* (**98**) and the *Heniochus acuminatus*. The one illustrated here (**97**) is a very rare aberration and, in addition, very spectacular because its banner is divided into several sheets. *Carnaval sous la mer* has already shown (on page 109) a normal *Heniochus,* and next to it quite an astonishing anomaly in a dorsal fin with the banner divided in four parts, starting from the base. However, that was without a doubt a congenital case[121]. X-rays taken of this fish allowed us to reach the conclusion that such internal deformities could only have been due to an abberation in the egg at a given phase of its development.

In **97**, on the other hand, the divisions are superficial and only start at a certain height on the banner. These secondary expansions can be attributed to accidental external causes. A natural suspicion might be that the banner must have become caught in a tangle of algae or corals, or it might even have been damaged by a fish attacking it. In fact, this type of anomaly can be obtained experimentally, with micro-surgical scissors, if one carries out a slight incision in the membrane at the spot where it adheres to the spine.

A few *Chaetodon* presented us some serious feeding problems, as is the case for *Chaetodon ornatissimus* (**101**) and *Chaetodon reticulatus* (**102**). These two superb fish are not very common in our region and have never survived more than about a fortnight with us. They feed by scraping the surface of certain species of corals, especially some *Porites* with minute polyps. It is easy to distinguish the multiple bite marks covering the whole surface of these corals, and the fish refuse any of the different foods that are quite acceptable to many other species in the Aquarium. Certainly other *Chaetodon,* like the C. *plebeius* and the C. *unimaculatus,* are great coral polyp gourmands — not to mention *Goniopora* and *Alveopora* — but if they don't have any at their disposal, they quite happily adapt to ordinary food (fish flesh, crabs and mollusks). We

can only keep the C. *ornatissimus* and the C. *reticulatus* by constantly renewing the corals they like to scrape each day, but this daily upkeep creates many problems — particularly financial.

Gurnard
(Dactyloptera orientalis)

The flying gurnard is a striking creature, notable for its enormously developed wing-like pectoral fin. In all the books this name is spelt *Dactyloptena,*[122] perhaps caused initially by an error in printing that all authors have subsequently repeated. In fact, the term should be *Dactyloptera* because *dactylos* means finger and *pteron* wing. Several lower dorsal rays of its pectoral fin are free and point downwards to scratch the sand. When stretched out this fin looks like huge wings. When handling prepared and dried specimens, the feeling of this fine sail is like touching the membrane of the wings of a bat. However, the wings of the fish are greenish-blue to purple in color and profusely ornate with numerous orange-edged spots. The comment from visitors observing its movements is: "Oh, its just like an aeroplane!" The resemblance is certainly quite striking, with its perfectly aerodynamic fuselage and retractable undercarriage: When "touching down", after several remarkable sweeping turns on its "wings", it lowers its ventral fins and "lands" with finesse. And its "wings" are geometrically variable (**107**). In addition it has a sort of antenna, none other than a retractable first dorsal ray which can be lowered at will into a deep groove (what aviation technicians call the sabre antenna). Yes, the comparison with a modern aeroplane is most apt.[123]

Taking comparison a little further, here is another quite amusing resemblance: New Caledonia has a famous endemic bird which is unfortunately rapidly disappearing — the cagou (*Rhinochaetus jubatus*). It can barely fly and when

---

121 Catala, R. *Sur un cas tératologique remarquable chez un Chaetodontidé du genre Heniochus.* Bulletin de la Société Zoologique de France, pp. 108–111, l pl., Paris 1949.
122 Now (1976) called *Cephala canthus orientalis* by some authors.
123 It was Bernard Conseil (a pilot with UTA) who provided the technical terms to caption these very characteristic shots.

chased — most often by wild dogs — its defence reflexes consist of flattening to the ground, opening its wings to their maximum and erecting its crest (**104**). If you observe a gurnard while a large fish passes by above, you will be struck by the analogy in behavior: it spreads its splendid fins over the bottom, and at the same time raises its dorsal antenna in a menacing posture.

At rest, and if undisturbed, its "wings" are folded close against the body and when it is in search of food it only half opens them out. Scratching the ground with its "fingers" with small, jerky, rapid movements, it forages about until it has unearthed a small worm or other suitable prey; these scratching and picking movements take place alternately to the right and left, very much like a hen in search of food.

In nature, gurnards always live on large areas of sand and in water that is not too deep. Some can be found at a depth of 40 meters (an obervation by P. Laboute), but we also regularly see them in water that is less than two meters deep. The largest of the captured specimens can reach about half a meter, from the tip of one "wing" to the other, with a body which is less than 30 centimeters long and about six centimeters wide.

We have never been able to keep gurnards alive for very long in captivity, scarcely longer than four or five weeks! Although they scraped well, they were not able to pick away often enough because, even in the largest tank in the Aquarium, a sandy surface which is ten meters long by three meters wide is really a restricted area for them to prospect. And then it's always the same sand, whereas in nature these creatures are able to cover large areas where they are free to choose the food that best suits them. Moreover, in the wild there are so few of them that there isn't a great deal of competition from the other fish belonging to different families. In the far distance there might be a sole or a flounder, or even a few pairs of *Gobius* or *Gergobius* which, although they are great excavators of sand, only occupy a restricted living area because they do not dare go too far away from their underground galleries.

For a long time we had lost all hope of keeping these beautiful gurnards alive unless we could find a substitute food. Then, in August 1967 Christiane Herve caught a sub-adult in the Baie des Citrons, and this specimen taught us quite a

lot. To prepare for photography, we put it into the laboratory and gave it a complete tank to itself. A few hours after its arrival it was already scraping away but unable to find a great deal to eat. We therefore began to try out all sorts of food on it, but with no results. Growing tired of this, but without much hope, I poured about 30 minute whitebait, (*Lebistes*) into its tank. We capture them by the thousands in the marshlands each week as food for all the carnivorous fish in the Aquarium.

For the first two days our gurnard didn't even appear to notice the presence of this fry around it, no matter how much they wriggled. But on the third day I observed from a distance that it was trying to swallow some of the smaller *Lebistes* as they passed by. It was as if it became anxious when we were too close: as soon as we moved far enough away it would set about its task again. From that point on we understood why these gurnards had never survived for long in the large tanks; the presence of other fish put them always on the alert. Today, two weeks later, it is moving around in front of us without the slightest fear.

What is interesting to note in this small observation is the relatively rapid adaptation to a type of food which the gurnards are absolutely not accustomed to catching. Moreover, its first attempts were extremely clumsy. But then, little by little, it understood that the best method to capture them was to push them back into a corner of the tank and subsequently became very skilful.

One day we were unable to provide it with whitebait, due to torrential rain and flooding in the marshlands, so we substituted them with pieces of fish and clam flesh; it took to them very quickly. But here again it is interesting to note that, at the beginning at least, it retained its habit of picking. It could see these small pieces descending quite well, but, instead of swallowing them immediately, it would pick them first. Today it knows what food is all about and catches our offerings straight away. What gluttony! We have this on film.

I have described the graceful movement of this fish, the spread of its pectoral fins when they open out, the sweeping runs it makes with its wings open, and its landing. However, the gurnard is not related to the true flying fish which leave the water with such vigor, spread their fins and thus carry out gliding flights for several tens of

109 and 110

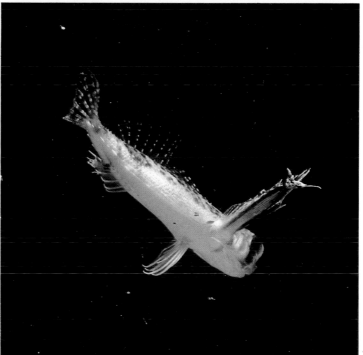

111 and 112

113 and 114

295

seconds. Despite having everything that would permit them to fly, gurnards do not move out of the water, contrary to what some authors have said. In fact they are more closely related to the red gurnard and *Trigla* of our cold seas.

Blennidae — Blennies

The blennies include the genera *Blennius, Istiblennius, Salarias, Astrosalarias, Graviceps,* etc. and are modest-size fish that very rarely reach ten centimeters. The appearance of certain species is remarkable because of the complexity of the designs made up of multiple lines, bands, spots or arabesques. Others have a very strong, more uniform coloring which is enhanced according to light conditions. Above their long and supple body stands a large dorsal fin which gives the blennies a very elegant look. As for their facial features, they nearly always resemble a funny mask which becomes even more comical in those that have amusing little tufts (**117**) above the eyes. Today I regret not having taken close-up photographs of all our blennies before placing them in the public tanks. What an interesting family album it would have been! Particularly so because certain features resembled famous men. I only wish I had found the time to film the following scene, which made the first visitors to the Aquarium laugh so much: a perforated brick had been placed in one of the tanks and several blennies had installed themselves in the various cavities with their heads sticking out a little. They looked like little busybodies at the windows of their apartments. In nature they utilize any rocks or old masses of dead coral which are riddled with holes and galleries as their individual homes.

Even though blennies are naturally very active, they never swim around for a long time. They scurry around in little jumps, and if they have to go from one cluster of alga to another, they do so in short journeys. Finally, if they are exploring coral or gorgonian heads, they do so in jerky movements. Many times, while watching them, I was reminded of little birds jumping from one bush to another and then suddenly stopping to perch on the end of a branch, not moving for a long time and inspecting the surrounding area (**116**). The spectacle of blennies feeding is always

very enjoyable, because they tackle this activity with a type of frenzy. Having so often observed them scraping away at thin algae like *Padina, Pocokiella* or *Ulva* with rapid pecks, I always wondered why their mouths attacked these seaweeds with such brutality and I was astonished that the violent impact never led to a laceration of the fragile plant. Examining the algae under the magnifying glass, I could not see any trace of damage. So rapid is the rhythm of the head movements, hitting these nutritive seaweeds in all directions, that to study it I would have needed special material and, above all, the time to film everything in fast-forward and then to play it back in slow-motion.

When I isolated a couple of blennies in a small tank, and the algae was wearing a little thin, I noticed that my fish would go and frantically scrape against the glass panes on which micro-algae were permanently growing. That gave me the following idea: After putting the blennies into a temporary container, I cleaned out the tank completely, from the sand bed to the glass panes. Then I stuck a sheet of blue cardboard on the back pane. Because the blennies would have nothing to eat, they would be obliged to scrape the micro-algae from the cardboard as it grew, and they would have to leave some traces for me to examine.

Illustration **118** shows how my cardboard looked the very next morning. These buccal imprints shows that the fish presses down with its lower jaw-bone, allowing the upper one to scrape from top to bottom. One can therefore understand their apparent brutal behavior when feeding. Under the magnifying glass these imprints also show the regularity of pressure exerted by the fine teeth, which leave perfectly clear marks on the paper.

When a new species of blenny was brought to me, I would put it through the same paper-scraping test during one night. The comparison of dental imprints was always very interesting, but unfortunately I never had the time to make up a complete dental card-index for each species — a reference which would have been original and scientifically profitable.

I was always fascinated by the study of animal behavior, but I never had a liking for the study of systematics and taxonomy. In fact one might say that I was allergic to it. Not everybody has the opportunity to be a Bruno Condé who is

115 *Blennies salarias sp.* on a jumble of algae.

116 *Blennies astrosalarias sp.* perched on a branch like a bird.

117 and **118** *Blennies*. A close-up of the head. These are the two jaws which have left imprints on the submerged cardboard in 118. The thin mark is from the lower maxilla, which is rested on, while the upper maxilla scrapes from top to bottom.

115 and 116

117 and 118

119 *Runula taeniatus.*
Looking upwards towards the surface to observe eventual victims with a smooth skin (trevally, boxfish, etc ...)

120 *Runula (Aspidontus) rhinorynchus.* Notice the position of the mouth below, and set back from, the snout.

121 *Fissilabrus (Labroïdes) dimidiatus.* With this little cleaner, the jaws point at the tip of its snout, like a beak.

122 *Runula taeniatus.* Observing while retreating in the tube of a polychaete worm.

123 *Runula taeniatus.* Blow struck, it retreats, tail first.

124 *Runula taeniatus.* Lightning departure towards its chosen victim.

119

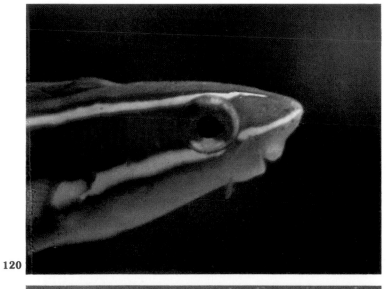

120

121 and 122

123

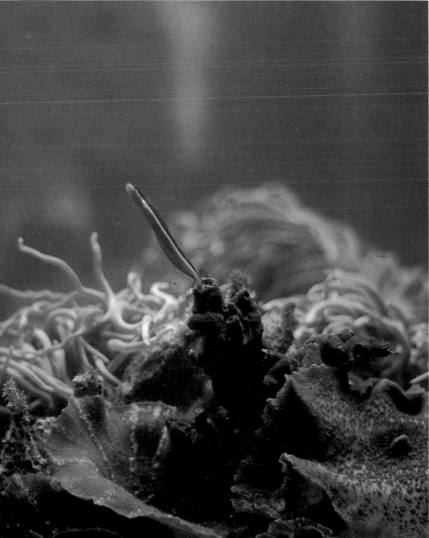

124

able to master both taxonomy and biology with equal skills. This friend clearly explained to me all the anatomical similarities that led taxonomists to conclude that fish called *Pescadorichthys*[124] belong in the Blennidae family. But my observations show me that their behavior and manner of living has nothing in common with that of blennies. Blennies are poor swimmers, remaining on the bottom, moving about in very restricted areas and feeding off small and large algae. On the contrary, the *Pescadorichthys* (**129**) constantly moves around in midwater all day[125] only fleeing towards the bottom when it needs to take refuge in one of its nocturnal hiding spots when trying to escape being captured by us. This is an induced reaction and one that should not be taken into account when studying its normal behavior. I should mention here, while on the topic of the capture of these *Pescadorichthys*, when the little nylon net has one covered it will defend itself and not hesitate to severely bite the hand that tries to seize it. However, if the net has closed up on the blenny, it will be quite frightened and inoffensive, never showing the slightest agression.

There are other differences in reactions, and even though they might be experimental, they are still of interest to students of fish behavior. The blennies will look at themselves with complacency in front of a mirror, and will nearly always carry out graceful undulations of their long body to highlight their opulent fins. They will sometimes lean to one side and then the other, posturing. On the contrary, the mirror test on the *Pescadorichthys* will not cause any excitation of interest, surprise or fear.

There are also differences in eating habits. Compared with blennies, one will never see a

124 Now called *Meiacanthus atrodorsalis*.
125 In their remarkable work (December 1976) on the fish of New Caledonia and the New Hebrides (3), Fourmanoir and Laboute tell us that "the very active movement (of this fish) is explained by the presence of a swim bladder, an organ which is generally absent among other blennies". It is evident that a fish provided with a swim bladder, by definition, is more apt to spend the major part of its time in midwater and it is quite logical for species which do not possess such an organ to spend their time on the bottom. However, this anatomical characteristic (which astonishes me in my ignorance of the secrets of taxonomy and which seems to be of value in systemic differentation) does not invalidate the biological observations which I made before knowing this specific characteristic.

Pescadorichthys, either at sea or in the Aquarium, rummaging in a clump of algae or in a rock hollow. It comes and goes, in midwater, capturing suspended micro-plankton. Aquarists, who could procure specimens of this ravishing species, might like to note that they can gradually get used to feeding on an ultra-fine purée of flesh of fish, crabs, clams and other bivalves, even miniscule worms, provided that this can be seized in midwater — something which must not be too common in the wild.

Another characteristic of the *Pescadorichthys,* which raises admiration in enthusiasts, is its ability to stop dead: many visitors remark: "If only my car had brakes like that!" It would be very interesting to film these stops at thousands of frames a second — just as one does in the study of bird flight — to see in slow-motion the precise action of the fins which provides these sudden stops so efficiently.

Other small fish which have been placed in the Blennidae family include the *Runula* (*Aspidontus*) — certain species of which are pure gems. Here again, behavior and taxonomy are in flagrant contradiction because *Runula* are extraordinarily rapid swimmers. Whether we are talking about *Runula rhinorynchus* (**120**) or *R. taeniatus* (**119**), we are dealing with beasts of prey, always up to mischief. One minute they are marking time in the cover of a rock fissure, the next they suddenly take off like an arrow towards a fish with very smooth skin or without scales (such as a trevally or boxfish) and, with their sharp teeth, tear out a little piece of skin or even a little of their protective mucus then, returning to their base, prepare for a new lightning raid. Things happened at such speed that the victim doesn't see this little torpedo coming, and when it bites it is too late. Our good blennies on the ground must have the same experience that we do when a jet roars overhead.

Our *Runula* puts its head outside its gallery (**122**), inspects the horizons and abruptly takes off at full tilt (**124**). In the twinkling of an eye it covers several meters, bites one of its victims and comes back to its original place of observation. The whole operation takes place so rapidly that if people are not warned they would never be able to understand what was taking place. Some visitors return again and again to wait for the moment when this little *Runula,* returning to its

gallery, would suddenly stop and do a semi-turn on itself to slide backwards into its tubular home, tail first. Its cautious and very studied penetration was always an amazing sight (**123**).

At sea these same *Runula* not only bite trevally, boxfish and whitefish (*Gerres* and *Leiognathus*), but in general all fish with very fine skin.

Many authors have written that *Runula* take advantage of the fact that they resemble the small cleaning fish *Fissilabrus dimidiatus* (or *Labroides dimidiatus*)[126] to take advantage of their victims and to approach them easily. Certainly the idea of these cleaners-in-disguise is very attractive and I must admit having believed it at first. However, having made many observations over the years, both at sea and at the Aquarium, I have revised my opinion.

Not many laymen know about the *Runulas'* reputation as false-cleaners and will of course confuse them with the true cleaner fish, *Fissilabrus,* and its incessant cleaning work. A visitor whom I left in front of our largest tank came up to tell me afterwards: "I saw the little cleaner bore into one of your beautiful trevally at a crazy speed to get rid of a parasite on it; however, the trevally didn't seem too pleased about it."

I explained: "What you saw is the famous false-cleaner biting the trevally to take a piece of flesh from it." Back in front of the large tank again, he was then able to observe the difference in attitude and behavior between the real and false cleaners. He could see the *Fissilabrus* moving continuously, calmly going from one fish to another (**128** and **138**), sometimes lingering longer on one to give it a complete sanitary inspection (**43**). The visitor admired how the client facilitated things for the cleaner by completely stretching out its fins while opening its gills and mouth to the maximum. He also noticed how fish really needing a thorough cleaning stay in the same spot to make it easier. In the meantime another fish, also desiring the attentions of the *Fissilabrus,* would come and place itself in an oblique or vertical provocative position (**43**), as if calling it to come across. At this affectionate invitation, the small cleaner would always swim across. And I

126   Refer to *Carnaval sous la mer,* pp. 104–107 and figs. 41, 42, 43.

125 and **126** *Platycephalus longiceps*. The large, protruding and very mobile eye (in 126 it is looking towards the bottom). The ramified cirres, looking like eyelashes, are situated on the internal face of the cornea.

125

126

pointed out to the visitor: "You can clearly see that while the *Fissilabrus* is going about its successive cleaning jobs with so much applications, the *Runula* is down there at the other end of the tank, lying in wait (**122**). It is waiting for the moment when the shoal of trevally comes by." And I added: "Now look at the major differences between these two fish. The *Runula* is clearly more slender and undulating, with astonishing flexibility. You have just seen it touch the tip of its caudal fin with its head, so it almost forms a perfect circle. Even though the *Fissilabrus* is very supple, it never plays snake, trying to bite its own tail. Again, look at the mouth of the *Runula,* positioned under the head (**120**) — amusingly reminiscent of the mouths of sharks — and now look at the small mouth of the *Fissilabrus* which is situated at the end of the snout (**121**)."

My visitor — like many others before and after him — soon knew how to recognize the differences in the separate attitudes and actions of these two fish. I have deliberately made this comment in order to introduce the following philosophy: After the human eye has been a little forewarned, it can make out major differences between the fish. But the fish themselves, with their marvellous instinct and with their innate experience, know how to recognize one another, especially in their own close surroundings. Since their juvenile stage — if not since birth — these fish have had the ability to distinguish between the organism that is dangerous, the one that is inoffensive and the one that is necessary for their well-being, like the little cleaning fish which is useful for removing parasites. These fish are provided along their lateral line with as many ultra-fine sensory "ears" as scales, so how could they confuse the vibrations caused by an "arrow", which is the *Runula,* with a little "dancer", which is the *Fissilabrus*? The one is totally undesirable and its only impact on its victims is the flashing speed of its attack (**124**), whereas the other is delicate and careful in its cautious contact with its voluntary patients.

I had already drafted this chapter in 1974 but quite recently (1977) I discovered additional curious observations about *Runula*: a group of white fish (*Gerres*), about six centimeters long, had been placed in a large tank. They kept close to a corner of the tank, hard up against the pane,

127

128

129

302

and would only briefly move out to pick a little at the twice-daily feeding times. In this there was nothing extraordinary. What did stand out was their dwarfism. Despite the huge capacity of the tank, carrying more than 4,000 liters of running sea-water, the size of these little creatures had not increased. Then suddenly, for a certain period, they began to grow regularly. This dramatic growth coincided exactly with the accidental disappearance (through an overflow pipe) of a *Runula* which had been in the tank for several months before their arrival. I think that the conclusions are obvious enough.

After seeing my film *Carnaval sous la mer*, André Maurois was so surprised by the behavior of certain fish that he wrote a very entertaining article which appeared in the *Nouvelles Litteraires*. I have great pleasure in quoting a few lines from it:

"Even more surprising was the *Fissilabrus*, the "doctor" fish. Very small, it controls each fish's sanitary state. One sees it sliding its pointed muzzle deep into the throat of a puffer fish, or under the gills of a rare *Coradion*. Its patients allow this to happen with docility, because it picks away the parasites and minute crustacea and gets rid of them, while it itself feeds and gets something out of it. I was wondering, as I watched this little cleaner working with such astonishing activity, whether a scholar from the star Sirius, observing our planet under an ultra-telescope, would marvel at our country doctors, as we admire the fish-doctor. 'Astonishing creatures', he might say, 'who, from morning to evening, and often at night, go from place to place, cleaning humans' ..."

No one could apply the same comparison to a *Runula*! And here are my last thoughts on this subject: Would fish exist that were so ignorant of their surroundings in their own marine environment that they could not distinguish between a devoted country doctor and a ruthless terrorist?

The Antennarius — Angler fish

In *Carnaval sous la mer* I wrote briefly about these strange fish, the largest of which is the size of two fists. Their pectoral fins take the form of thick paws like miniature elephant feet. As for the gill covers, they are reduced to simple tubes situated at the base of these pectoral fins.

These rough-skinned *Antennarius* are absolutely inoffensive creatures, contrary to what most visitors imagine as they mistake them for dangerous scorpion-fish. To the touch and to the eyes these fish resemble a mass of mossy rubber. Their eyes are tiny pinheads and are very difficult to distinguish. However, the most remarkable characteristic of the *Antennarius* is certainly its fishing device which consists of a very fine fishing rod implanted above, and a little behind, the mouth. When at rest, the rod and the thread-like appendix called illicium (which means bait), rests close against the skin, only visible to a trained eye. The tip of this rod carries a small white sphere, barely distinguishable amongst the reddish and pale spots sprinkled all over the body (**130**). But if one or more fish swim nearby, the rod immediately swings into action, jumping with vertical oscillations or back and forth gyrations. This continuous agitation — sometimes faster and sometimes slower — makes the leaves of the small terminal sphere open out (**131**).

Intrigued by this jumping lure, the fish try to take hold of it and are immediately swallowed into the wide mouth of the *Antennarius*. So powerful and rapid is the suction that we sometimes wondered how the rod and lure never got caught up with the prey. Suction and swallowing of the prey take about one fiftieth of a second. These little fish do not have time to understand what has happened to them. As for the *Antennarius,* it remains perfectly still ... except for its stomach which moves with the dying spasms of the prey, desperately trying to escape. But the gastric juices do not take long to act.

The fat lump *Antennarius* can survive for sometime on an empty stomach because in the wild it is not every day that he has the windfall of a capture.

Sometimes, when we give it a living fish which either ignores the lure or is not in a good position to be swallowed, the *Antennarius* will decide to move. It leans on its large "paws", advancing millimeter by millimeter with an incredible slowness which is enough to send the most patient observer into despair. However, it is extremely rare that so much phlegmatic perserverance by *Antennarius* and by ourselves is not amply rewarded.

In figure 6 of plate XXIV of *Carnaval sous la mer,* the fishing lure of *Antennarius commersoni* could not be seen. At that time I had not learnt all the ropes in order to obtain this type of shot. The camera would either not be ready at the right moment, or perhaps the agitation of the rod and its lure would not take place for several hours. Also the physical transportation of the fish to a special tank influenced its normal behavior for some time. It was therefore necessary to train it for conditioned reflex action and we settled into a very long training period. Each day, at a regular time, we would pour about ten whitebait (*Lebistes*) into the tank. With our nails we would then give little taps on the window pane as soon as the rod and lure began to operate. After some time tapping on the glass was enough to start the movements of its fishing device, even if we didn't then give it fish. But the conditioned reflex action would be lost in a few days unless we reinforced the tapping on the pane by throwing in prey. And then again, it would be unfair not to feed it! Photograph **131** shows how the fishing rod and lure are opened out.

There is one last comment I would like to make on the *Antennarius.* Some are red, some black, others gray and greenish etc, and for a long time it was believed that these diverse colors denoted different species. But that is not so. We placed a scarlet-red *Antennarius* (the species that was dedicated to the famous naturalist explorer, Commerson) in a tank containing some spherical red sponges (*Axinissia* or *Clathria*). The camouflage of the fish with these sponges was so effective that few people were able to distinguish the *Antennarius* themselves. Then one day we took out all the red sponges and replaced them by a black species such as *Dendrilla nigra* or *Megalopastas.* In less than two weeks the *Antennarius commersoni* had become black (except for the rod and lure and a few small spots which always keep their white color). If we conducted the operation in reverse, the *Antennarius* would become red in the same lapse of time. Moreover, it was not necessary to use sponges to obtain similar adaptations: some black rocks were sufficient.

Even though the science of taxonomists is sometimes as confusing as it is subtle (for me, at least), it is quite possible that "my" *Antennarius commersoni,* as I identified it in the classic work

by J.L.B. Smith[127], might be the same species as the *Antennarius moluccensis* illustrated by P. Fourmanoir and P. Laboute in their remarkable work[128].

Whatever the identity, the different colors of the numerous *Antennarius* which were guests for more than 20 years in our tanks were clearly nothing to do with their age. Their remarkable camouflage is always dependent on the surroundings in which they find themselves. The only small point that I would like to argue with some authors is their tendency to think that a black *Antennarius* on a background of clear coral is "as if it wanted to mime the shadow of a cave". My dear old teacher and friend, Maurice Caullery, once said to me: "In biology, always be cautious what you claim in the delirium of interpretation." Being the same age today as he was then, I would dare to give the same serious advice to fight against this anthropomorphism which could lead to non-scientific notions — fun though they be.

Boxfish

The boxfish hardly measure up to the usual concept that we have of the fish form and I must ask myself not "why" but "how" did nature arrive at such fantasies? I can imagine that all the fish looking at us through the glass pane of their tanks probably ask themselves the same question!

And I then imagine a facetious Creator, having become tired of forming so many fish whose *exterior* appearance is about the same, saying to himself: "Now what if I changed something a little, just to have some fun?" So he sat at his large work bench and fabricated little polyhedral boxes, of quite hard material, then pierced them with just enough holes for the eyes, mouth and fins and added — just to put a bit more imagination into it — either a solid blade on the back of one, or horns in front, and thought, why not add two others at the back while I am at it? And that gave him little toys which, once put

127 Smith, J.L.B. *The Sea Fishes of Southern Africa.* 1950.
128 Fourmanoir, P. and P. Laboute *Poissons de Nouvelle – Calédonie et des Nouvelles-Hébrides*, Les Editions du Pacifique, 1976.

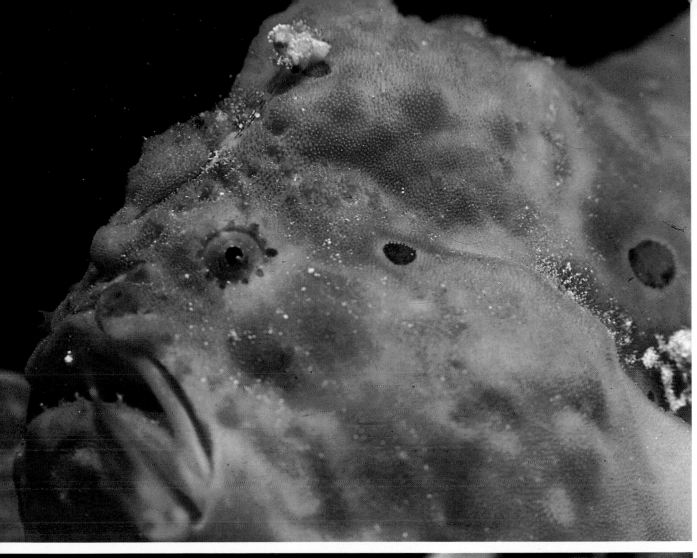

130 *Antennarius pictus* (Angler-fish). The fishing appendage (*illicium*) is pressed against the skin. The white lure (fleshy layers) is similar in form and color to the few white spots that the body has (to the right). There is also a similarity between the round spots and the eye.

130

131 *Antennarius commersoni*. Fishing rod and lure in action to attract fish (sometimes nearly as large as the lure).

131

132 and **133** *Tetrosomus gibbosus*. This boxfish is in triangular sections. The large spikes bordering the ventral osseous patch are not venomous. In the photo showing profile, note the insertion of the caudal peduncle in the "main box".

134 and **135** *Ostracion cubicus*, (juvenile) face and profile. Small playthings which are quite likeable, but if one of them happens to die in a tank, and the death goes unnoticed, watch out for general poisoning — the extreme virulence of which will quickly wipe out all the other fish. Because of this, all boxfish are dangerous residents in aquaria.

136 *Lactoria cornuta*, in profile, seen here resting on *Padina* algae. These gentle horned animals have a lot of personality. The pointed horns in the front and back play almost no attacking or defensive roles. They remind one a little of the immense, but useless, appendages of certain male beetles.

137 *Lactoria cornuta*. It isn't one of them looking at itself in the mirror, but a couple exchanging "secrets". They are "knitting" (refer to anecdotal text).

134 and 135

306   **136 and 137**

into the water, began to move about with as much ease as the other fish. I am referring to *Lactoria cornuta* (**136** and **137**), *Ostracion cubicus* (**134** and **135**), *Ostracion lentiginous* (**128**) and *Tetrosomus gibbosus* **132** and **133**).

These unusual little creatures are quite likable and have generally placid habits. At sea they prefer the muddy-sandy areas which are not too deep and sometimes fishermen accidently capture them with their trawl nets. But one often meets them on the barrier reef and fringe reef areas, particular in the lee of the little islands of the lagoon. In the Aquarium they enjoy the luxury of the very spacious tanks where they can dawdle at leisure. A couple of *Lactoria cornuta* always offer the patient observer either amusing or somnolent scenes, depending on the time of the day, because these gentle horned creatures alternate between play-acting, with appropriate postures, or periods of prolonged rest. In the large tank filled with corals, sponges, gorgonians and other colonial animals, they prefer to snuggle into the soft folds of the large mushroom-shaped soft-corals, *Sarcophytes*. Sometimes they play at scaring themselves, or is it a game of love? They twist and turn on themselves, come close together, move away for a moment then quickly rejoin to tangle horns. A young boy whom I asked how the two recently-arrived *Lactoria* were getting on, replied: "Everything is fine, they are knitting." However, all these games of hide-and-seek, leap-frog and catch-me-if-you-can, stop immediately if certain familiar noises announce feeding time. That is not the moment to go browsing over the algal coatings which line the concrete walls, because what they get is their favorite food: shellfish flesh, whitebait or clams. Because other fish can snap up this choice food before them, we feed them by hand. But, in their eagerness to eat, how many times have these little *Lactoria* literally bitten the fingers that feed them.

If it were not for the keen interest shown by aquarists, and for the amusement of visitors, we wouldn't keep boxfish by choice since they are sometimes a source of trouble and disappointment. These difficult creatures are very vulnerable to eye infections. With this gradual loss of vision, they become less able to feed themselves and die in a few weeks. Nearly all the boxfish are affected by this disease and very few

escape, but those that do pass the hurdle are immunized and live happily for a very long time.

Another serious inconvenience occurs when a boxfish dies in a tank and lies hidden behind a coral or in a rock crevice for a time. Its demise becomes a mortal danger for the other occupants, no matter what species they belong to. Even before decomposition they poison the water and, although this is continually and abundantly renewed, the poison spares almost no one.

For a long time writers have pointed out that boxfish have fatally poisoned people who have cooked them with other perfectly edible fish. Moreover, the same observation can be made about pufferfish. But one wonders what gastronomic perversion leads people to cook boxfish at all because, apart from the terribly toxic viscera, they are only skin and bone. As one has read in the section on false-cleaners, this skin is the object of frequent attacks by the ferocious *Runula*.

There is one last observation to be made regarding the eyes of the boxfish — especially those of the *Ostracion cubicus* (**134** and **135**). Under ultra-violet rays we saw a superb golden-yellow fluorescence appearing. It was only by chance that we realized that with this irradiation we were helping to cure those sore eyes. The eyes of the other fish revealed nothing similar to us. This is yet another field of experiment to challenge the intellect of a specialized researcher.

Pufferfish are the close relatives of the boxfish. So many works have highlighted them that I will restrict myself to illustrating an *Arothron mappa* (**138**), accompanying a small cleaner fish, *Fissilabrus*. There is another fish that is able to puff up like a balloon — the *Canthigaster ocellicinctus* (**151**). *Canthigaster* are small and quite amusing creatures, because when they are afraid themselves, or wanting to frighten others, they suddenly swell up. Their eyes remind us of the beauty of the eyes of certain tree-frogs which display the same vivid green color. Although their behavior is much like that of the boxfish, fortunately they are more hardy and able to resist disease. With more research there would be quite a long chapter to write about their captivating way of life, and I hope that others will be able to do so one day.

138 An *Arothron mappa* (balloon-fish), watchfully accompanied by two *Fissilabrus* cleaning fish.

139 A *Synanceia verrucosa* (stonefish) out in the open, but merging with the stones around it. The 13 deadly spines, sheathed in a fleshy dorsal groove, are invisible.

140 A *Synanceia verrucosa* in its most frequent position, buried in the muddy sand bottom. One can barely make out its closed mouth (in a circular area) and the two ocular globes (same position as in 139).

Some remarkable scorpion-fish

In the few pages of *Carnaval sous la mer* dedicated to the venomous scorpion-fish belonging to the order Cataphracti, I pointed out that the most dangerous of the lot is the *Synanceia verrucosa*. This hideous creature, commonly called the stonefish, is not suited to swimming and often remains buried under the sand leaving only its tiny eyes and the closed, arc-shaped mouth visible (**140**). Even if it didn't bury itself, one could easily overlook it because of its astonishing mimicry which blends in with the surrounding stones in perfect camouflage (**139**). The dorsal fin of this stonefish carries 13 sheathed spines which cannot be easily distinguished. At the base of each spine are two poison glands whose toxicity is so high that it has caused human deaths many times. The accidents were nearly always due to the extreme carelessness of people walking barefoot on a reef at low tide, or only wearing shoes with thin soles which are not enough to prevent the spines penetrating. And the chance of confusing these stonefish with the surrounding stones increases even more if the water is clouded by the breeze. It could even be the hand of a person looking for shells that is stung when moving this "stone".

In *Carnaval sous la mer* I explained why the stings of these stonefish were mostly fatal, and how atrociously the victims suffer. Since then, excellent research carried out in Australia has led to the production of a very good serum named "Stonefish antivenene". Unless you happen to be close to a medical center carrying this precious antidote, every beachcomber prospecting on a reef should always carry the serum and a syringe with him — a precaution which, I suppose, is very rarely taken.

Like other scorpion-fish, the stonefish only feeds on living prey. Woe betide the passing fish which is instantly sucked in and swallowed, even if it is as big as the stonefish itself. Films taken at 64 frames a second only show two blurred images for the whole operation of drawing in and swallowing. My dear friend, Jean Painlevé, was disappointed with a special camera which he invented to take shots at 200 frames a second: he soon realized that one would need to shoot at 1,000 frames a second to be able to obtain a really detailed image of the action in slow motion. But our visitors watch this death scene with morbid fascination.

I would seriously recommend that thousands of aquarists should each procure one specimen of stonefish and that would leave many less on the reefs. In captivity, survival of this creature poses fewer problems than for many other species. It is an animal whose oxygen requirements are modest and, since it is nearly always immobile, it can live in a very restricted space. And it only needs infrequent meals — provided the fish is of a decent size — to keep alive.

The stonefish seen in our tanks today by visitors have been there for more than 15 years. The first ones that we kept died of overfeeding — hypertrophic cirrhosis. With the reflex action of sucking in and swallowing working with nearly each shot, we thought we were doing the right thing by serving them a daily meal, but two meals a week have proved to be sufficient.

For the interest and curiosity of the aquarist, I will say a word about the sloughing off of the stonefish's skin. It happens in two stages. If a stonefish has just been brought in from the inner zone of the barrier reef, it is usually pale colored with similar tonings to the pinkish calcareous algae, or the light colored-sponges. Once installed in one of the Aquarium tanks, the necessity for camouflage leads them to change their skin in a few days. Swelling movements, followed by abrupt deflations, makes the old skin flake off in large pieces. Then it buries itself under the sand, leaving only the mouth and eyes visible. At this stage micro-elements from this muddy-sand habitat gradually attach themselves to the mucus covering of the skin.

This is where the second stage comes in. Some algae from different families grow on these stonefish and copepods, worms and lace corals take up residence in the tangle that they end up forming. After a while this microcosm becomes too much for the fish which then successively sheds large strips or small fragments of skin.

Stonefish are not the only scorpion-fish to change their skin like this and we have noticed that the chicken scorpion-fish (*Brachyrus zebra*[129]) sloughs it off in small scales, just like we peel after getting sunburnt.

The most astonishing species of scorpion-fish in the world is quite certainly the *Rhinopias*,

---

129 Refer to *Carnaval sous la mer*, color plate XXIV, fig. 5

141 *Rhinopias aphanes* (ex *frondosa*). First specimen found in 1964 at a depth of 30 meters and which was scarcely visible in the middle of algae of the same color. This scorpionfish has been photographed in the Aquarium, free of all the things that would have hindered an examination of its extremely complicated designs. Photographs 146 and 147 are close-up studies of the same specimen.

142 *Rhinopias aphanes*. A second specimen captured in the same area in 1973 with different coloration (perhaps an adaptation to a sea bed of algae or sponges carrying this same pinkish-brown shade).

143 *Rhinopias aphanes*. The great beauty of the dorsal fins where the areas that are not colored are translucent.

144 *Rhinopias aphanes* face on. In the jumble of "horns" (some of which look like those of a stag), in the middle of this bush of thorns, and among so many spots and lines decorating the body and fins, the location of the eyes and the branchial tube is not distinguishable. As for the mouth (which is able to distend considerably when swallowing prey), it seems to be a whitish band in a circular area, but this is only a design on the lower lip.

145 *Rhinopias aphanes* in profile. The eye, which is the same pinkish-brown color as the skin, is situated just at the base of the high plumes of horns above one of the whitish spots (the "false eyes" that one finds on other scorpionfish such as the *Inimicus*).

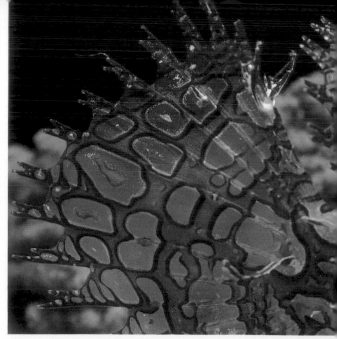

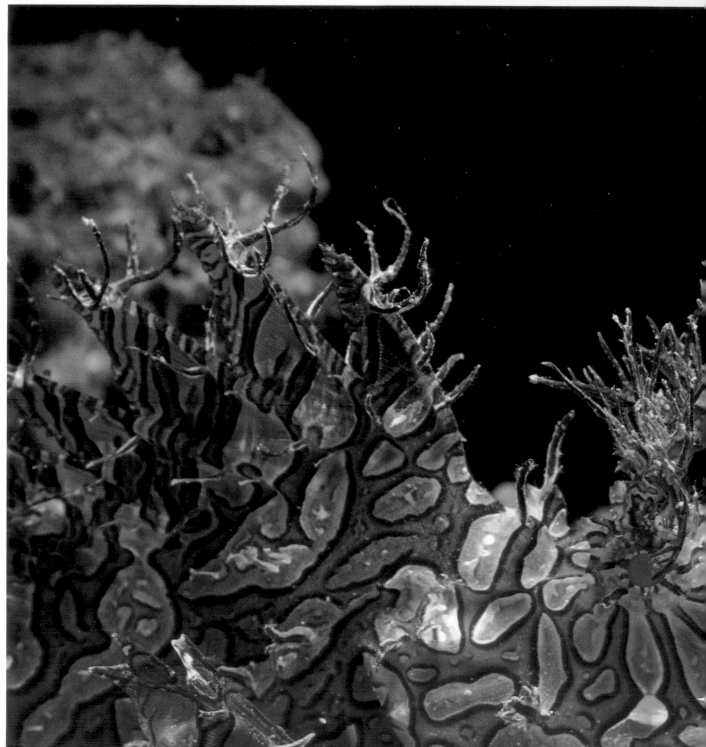

144

discovered for the first time in 1964 by Yves Merlet and Claude Conseil who captured it at a depth of 30 meters in the outer passage through Great Reef near Nouméa. This species was at first named *frondosa,* which suitably describes this astonishing thorn bush, but its name was altered to *aphanes* for reasons of taxonomy which I cannot go into in this popular work[130].

Such a species must have been very rare since it was only known at the time from this single specimen (as were the other species of the genus recorded from different regions of the globe). In fact, it took nearly 10 years for Bernard Conseil and his team-mate Alain Coqueugnot to capture a second, but quite differently colored specimen, at the same depth. Photograph **141** shows the profile of the first specimen; photograph **146** is a close-up of its head highlighting the beauty of the eye; the next photograph, **147**, gives details of the pectoral fin looking like a stained-glass window. The second specimen can be seen in profile in **142** and then from the front in **144**. The eye is the same pinkish color as most of the designs that surround it and can scarcely be distinguished. Finally, photograph **143** allows us to admire the beauty of its dorsal fins.

A species which English authors call the "false-stonefish", *Scorpaenopsis gibbosa* (**150**), belongs to the same order of Cataphracti. Its general look really has nothing to astound us, but it has hidden beauties. Observing it one day about to gobble down some small mullet, I was very surprised to see that when it rolled over on one side the surface of its ordinarily-hidden pectoral fin is tinted with superb colors. When this fin is properly stretched out it looks like a butterfly wing (**149**).

Even though it is quite astonishingly ugly, I will not repeat my photograph of the hallucinating facial features of another scorpion-fish — well named *Inimicus* — because it was featured in *Carnaval sous la mer* (colour plate XXIV, fig. 3). There I had drawn attention to the white spots which, on a very dark background, simulate eyes. The real eyes are, in fact, above and at a distance from these spots, and are

---

130   For those who are particularly interested in this, I thoroughly recommend the remarkable study made by Professor B. Condé in the *Revue Française d'Aquariologie*, third year, no. 2, second term, Nancy, 1976.

145

masked by the general coloring of the animal. My full-length color film, *Carnaval sous la mer*, also shows this terrifying "death mask", and in one sequence it fills up the whole screen. Even though the stings inflicted by the spines are not fatal, they are horribly painful. I can speak from experience!

I will end this chapter with comments on the *Erosa erosa* (**148**), a species which really has nothing going for it. I would not even have featured it here except that I have not seen it illustrated by any other author. Moreover, it isn't only for the avid aquarist that I mention it, but a little ... *"ad usum delphini"*, in other words, for those who will eventually take over our long and arduous task at the Aquarium. Under the circumstances, I always mistrusted this *Erosa*; in spite of its inoffensive air, this scorpion-fish should only be handled with the tip of a pair of tongs. My grudge against this abominable scorpion-fish occurred because one of our favorite *Syngnathus*, which lived in its company, dropped its guard one day and it only took the *Erosa* one mouthful to swallow it. An old friend, who made a film called The Vampire, witnessed the event and said: "Good God! How unpleasant it is!" And it looks so horrible too — one might call it "excessively beastly". Some ichthyologists could perhaps explain *Erosa's* bizarre post-cephalic depression to us. It is as if it has less of what a *Scorpaenopsis gibbosa* (**150**) has too much of! I should have asked my friend Fourmanoir this question, because he was the one who told me it was called *Erosa* (from "erosus" which means "corroded" or "eaten away" and not from "Eros" — "love"!). Fortunately for me this species had already been named, otherwise this distinguished expert who had previously named a small deep water *Apogon* after me (*Apogon catalai,* **64**), was considering giving my name to this odious creature! I would have been very sad to have been marked with such paternity till the end of my days!

Portraits

Honour to whom honour is due, so first of all here is a *Cheilinus undulatus* (**154** and **155**), the largest of the labrids which is very widely represented throughout the Indo-Pacific area. In New Caledonia it is generally called "Napoleon", not because it resembles the

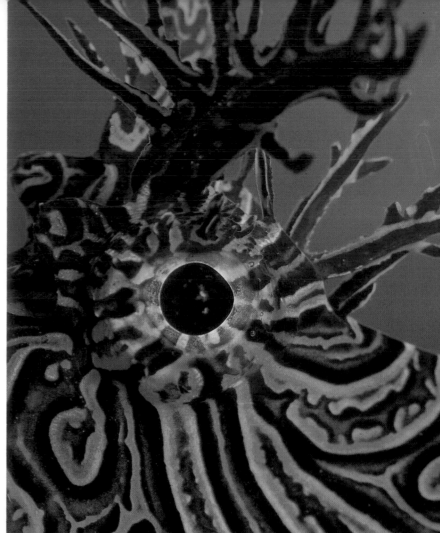

146

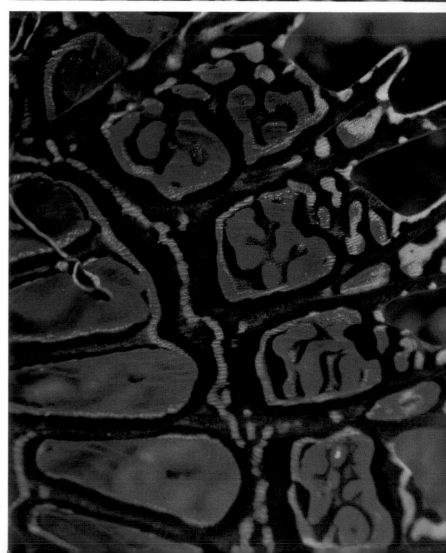

147

146 *Rhinopias aphanes*. A close-up of the first specimen, studying the eye, bands and soft rays.

147 *Rhinopias aphanes*. A close-up of the fin of the first specimen. The spaces without designs are translucent. In beautiful sunlight you might say they looked like precious stained-glass windows.

148 *Erosa erosa*. Poor thing! Nature has completely disinherited it (at least to our eyes).

149 *Scorpaenopsis gibbosa*. The ventral face reveals quite unexpected colors so the fins resemble butterfly wings.

150 *Scorpaenopsis gibbosa*, on a rocky bottom. The mouth is half-open. The spines of this gruesome stonefish can inflict a terribly painful wound.

149

150

"Little Corporal", or because of his hat, as many believe. I was told that it was quite simply because a family called Napoleon, who lived in the north of the island, specialized in catching this fish. According to the great ichthyologist, J.L.B. Smith, its size can reach two meters. Local fishermen have confirmed that they have caught specimens weighing more than 100 kilograms. E.M. Grant, in his excellent Australian book[131] quotes that it is likely for a "Hump-headed Maori wrasse" to weigh 420 pounds (about 200 kilograms).

Once they reach adulthood the frontal hump begins to appear on the head of these fish, and this gradually increases as they grow older (**155**).

I wonder what age specimens weighing between 150 and 200 kilograms could be: 40, 50, 60 years old — or even more? If the underwater spearfishermen had tried to capture them for the purpose of tagging and then letting them go, instead of killing them, we would have had some valuable information regarding their longevity. The large adults have scales as large as the palm of our hand. The pink bands with which they are adorned give them a distinctive pattern, which is heightened even more by a complete network of lines coloring the head, cheek and neck.

So many authors have written on how the *Cheilinus* behave at sea that there is no need to paraphrase: but I would like to deplore the fact, once again, that many underwater hunters seek and kill this very noble animal as a trophy. There is no need to kill such animals that are so tame and confident that they swim right up to humans. I will always remember two large photographs which appeared in the local daily paper and which professed to show the "prowess of a hunter" standing alongside his equal-sized victim. The two heads were next to each other, side by side. Even though it had been slaughtered, the animal still retained all its nobility. I would certainly have argued differently if the killer had measured himself against a shark (a really dangerous one). But a placid "Napoleon" — what glory!

I am not ridiculing leisure merely for the sake of sentimentality. My emotions are something completely different. It is a love of all the beautiful wonders of Nature. To see one of these splendid creatures senselessly destroyed makes my heart

131 Grant, E.M. *Guide to Fishes*. The Coordinator-General's Department, Brisbane, 1975.

bleed as much as when I was in the primeval
forests of Madagascar and saw large Brazilian
rosewoods and many other great "lords of the
forest" being put to death by men, quite often to
no better purpose than the slaughter of the *Cheilinus*.

In the Aquarium we have several *Cheilinus*.
Some are still very young, but one of our favorites
has grown in a large tank for more than 15 years,
and is by far the largest fish in the building. It is the
one featured in this book. Famous in more ways
than one, it is, *"urbi et orbi"*, one of the best
memories that visitors take away with them.

They are quite astounded that this enormous
fish of one and a half meters is able to remain so
still for many hours lying on the sand against the
glass pane. In fact, the behavior of this
magnificent creature is very interesting: when
there are no visitors in the public gallery it moves
about in the large space of its tank, but as soon as
the first visitors arrive the *Cheilinus* stops
swimming and places itself at the window, staring
at everyone with its large eye which seems to be
mounted on a ball-and-socket joint.

Someone once said: "He is a great show-off"
but the truth is that, like many other fish, he has
unflagging curiosity.[132] When there are no more
visitors, "Monsieur" starts going around again,
with a little more purpose if the hour has come for
the extra tit-bits brought by his admiring lady
keeper who has the same rapport with him as
when her own dogs welcome her at home. This
reciprocal affection is further confirmed when she
descends into the vast tank, equipped with mask
and snorkel. He then swims very close to her,
even if she doesn't offer him shellfish or crabs. He
remains beside her and allows himself to be
caressed; she sometimes amuses herself by sliding
a finger under his large half-open gill cover to
very softly stroke his gills. She also does this with
other fish, like the *Lepidaplois*[133] for example, so
one can assume that the reason why these fish so
gladly allow their gills to be stroked is that they
feel the same sensation as when being cleaned by
the small *Fissilabrus* fish.

Having spoken about the curiosity of
"Napoleon", and having just mentioned the
Lepidaplois, I must again refer to what I formerly
called the mirror test. I had already featured a few

132   The final photograph in this chapter dedicated to Fish is
also quite eloquent and allows us to illustrate a double curiosity.
133   Refer to *Carnaval sous la mer*, p. 116.

151

152

153

151 *Canthigaster ocellicinctus* which is capable of puffing itself up and deflating at will. Its eyes are circled in green like those of certain tree frogs.

152 *Acanthurus dussumieri*. (Surgeon-fish). In the Aquarium, it scrapes away for a long time on the concrete partitions of the large tanks on which numerous algae grow.

153 *Acanthurus dussumieri*. On both sides of the caudal peduncle, a white stylet which is hard and fearfully sharp, frees itself at will from its groove and can inflict deep gashes — hence the common name Surgeon-fish.

154 and **155** *Cheilinus undulatus*. The largest of the labridae. It can reach a length of two meters and a weight of 200 kilograms. This lord is so peaceful and gentle that it should be forbidden to feature it among underwater hunting trophies.

154

155

reactions of a Trigger fish looking at itself in the mirror in *Carnaval sous la mer*. Here I will only show a *Lepidaplois* (*Bodianus*) *axillaris* (**96**) studying itself in a small round mirror placed on the visitor's side of the tank. Next to it, other fish such as the superb blue *Paracanthurus teuthis* wait their turn.

Illustration **93** shows a superb *Variola louti* grouper (called swallow loach or *loehe hirondelle* in New Caledonia). You must not think that the four beautiful *Platax orbicularis* which face us are at its funeral vigil because this loach is in excellent health. How many times did we notice these *Variola* lolling around just like that, lying on their sides with the pectoral fins sometimes haphazardly leaning against the glass slab. What can this posture mean? I will not be the one to tell you. I will always regret not having really succeeded in taking a shot of the *Variola* lying down like that, with a nonchalant fin leaning on a rock — a very Recamier pose!

The *Platax* featured here were installed in the Aquarium when they were very young (at the stage shown in photograph **159**). A representative of this pretty species has been with us since October 1956, the year the Aquarium opened, which means that as I write these lines it has been here for 20 years and four months. It is the veteran of all our fish and seems happy enough to live on for a long time yet.

Another very beautiful portrait is that of an *Acanthurus dussumieri* (**152**). Photograph **153** shows a close up of the razor-sharp knife on this beautiful surgeon fish. Nearly every year in the very large tank one of these fish comes into conflict with a *Platax*, inflicting long gashes down its sides with that dangerous weapon. One needs all the natural resistance of the *Platax* to survive the loss of the blood caused from such a deep cut. It is so upsetting that we always say: "This time it cannot survive" But then, in less than a month, the wounds heal without leaving any scars. What health!

Some people suggest: "Why not put the *Platax* that are exposed to such attacks into different tanks?" Quite simply because our physical attempts to capture strong and determined fish in our large tanks are usually not successful. Our efforts also cause immediate panic among all the other fish, causing more or less serious injury to them, and some would even succumb to infections from the resultant bruises.

156

157

158

156 *Cromileptes altivelis*. Juvenile grouper-trout. Its long snout makes it a "different" rock cod, not having any resemblance to the other Serranidae. Here, it can be seen in front of an encrusting *Cliona schmidti* sponge.

157 and **158** A *Priacanthus hamrur*, commonly called "lantern-fish" because of a strange reflection at the back of the eye. It seems that nobody has identified the optical mechanism which causes this.

159 A sub-adult *Platax orbicularis*. The very young individuals are almost as perfectly round as a coin.

160 An adult *Pomacanthus semicirculatus*. One of the oldest residents in the Aquarium.

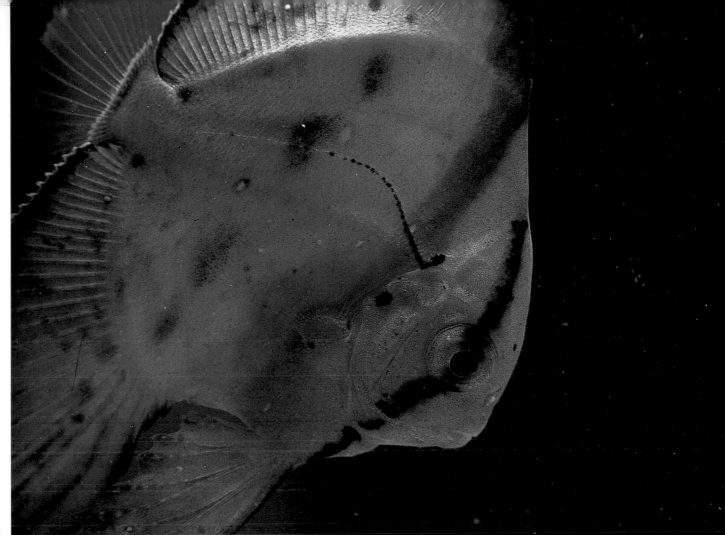

159

160

Priacanthus hamrur (lantern-fish)

The common name given by the fishermen in New Caledonia to this superb fish (**157** and **158**) refers to the strange luminous reflections at the back of its eyes. Despite all our attempts, we have not been able to photograph this glow which no other fish demonstrates. What a lovely research topic this would be for an anatomist interested in animal eyes. Obviously it is a play on light and only appears under certain incidences, but it would be interesting to find out the cause.

Like other refractory species in captivity, these lantern-fish were very difficult to keep in the Aquarium. No food tempted them, in spite of their extensive *à la carte* choice, so after a few days they would die. Our attempts were so disappointing that if any fishermen brought us some, or if we found them in our nets, we would immediately give them back their liberty by releasing them to sea.

Cromileptes altivelis

Visitors who have a good knowledge of coral fish will be somewhat surprised to learn that this species belongs to the family Serranidae. In fact, its compressed body, as well as its long and pointed snout — especially at the adult stage — does not resemble the normal grouper. This fish is not rare and the professional fishermen in New Caledonia call it grouper-trout. They catch it on a hand line and one seldom sees it on the market stalls because its flesh is delicious.

Cromileptes altivelis is featured in many ichthyological works, but since the coat of the juvenile is much more striking than that of the adult, I illustrate this pretty creature here (**156**) moving about in front of a violet sponge (*Cliona schmidti*). Our attempts to capture the juvenile *Cromileptes* are not always crowned with success, so able are they at threading their way through the branching corals or amongst the heaps of dead coral debris. Slow and gentle movements of the hand are necessary to avoid hurting these delicate little creatures. One can never lose sight of these wriggling little fish however, since through all the operation they never stop waving their fins, stretching out like high sails (from which the species gets its name of *altivelis*). This continual undulating movement brings to mind the grace of the transparent veil that a dancer swirls around her. Whatever the color of the coral or sponge that the fish swims past, the translucent dorsal fin seems to take on the color of its backdrop.

Once they reach a size of about 10 centimeters the activity of their veils is very reduced. They like to keep sheltered from the daylight and remain most of the time under rock undercuts, in caves or in the shade of large coral heads.

Finally, a few other fish pictures justly deserve to be featured here. I have chosen those of the juvenile *Platax orbicularis* (**159**) and, because the image is remarkably alive, the portrait of an adult *Pomacanthus semi-circulatus* (**160**) — one of the oldest fish in the Aquarium.

Shell Collectors and Vandalism

All the small bays around Noumea were underwater paradises in 1946. Each bay has its own particular shape determined by its position on the island anad its orientation to prevailing trade-winds and ocean currents.

Only a few minutes from the center of town some incredibly diverse habitats of exceptional value were available to naturalists and research workers. But today all this has disappeared. Some might say: "It is the inevitable consequence of demographic growth and all the development works that follow: in a word — the ransom of progress." An easy argument, but under the circumstances nearly always incorrect. I would like to give a few typical examples.

The bay called Orphelinat was not subjected to any new development for more than 10 years and its coastal borders abounded in magnificent feather worms which had hollowed out their galleries in living corals or coral rocks. At the time when I was filming my documentary, *Carnaval sous la mer*, I had no need to go any further than this bay to find the *Spirobranchus* opening out their superb, multi-colored bouquets. The muddy-sand area of this small bay was full of boxfish, puffer fish, angler fish, gurnards, etc. But the most beautiful richness of this habitat was contributed by the great diversity of mollusks. including very rare species. You only have to leaf through Jean Risbec's *Mollusques nudibranches de la Nouvelle-Calédonie* to see page after page mentioning Orphelinat bay as the unique locality for numerous sea-slugs of the genera *Noumea, Cadlinella, Risbeckia, Vayssierea,* etc. And you might well ask how many other important gastropods have also disappeared from this special biological region?

I witnessed another example only a few kilometers away on the large reef called Ricaudy. It was truly a living museum with all the invertebrate groups represented in an astonishing profusion in less than one meter of water at high tide. Adult and juvenile fish of many families, genera and species, swam amongst the large seaweeds where one could also admire a great variety of algae — *Laurentia, Caulerpa, Enteromorpha, Plocanium, Dasycladus, Acetabularia,* etc — "fixed" to the rocks and stones (it will soon be understood why I stress fixed).

At very low tides this reef is completely exposed and dried out, with the exception of a few depressions forming large and small pools where many organisms group together, waiting for the return of the tide.

I still remember about 20 American scientists who came to visit the Institut Français d'Oceanie (today called the ORSTOM of Noumea) for a few days in 1959. Flabbergasted by such abundant marine life, they filled their notebooks with jottings ... but collected nothing. What would they see if they came back today? A desert. Now there, just as in many other areas around the island, no modifying development has taken place and there are no harmful toxic products to blame for the denudement.

I would need a complete book to talk about every area where such biological imbalances have been produced around Noumea, but I will restrict myself to mentioning just one more, the bay called Isoles, so-called because of the three small rocky islets situated only a few hundred meters from the coast. In very shallow waters in a small area of less than one hectare there was the most astonishing assemblage of marine reef species that we had ever seen during our 30 years of coastal underwater explorations.

When the Aquarium had just opened my great friend Jean Rolland (who was a technical college teacher) showed the greatest dedication and most constant perseverance in all our activities and also proved himself to be an excellent connoisseur of inshore fauna. It was he who suggested that we go and prospect the small bays of Magenta one November day in 1956. I can still see the old jeep with its trailer carrying a galvanized tank fitted with compressed air diffusers which enabled us to bring back live invertebrates and fish to enrich the tanks at the Aquarium. Since Magenta was uninhabited at that time we could only drive as far as a small beach. The first area wasn't very attractive: muddy sand with layers of *Cymodocea* "grass" here and there, abundant starfish, hermit-crabs and other crabs, a few small horseshoe clams (*Hippopus*) which closed up as soon as we approached, plus the usual sea-urchins. As soon as the water was deep enough so that our stomachs did not rub against *Actinodendron*, those famous "cauliflowers" which sting atrociously, we put on our masks and snorkels. Pushing ourselves along with gloved hands we noted all the organisms most worthy of interest. The first small formations of corals soon appeared — minute colonies alternating with numerous mushroom corals, *Fungia*. After about 60 meters we arrived at the edge of a great forest of branching staghorn coral, the fragile *Acropora* with blue tips. There an extraordinary spectacle awaited us. We had seen coral formations of all types over the past 10 years but these *Acropora* were so tight, their ramifications so interwoven, that they formed a real network. In the middle of this tangle was a dense mixed school of fish of the genera *Apogon*, *Zoramia* with violet eyes like precious stones scintillating with fire, *Aspicis* with enormous eyes, easily recognizable because of the large black band around the base of their tail, *Archamia* with the brilliant line stretching across from one eye to the other, *Lovamia cheilodipterus* and many, many more. What pen could describe this spectacle, what brush would be able to paint the subtlety of those colors? As well as the masses of *Apogon*, numerous *Chaetodon*, *Zanclus* and many other species moved around the tips of the corals. A real ballet!

As we stood up and took off our masks and snorkels, we were both equally flabbergasted at the sight of the many marvels in this well-stocked paradise. Rolland said: "I was wanting to point out two *Apogon*. Did you recognize them?"

"One of them, yes, it was an *Apogon orbicularis*" (photographs **61** and **63**). "Many books have suggested that it is quite common in several regions of the Pacific, but I had never seen it alive before. The other one I don't know. There was only one pair."

"What are we going to do now?"

"I think we should come back when the tide is higher and go over this reef of high *Acropora* clumps again. Today we would risk breaking too many things because of the tips of the staghorns are practically at water level.

"While waiting, I suggest a search around the edges to get an idea of the extent of this population. You go to the left, I'll go to the right and we will meet on the other side."

"Well?"

"It doesn't go too far."

That partially explains why there was such an incredible density of *Apogon* in so restricted a space. Nearby was a very dense clump of

Millepora[134] where the fish were quite scattered, but luckily, there was also another pair of this unidentified *Apogon* that intrigued us so much. We captured it without difficulty and it turned out to be a new species which Dr. Gilbert Whitley, an expert from the Australian Museum, dedicated to the city of Noumea. Since then this *Apogon noumeae* has never been reported to us at this or at any other locality, either in New Caledonia or elsewhere.

During the next three years we returned several times to this little bay in Magenta and learnt the characteristic features of each zone throughout the whole area. Homogenous coral zone, hydro-coral zone, rock and pebble zone richly populated with algae, muddy zone of *Rhizophora* mangroves and sandy-muddy zone of *Cymodocea* and *Halophila*. This last zone, the closest to the shore, was very rich in *Gergobius*, fish excavators of the most complicated tunnels, *Synanceia* stonefish, *Inimicus*, mimics of stones, gurnards, *Ostracion* boxfish, *Lactoria* and *Tetrosomus* swimming around a few centimeters from the bottom. At a higher level, young trevally were chasing *Fimbriclupea* sardines and *Pranesus* priest fish over the banks, while on the surface, groups of small squid always offered a glorious spectacle by continuously undulating the iridescent fringes of their diaphanous mantles.

We investigated many other regions, but we never found such a diversity of habitats in such a restricted space anywhere else. But today the biological balance of this true sanctuary is broken forever.

Here, as in the other examples noted, the cause of this imbalance in the coastal regions has been the frenzy of profit-seeking by people who deal in shells. To be more precise, it is because of the irresponsible way in which they maximise their collecting sprees in the shortest time possible.

I do not want to lay blame on responsible, serious collectors. They are quite content with only a few carefully-collected examples of each species, knowing that excessive collection would signal the beginning of imbalance. They also

---

134 Commonly called "electric coral" because of the very lively stings inflicted by the nematocysts. (see *Carnaval sous la mer*, pp. 21–22 and figs. 11 and 12), microscopic cells that are highly toxic, these *Millepora* are not corals but hydro-corals.

know that for numerous species, even given the best possible ecological conditions, only one or two dozen adult individuals successfully survive from the hundreds of egg masses laid and the thousands of eggs hatched from them.

No, the main culprits are those who will stop at nothing to make money, ignoring all the permanent consequences of their greed. For example, they think nothing of using crowbars and even car jacks to break up the large, tabular *Acropora* and other corals that have taken many decades to achieve their large forms.

Under the cover of these corals and rocks, multitudes of shellfish are sheltered from the blistering sun. But that is not all! In these havens are all the thousands of egg masses of fish, mollusks, crustacea, echinoderms, etc. All these embryos of life are destined to annihilation when their coral shelter is upturned and they are abruptly laid in the open because the millions of eggs will soon be the victims of any predators which are fond of this "caviar". And those eggs that escape the banquet will end up being torn away by the returning tide. The innumerable polyps that have built the corals themselves will die, leaving behind only gray, slowly-disintegrating calcareous skeletons.

Some very rich people even employ full-time collectors to exploit the reefs, turning over stones, breaking up rocks and massacring the beautiful coral. All to gain more money from the sales of shells to specialized shops in large cities overseas. Nature, that should be everyone's benefactor, has had to submit to desecration by a few traffickers for their exclusive and sordid profit.

Less than 10 years ago, one of these "professionals" completely swept up a whole population of *Cassis* helmet shells (Mollusks **74**)[135] from a very restricted habitat in less than 15 meters of water. He very quickly sold close to 25 specimens on the beach itself and in the center of town. This sale was conducted shamelessly in less than two hours and would have netted him a small fortune.

Another "pirate" was even more outrageous with his comment: "All I am interested in is making the value of the shells as high as possible. I therefore deliberately rarify the species and that increases the total value of my stock in hand."

The only consideration such greedy people show for these incredible marine creatures is their money value. What importance does beauty have? What importance is there for the respect that one owes to these jewels of nature? The following anecdote is very significant.

On a short dive, my wife was swimming in less than three meters of water above a pair of sand excavator fish. There is still so much information to be gleaned on the behavior of these *Gergobius* that they can never be observed enough.[136] Their shelter was a giant empty *Tridacna* clam shell resting on the sand. She very gently lifted up the edge of their shelter for just a moment, enough time to see how many galleries diverged from their "living-room". Then she felt a small object fall into her hands. It was a very rare porcelain-shell. The shell was empty, but still in a perfect condition and with all its original brilliance. We have never collected shells, and are only interested in identifying those which we can keep alive in the Aquarium, so she showed her find to a fanatical collector.

"Do you recognize this rare species?"

"Rare! You can say that again. The minimum amount you will get for that is 15,000F."[137]

"I'm not asking you how much it is worth, but what its name is?"

"It is a *Cypraea stolida*."

He also added the word "niger"[138] and then very quickly returned to his single preoccupation adding: "Certain varieties of *C. stolida* can earn you double or even triple that amount."

Photograph **88** in Mollusks was taken thanks to a living specimen loaned to me by another fanatic who barely gave me time to photograph it. I asked him what he intended to do with it.

"Sell it of course! It is going to fetch me around about ..."

At night — and especially on nights when there is no moon — most of these gastropods leave their shelters or emerge from under the surface of the sand. This is when the shell hunters go to town; and with the use of powerful

---

135 A reminder in passing that the *Cassis cornuta* is one of the species of gastropods which, like the conchs (*Charonia tritonis*), feeds on the dangerous starfish *Acanthaster planci*, a great destroyer of coral.

136 Refer to chapter on Fish, photograph 55 and following plate.

137 This sum is in Pacific francs and equals US$120.

138 A few New Caledonian shellfish show very curious coloration which is more or less intense and which is quite often acompanied by a strange deformation of the two extremities (see chapter on Mollusks).

underwater torches they collect everything that can be turned into profit. Such depletions lead to the worst imbalances and to the growing scarcity of certain species! This is so bad that one even fears that they will disappear completely[139]. At the moment I am thinking about the threat of extinction to nautilus shells. Currently there is quite considerable research interest in their physiology, the implications of which go well beyond simple knowledge of mollusks.

Professor Arthur Martin, of the University of Washington, has come to Noumea several times to carry out remarkable research at the Aquarium laboratory. For his tasks he required a few dozen specimens each month for less than a three month period: this therefore did not risk causing any imbalance to the "stock", and any danger was further minimized by collecting the supplies far away from each other. In order to capture these nautilus shells, special traps were set by very experienced divers at depths between 25 and 50 meters. One diver took advantage of the training and went on to form his own team to exploit shells for commercial gain. But while we always limited our captures strictly to the needs of Professor Martin, this commercial team established a savage program.

There is only a small percentage of perfectly intact shells that are saleable because most of them have imperfections following repair or are broken on the edges of their last chamber. One can therefore imagine the number of nautilus shells these traffickers must catch to find a perfect one. Still, if the lives of the unsaleable ones had been spared, the damage to the whole population would not be so great. But this is not the case. Firstly, they are not sorted as soon as the traps are brought up, but much later when all the animals are dead. Secondly, we know that if the traps are left down longer than 24 hours, most of the nautilus shells turn on each other in merciless cannibalism. But what do these greedy people care, because all that interests them is the shell.

Think about it then! It seems that an intact nautilus shell sells for more than 2000F. in the souvenir shops where precious shells are exhibited for sale.

In his admirable book, *Avant que nature meure*[140], my friend Jean Dorst from the Institut and Director of the Museum d' Histoire Naturelle in Paris, quotes typical examples of the growing scarcity of several species of European butterflies which, he writes, "are collected non-stop, not only to be sold at good prices to collectors, but also for more corrupt exploitation: coated in plastic they make ashtrays, paperweights and key-holders[141]. Some very localized beetles are also subject to such intensive hunts that their populations diminish each season."

Jean Dorst adds: "This vandalism ... is driving these endemics with very limited distribution towards extinction. Moreover, this excessive collection has, in many cases, resulted in strong legislative measures" (particularly in Switzerland and Germany for certain insects).

Many authors have written in anguish about such degradation. I will restrict myself to quote one more by Isobel Bennett in her magnificent book on Australia's Great Barrier Reef[142].

"Those historic days have gone but the present upsurge in popularity of shell collecting, very unfortunately, has brought in its wake the ruthless commercial collector. The great fascination, the stimulation and aesthetic reward, of a private collection should lie in the personal gathering of the shells by its owner. The appreciation of the living animal which created the shell and a knowledge of its habitat and perhaps its life history, must surely lead to a greater awareness of the destructive consequences, to the habitat, and to the animal, of careless and indiscriminate collecting and, hopefully, to a strong desire to further in every way the preservation and conservation of both.

"The devastation which can be caused by one small boatload of people during the few hours of one low spring tide on a reef flat can be quite appalling. By their thoughtless depredation the whole productivity of that reef flat, and the natural habitat of thousands upon thousands of its

139   That, among other things, is what the unfortunately famous commentary of the Cousteau film *500 millions d'années sous la mer* should have said, instead of its deplorable untruths and errors. On this topic — and that of sea snakes — see what I have written in the Epilogue of this book.

140   Dorst, Jean. *Avant que nature meure*, Delachaux et Niestlé, Neuchatel, Switzerland, 1970.

141   With regards to the Caledonian lagoon, we could also add necklaces. In Tahiti, in fact, the use of shell necklaces greatly increased because of the importance of the tourist trade. Teams of Tahitians residing in Noumea send quantities of shells to Papeete where the same species has become too rare to satisfy demand. With the Tahitians being such excellent divers, one can easily imagine the consequences that these catches bring about. In this particular case it is the quantity collected that matters.

142   Bennett, Isobel. *The Great Barrier Reef*. P. 126.

inhabitants, can literally be ruined in a matter of hours. To appreciate the truth of this statement fully one must have traversed such a reef — far from human habitation and the normal shipping lanes — where the trail of destruction across the reef was glaringly apparent and easy to follow. Boulders, not one, but many hundreds, had been overturned in the blazing tropical sun. They once gave life and protection to untold numbers of plants and animals, large and small, and, in the spring breeding season to millions of eggs. Multiply this by a few more boats and a few low spring tides, and the result is not difficult to imagine. Only when the full significance of the very simple act of turning back a boulder is realized by *all* visitors to a reef, will there be any future for many of its marine inhabitants."

The few examples of destruction that I have given for New Caledonia fully confirm the pessimistic view of Isobel Bennett whose scientific authority gives unquestionable value to the statement I have just quoted from her book.

Some people have said to me: "But you who knew ... why didn't you warn the authorities and so avoid such depradation, not only for living fossils such as the nautilus shells, but also because of the havoc caused to coral formations everywhere."

Two answers will suffice. The first is the practical difficulty of imposing the rules and regulations that would become law. How does one put them into practice? You cannot put a policeman on duty, day and night, in every area under threat, nor provide a flotilla of boats which would be necessary to efficiently patrol the entire lagoon in New Caledonia.

The second aspect is more personal. I have learnt repeatedly of the futility of such legal intervention and I have not the slightest illusions. A small anecdote that occured some years ago illustrates the point.

In 1947 I was given the very impressive title of Membre du Conseil Supérieur pour la Protection de la Nature en Nouvelle-Calédonie and I thought that I could be very useful to this cause. How naive I was! I was asked to carry out a study, which appeared in 1948 in the journal *Pro Natura*[143], published in Switzerland by the International Union for the Protection of Nature. In the chapter dealing with the incredible richness of marine animal life, I vigorously protested against the then widespread practice of dynamiting in the lagoon. The boomerang that I thus launched very quickly backfired on me. Those same men who had conferred the honorable duty on me hastened to remove me from office and one of the more sinister ones made this cynical comment: "He didn't know how to play the game." I translate that as: "The game of cowardliness". The writer-philosopher who said: "If I had a hand full of truths, I would be very careful to make sure I didn't open it out" was so right.

What of conservation? Fortunately an Association pour la Sauvegarde de la Nature now exists. But it is now too late for most of the bays in Noumea, which in earlier times I had regarded as typical. The imbalance that they have all suffered is, in today's language, irreversible. However, if we look only at the case of nautilus shells there is still time to intervene. In the bulletin *La Sauvegarde de la Nature en Nouvelle-Calédonie*, I wrote: "In less than two years the physiologists who regularly visited Noumea to continue their research programs noted a considerable reduction in the "stock" of nautilus in areas where they used to find them easily. The very careful and necessary collecting of nautilus shells by these men of science had had no observed effect on depletion. We come to only one conclusion: the systematic destruction of nautilus shells for commercial purposes is criminal."

Even if legal measures were taken — and given that their rigorous application was possible — the pillagers of nature would treat it as a joke as their fines would only slightly curtail their profits and they would begin again the very next day. I firmly believe that the best, if not the only, effective measure is to simply forbid all export of shells (except for strictly scientific purposes) and to also ban all sales in shops. I have been told that this is being done in New Guinea for butterflies and birds of paradise. Because trading had seriously reduced their populations, it was feared that certain endemic species that were already not so common would become extinct.

Unless the Association for the Protection of Nature, and the committee of wise people presiding over the responsibilities, have the authority and weight to make sure that such legislation will work, then one must lose all hope.

---

143 *Pro Natura*. vol. 1, no. 2, Basel, October, 1948, pp. 77–85.

Thus concludes this kaleidoscope of marine organisms. As rich as it is, this book's content has only been able to give quite a modest idea of the wonders that live in the Aquarium of Noumea and the lagoon. I would like to point out that the great majority of organisms illustrated here were collected in a section of the lagoon close to Noumea and only between five and 22 kilometers away from the Aquarium.

One of the closest habitats was only a few minutes journey by boat, at a bay called Nickel where, at an average depth of about 18 meters, the sea bed is covered with an astonishing profusion of all sorts of invertebrates (hard corals, soft-corals, stony corals and many other animal colonies). Yet these organisms flourish only a few hundred meters from the factory treating the nickel ore and are therefore subject to the influence of quantities of submerged waste. I have specially stated that for the information of certain systematic "knockers" of the lagoon in Noumea who apparently do not believe that there is a rich marine community in Nickel Bay.

In writing this book I have had to criticize a few vandals who, for sordidly lucrative shell reasons, inflict drastic damage on the small bays in Noumea, which until quite recently were still intact biological paradises. However, as regrettable as they might be, these degradations only concern very localized habitats which are almost insignificant when compared to the immensity of the whole lagoon. Also, it would be ludicrous to let readers believe that this lagoon has become "a dying sea, a coral cemetery where only venomous snakes multiply ... and where in New Caledonia the world of corals, which was formerly the cradle of life, is now but a cemetery, ... haunted by a sinister and dangerous survivor slithering through sponge, seaweed and dead coral bodies."[144]

After Cousteau's film, *500 millions d'années sous la mer*, was shown in 1973, many visitors to the Aquarium asked: "Do you get all these wonders sent over from the Great Barrier Reef in Australia?" Now, I ask you — why would we go so far away for organisms that we have right on our doorstep and which are in great abundance in the Noumea lagoon?

These people had been led to believe that "because, from a recent film by Cousteau we got the depressing impression that your lagoon had become a dead world where only a quantity of dangerous snakes existed." Many of these people would add: "That film has greatly discredited your lagoon".

In the press articles about this film that appeared at the time,[145] much was written about the fact that there would be a few misconceptions to qualify in the documentary. Many readers already know of the severe criticism that it aroused in many places.[146] I must say how annoying it is that such excellent quality cinematographic shots, obtained at great cost and with perfect equipment, should be spoilt because of such a great number of glaring errors and so much ignorance of ecological, zoological and biological data. Of course, some people would expect me to criticize this extravagant commentary severely. But I have neither the time nor the desire to do so, and the present book has better things to say. What prompted me to repeat my complaints, already expressed by others, was the desire to re-established the truth about the admirable floristic and faunistic richness of our lagoon.

It is also appropriate to mention these famous sea snakes, recalling the very interesting observations by Professor P.H. Verkammen-Grandjean, from the Medical Center, San Francisco, at the University of California. He visited Noumea in March 1968 (well before Cousteau's team came in 1973), in the hope that we would be able to help him find "a few living specimens of this reptile". He was concerned that he had been unable to bring his diving equipment

144 Diolé, P. *"Odyssée sous-marine de l'équipe Cousteau. Le lagon pollué de Nouméa"* in Le Figaro, July 2, 1973.

145 Diolé, P. *"Odyssée sous-marine de l'équipe Cousteau. Le lagon pollué de Nouméa"* in Le Figaro, July 2, 1973. Descateaux C. *"Le serpent marin de Nouvelle-Calédonie a survécu à la pollution des mers par les déchets de nickel. Les survivants de la mer maudite"* in Télé 7 Jours, July 12, 1973.

146 Loison, Dr. G. *"L'imposture Cousteau"* in La France Australe, August 29, 1973 Arnold R. *"La morsure d'un membre de l'équipe Cousteau: une caisse mal arrimée"* in La France Australe, July 12, 1973 (another protest by a local diver on the subject of the article in Le Figaro). Professor Bruno Condé: *"Je dénoncerai en France la fumisterie Cousteau"* in La France Australe, November 6, 1973 (interview). Les nouvelles calédoniennes, October 12, 1973. *"Des experts jugent le film Cousteau est une imposture scientifique."*

with him but we immediately reassured him by saying that in one morning alone, and without getting our feet wet, we would be able to get him a good number of *Laticauda colubrina* (photograph **3**), because these snakes spent a long time warming themselves on the limestone slabs of the lagoon islets. We walked to Signal islet, one of the closest to our Aquarium, and easily caught more than 100 of these sea-snakes in only a few hours. Here is the essential part of a report that he sent us a short time after his return to San Francisco[147]:

"In three days of dissection on more than 100 *Laticauda colubrina*, I observed the remnants of partly digested moray eels in the digestive tracts of each snake. No snake was without moray eel and we found no other type of food. In this large sample four species of moray eels were able to be identified. In the posterior part of the moray eels, the part that was least digested, one could see the bite mark of the snake. These moray eels had all been swallowed head first, as is the habit of many other snakes apart from the *L. colubrina*. Given that moray eels are generally detested by fishermen because of their voracious destruction of fish, sea-snakes should be considered beneficial and consequently they should be protected.[148] As for being venomous, *L. colubrina* has an exaggerated reputation. Therefore, instead of being respected and returned with all care to the sea, it is generally killed by ignorant fishermen who find it in their nets." And Professor Verkammen-Grandjean adds: "It should also be noted that the species of the genus *Laticauda* are rather unaggressive snakes that can be tamed."

It is a fact that even in the water, these sea-snakes (*L. colubrina*, photograph **3**, *Aypisurus laevis*, photograph **2**) are naturally afraid and flee from the diver. The *Platurus* (photograph **1**) seem to be less frightened and often irritate divers by persistently accompanying them and even striking against the glass of their masks. However, I have often wondered whether this behavior is not due, quite simply, to the reflections of the face-mask and the shine of its metallic band which attracts them. Whatever the cause, I have not known any cases of these snakes "attacking" anyone, and I will add that one really has to want to be bitten for an accident to happen. Conclusion: we are quite far from the Dante-like descriptions that Diolé evoked in his commentary: "… these marine reptiles, with a diabolic vivacity, these mad

1   **2**

creatures, these ribbons with an open mouth whose bodies writhe like the lash of a whip!"[149]

There is every reason to writhe!

This book highlights the immense amount of research work and observation that still remains to be done inside this magnificent lagoon and all around the outer edge of the great coral reef which surrounds it for more than 800 kilometers, as well as around the islands inside the lagoon, the Loyalty Islands, the Isle of Pines and other marine Edens.

3

René Catala
The Aquarium of Noumea
Noumea, April 1977

147 Verkammen-Grandjean, P.H. "Is *Laticauda colubrina* a *factor of equilibrium in maraena populations?*" (this note was supported by U.S. Public Health Service Research Grant A1–03793 from the National Institute of Allergy and Infectious Diseases.
148 I wanted to highlight this passage.
149 Diolé, P. *"Odyssée sous-marine de l'équipe Cousteau"* in *Le Figaro*, July 2, 1973.

BIBLIOGRAPHY

Allan, Joyce
> *Australian Shells,*
> Georgian House, Melbourne 1942.

Babelt & Cayet
> *Le monde vivant des Atolls,*
> Société des Océanistes, Paris 1972.

Barnes, Robert
> *Invertebrate Zoology,*
> W.B. Sanders Company, Philadelphia 1968.

Bauchot, M.L. & R.
> *La vie des poissons,*
> Stock, Paris 1967.

Bennett, Isobel
> *The Great Barrier Reef,*
> Lansdowne Press, Melbourne 1971.

Boué, H. & R Chanton
> *Zoologie. Invertébrés.*
> G. Doin & Cie, Paris 1962.

Budker, P.
> *The Life of Sharks,*
> Weidenfeld and Nicolson, London 1971.

Bürgi, Alfred
> *Contribution à l'étude du comportement vis à vis d'objets étrangers chez les Majidae,*
> Bulletin Laboratoire Arago (Banyuls) vo. XIX, 1968.

Catala, R.
> *Effets de fluorescence provoqués sur des coraux par l'action des rayons ultra-violets,*
> Comptes rendus Acad. Sciences, Paris 1958.
>
> *Carnaval sous la mer,*
> Sicard, Paris 1964.
>
> *Etude sur l'économie des Iles Gilbert, Mission pour la Commission du Pacifique Sud,*
> Academy of Science National Research Council, Washington D.C. 1957.
>
> *Contribution à l'étude écologique des îlots coralliens du Pacifique Sud.*
> Bull. Biol. France et Belgique, Paris 1950.
>
> *Longévité d'organismes marins à l'Aquarium de Nouméa,*
> Bull. Museum, Paris 1970.
>
> *Poissons d'eau douce de Madagascar,*
> Revue Française d'Aquariologie, Nancy 1974.
>
> *Elevage de Carangues en captivité,*
> Revue Française d'Aquariologie, Nancy 1974.
>
> *L'Aquarium de Nouméa,*
> Atlas-Air France, Paris 1973.
>
> *Le nautile en danger,*
> Sauvegarde de la Nature néo-calédonienne, Nouméa 1975.
>
> *Sur un cas tératologique remarquable chez un Chaetodontidé du genre* Heniochus,
> Bulletin de la Sté Zool. de France, Paris 1949.

> *Accélération, par des chocs, de la métamorphose des chenilles de* Chrysiridia madagascariensis,
> Ac. Sc. CC VIII, Paris 1939.
>
> *The Aquarium of Noumea.*
> Australian Natural History, vol. 15, Sydney 1966.

Clark, Hubert
> *The Echinoderms, Fauna of Australia,*
> Carnegie Institution of Washington D.C., 1946.

Coleman, Neville
> *A Field Guide to Australian Marine Life,*
> Rigby Ltd. 1977.

Dakin, William, Elizabeth Pope, Isobel Bennett
> *Australian Sea Shores,*
> Angus and Robertson, Sydney 1959.

Dorst, Jean
> *Avant que nature meure,*
> Delachaux et Niestlé, Neuchatel, Switzerland 1970.

Figuier, L.
> *Zoophytes et Mollusques,*
> Hachette, Paris 1866.

Fisher, P.H.
> *Vie et moeurs des Mollusques,*
> Payot, Paris 1950.

Fourmanoir, P. & Laboute, P.
> *Poissons de Nouvelle-Calédonie et des Nouvelles-Hébrides,*
> Les Editions du Pacifique, 1976.

Garnaud, J.
> *Nouvelles données sur l'éthologie d'un Pomacentridae Amphiprion percula Lacepede.*
> Bull. Inst. Océanog., Monaco 1951.

Gillet, Keith & Frank McNeill
> *The Great Barrier Reef and Adjacent Isles,*
> Sydney 1959.

Grant, E.M.
> *Guide to Fishes,*
> The Coordinator-General's Department, Brisbane 1975.

Grassé, P.P.
> *Pages choisies. Le fait social et l'effet de groupe,*
> Ouvrage jubilaire, Masson, Paris 1967.
> *La Vie des Animaux,*
> Larousse, Paris 1969.

Grassé, P.P. & A. Tetry
> Zoologie I. Encyclopédie de la Pléiade,
> Tours 1963.

Guinot, D.
> *Les arthropodes, Panorama du Monde Animal,*
> Hachette, Paris, 1968-1974.

Halstead, B.
> *Poisonous and venomous marine animals,*
> United States Government Printing Office, Washington D.C., 1965.

Hyman, L. Henrietta
The Invertebrates,
McGraw-Hill Book Company, 1940.

Jussieu, B. de
Mémoire de quelques productions marines...
Manuscript and 4 plates, extract from Mémoires de
l'Académie, Paris 1742.

Martin, Arthur W. & Stucki I. Catala
The growth rate of Nautilus macromphalus,
Dept. of Zoology, Univ. of Washington, Seattle &
Aquarium of Noumea, New Caledonia and Peter D. Ward,
University of Columbus, Ohio, 1972/1976.

Pavans de Ceccati, M.
Les spongiaires. La Vie des Animaux,
Larousse, Paris 1969.

Peloux, Y.
Etude histologique des coraux fluorescents de profondeur,
Comptes rendus Acad. Sciences, Paris 1960.

Pope, E.
E.C. New Caledonia, The coral-ringed Island,
Australian Natural History, vol. XIV, Sydney 1962.

Pope, E. & F. Rowe
*A new genus and two new species in the family
Mithrodiidae (Echinodermata: Asteroidea) with comments
on the status of the species of Mithrodia Gray 1840,*
Australian Zool. 19(2), 1977.

Prince, J.N.
The molluscan eyestalk using as an example Pterocera
lambis, Ohio Univ. 1954.

Ranson, G.
La vie des huîtres,
Nouvelle Revue Française, Gallimard, Paris 1943.

Risbec, J.
*Mollusques nudibranches de la Nouvelle-Calédonie.
Faune de l'Union Française,*
Larousse, Paris 1953.

De l'anatomie des trois Strombidés,
Annales du Musée de Marseille T. XXI, 1927.

Roby
Le monde des nageoires,
Editions Albin Michel, Paris 1970.

Rostand, J.
Science fausse et fausses sciences,
Nouvelles Revue Française, Gallimard 1958.

Esquisse d'une histoire de la biologie,
Nouvelles Revue Française, Gallimard 1945.

Salvat, B. & Claude Rives
Coquillages de Polynésie,
Les Editions du Pacifique 1975.

Saville-Kent, W.
The Great Barrier Reef of Australia,
W.H. Allen & Co, London 1893.

Smith, J.L.B.
The Sea Fishes of Southern Africa,
Johannesburg 1950.

Stix, H.M. & R. Tucker Abbott
Les Coquillages,
Seghers, Paris 1969.

Tixier-Durivault, A.
Les octocoralliaires de Nouvelle-Caledonie,
Editions de la Fondation Singer-Polignac vol. IV, Paris
1970.

Tuzet, Odette
Spongiaires Zoologie,
Encyclopédie de la Pléiade 1963.

Wells, J.W.
Report of the Great Barrier Reef Committee,
vol. 6 p. 26.

Notes on Indo Pacific Scleractinian Corals. A new genus
Catalaphyllia,
Pacific Science, vol. XXV, July 1971.

Treatise on Inv. Paleontology, Coelenterates Geol.,
Sty. of America, Univers. of Kansas Press 1936.

The recent solitary Mussid Scleractinians Corals Leiden,
1964.

Willey, Arthur
Contribution to the Natural History of Pearly Nautilus,
Cambridge University Press, 1902.

Yonge, C.M.
A Year on the Great Barrier Reef,
Putnam, London 1930.

Zoo
Société Royale de Zoologie d'Anvers,
No 3, January 1960.

INDEX OF SCIENTIFIC NAMES

The numbers in bold refer to the text pages and the numbers preceded by letters relate to captions to the photographs. The letters are a key to the relevant chapters.

S = Sponges   Cr = Crustaceans
Co = Coelenterates   E = Echinoderms
M = Mollusks   F = Fish

Above: *Lutjanus sebae*

The photographs in this book are by the author and his wife,
with the exception of the following:

Coelenterates: *Physalia physalis* by F.G. Myers, Sydney
Tentacles of *Physalia* by F.G. Myers, Sydney
Micro-photo of nematocysts by Keith Gillet, Sydney
Mollusks: Aberrant shell shapes by G. Gaeta
from the collection of R. Lesage, Noumea
Echinoderms: X-rays of *Ophiarachna incrassata*
and *Euretaster insignis* by R. Abgrall, Paris
Fish: *Pomacanthus imperator* adult, *Lepidaplois perditio* and
Fissilabrus dimidiatus by B. Conseil, Noumea

Translated from the French by **Enzo Sirna**
General Editor, **William R. Reed**, M.I. Biol.
Scientific Editor, **Dr Ray George**, Ph.D. (W. Aust.)

Printed in Singapore
August 1986

FOLIO
574.92
C27
871321

Catala, René.
Treasures of the tropic
  seas
50.00

871321

Plainfield Public Library
Eighth St. at Park Ave.
Plainfield, NJ   07060